Winning

Omaha/8

Poker

Mark Tenner

Lou Krieger

Other ConJelCo titles:

Books

Internet Poker: How to Play and Beat Online Poker Games
by Lou Krieger and Kathleen Keller Watterson

Hold'em Excellence: From *Beginner to Winner*
by Lou Krieger

Las Vegas Blackjack Diary
by Stuart Perry

More Hold'em Excellence: a Winner for Life
by Lou Krieger

*Stepping Up: The Recreational Player's Guide to Beating
Casino Poker*
by Randy Burgess

Serious Poker
by Dan Kimberg

Video Poker—Optimum Play
by Dan Paymar

Winning Low-Limit Hold'em
by Lee Jones

Software

Blackjack Trainer for the Macintosh or Windows

Ken Elliott's CrapSim for DOS

StatKing for Windows

Winning

Omaha/8

Poker

Mark Tenner

Lou Krieger

 **ConJelCo**
Pittsburgh, Pennsylvania

Winning Omaha/8 Poker
Copyright © 2003 by Mark Tenner and Lou Krieger

Publisher's Cataloging-in-Publication Data

Tenner, Mark
Krieger, Lou

Winning Omaha/8 Poker
viii,252p. ; 22cm.
ISBN 1-886070-19-9
I. Title.

Library of Congress Control Number: 2003114916

First Edition

1 3 5 7 9 8 6 4 2

Cover design by Melissa Hayden

ConJelCo LLC
1460 Bennington Ave
Pittsburgh, PA 15217
[412] 621-6040
http://www.conjelco.com

Table of Contents

These days it seems like everyone is playing poker and talking about it, too. Poker has undergone a huge growth spurt during the first few years of the new millennium. It's everywhere: in casinos, on the Internet at online poker sites, and in regular weekly or monthly home games. It's even a big hit on television, where state-of-the art "lipstick cameras" allow viewers to see everyone's cards and mentally play along with the experts who compete for big bucks on the World Poker Tour and at the World Series of Poker. The influx of new players has created incredible opportunities for knowledgeable players. Never before have poker games been populated by so many inexperienced, unskilled players.

Some new players develop an interest in the game because they've seen it on television, and they're lured by the prospects of great action and big payoffs that poker can generate. Many of these new players like to gamble, and poker is an exciting form of gaming. Win or lose, these players view poker as a great form of entertainment.

Other new players are not content to linger in perpetual rookie status. They're lured not so much by the big gamble, but by the skill and decision-making that's part and parcel of playing poker the way it's meant to be played — as a game of skill, heart, and daring. Poker is an intellectual challenge to these players, and if properly pursued it's a challenge that can yield substantial financial rewards. Whether you're a new player or an experienced hand at the game, the fact that you purchased this book is proof positive that you're this type of player.

An abundance of new literature has accompanied the growth of poker. Most of the recent books, however, deal exclusively with tournaments and Texas hold'em. While these are certainly relevant and valuable, they don't cover everything that's going on in the poker world. One form of poker that continues to grow in popularity is Omaha eight-or-better high-low split, which everyone refers to as "Omaha-eight" when speaking about it, and abbreviates as "Omaha/8" in print.

You'll find an Omaha/8 game in virtually every cardroom, whether it's a brick and mortar card casino or an Internet based site located in cyberspace. And when you do find a game, take it from us: Most of the players in the game don't know what they're doing. Until now, only one definitive book on Omaha/8 existed — Ray Zee's "High-Low-Split Poker For Advanced Players." That's it. Just one. Contrast that to the multitude of works on hold'em and tournament play, and it's obvious that there's a gap in the poker literature crying out to be filled. With this book, Mark Tenner and Lou Krieger provide a much needed and useful tool for poker players interested in improving their game.

Omaha/8 is widely misunderstood. As a result, better players stand to make a significant profit in the game. We believe that a thorough reading of this text will dramatically speed up the learning curve for readers intent on studying — and learning — about Omaha/8. This book discusses traps to avoid, and believe us when we say this: Omaha/8 is a minefield of traps and potential pitfalls, and Tenner and Krieger show you how to deftly sidestep all of them. If you don't believe us, just take a tour of any Omaha/8 table and you'll see some players stepping on the same mines they've been detonating for years. They never seem to learn. But that's a catastrophe this book will help you avoid.

"Omaha Poker" deals with specifics. Hands are broken down piece-by-piece, giving you insight into the value of position, showing you how to play the blinds, explaining when to raise, and telling how to play multi-way versus shorthanded pots. And there's a lot more, too. Just take a look at the table of contents and see for yourself. Many of these areas have never been dealt with in print before, but are keys to success at Omaha/8. Until now, only experienced, highly successful Omaha/8 players knew much of the information presented in this book. Those experts learned the hard way. But by carefully reading and studying this book, Omaha/8 players — yes, even beginning players — will see immediate benefits in their game.

Linda Johnson and Mark Gregorich

October 2003

Linda Johnson, a World Series of Poker Razz champion, is also an expert Omaha player, and was formerly the publisher of Card Player Magazine. Mark Gregorich is an editor at Card Player Magazine, and was voted the best Omaha/8 player in the world in a recent poll.

Introduction

Omaha Poker has been called "the game of the future" by players and pundits alike. Omaha arrived hard on the heels of its cousin, Texas hold'em, which in recent years has surpassed seven-card stud as the world's most popular poker game. Omaha, for reasons we'll get into later, offers more action and excitement for many players. That's one of the factors that accounts for its rapid growth in popularity both as an anticipated staple of poker tournaments in the United States and Europe, and as a cash game played in most cardrooms and casinos.

Two forms of Omaha are commonly played. In America, the game of choice is generally Omaha hold'em, eight-or-better, high-low split, which we'll mercifully abbreviate from this point forward as Omaha/8. It usually features four rounds of fixed betting limits, and the betting limits on the latter two betting rounds are generally twice that of the first two. Because it's a split-pot game, the holder of the best high hand and the holder of the best low hand composed of five unpaired ranks of eight or lower (the best low hand is 5-4-3-2-ace) split the pot.

In Europe, Omaha is generally played high-only, and there's usually just one winner, unless two players have the same high hand. When Omaha is played high only, the betting is generally pot-limit, although there is nothing inherent in the game that mandates pot-limit rather than fixed-limit betting — it's just that in Europe, most poker is of the pot-limit variety.

Pot-limit poker can have exponential raising, since the rules allow you to match the wager of a bettor and then raise the total amount of money in the pot. So if there's twenty dollars in the pot, and your opponent makes a pot-sized bet, you can match his twenty and raise the size of the pot. In other words, if there's twenty dollars in the pot, and your opponent then bets twenty, you can make it — as we poker players like to say — "...eighty to go." Your opponent can then call your raise. He can also raise you, and if he's really confident about his hand, he might just make it $320 to go. As you can see, pot-limit raises get a lot of money into the pot in a hurry whenever two or more players have hands they like.

Poker has always been America's game. But it's changing these days, and in a big way too. The world is shrinking, it seems, and poker — like baseball and basketball — is fast becoming a world game. And you're as likely to find an Omaha game in Australia, Vienna, or London as you are in Los Angeles, Las Vegas, or even Omaha, Nebraska for that matter.

Poker conjures up a host of colorful, evocative images. When you think about poker, it's an easy nostalgic leap to the game played by gunfighters in saloons of the Old West — men like Wild Bill Hickok, Bat Masterson, and Doc Holliday — and a generation of quick witted and quick handed Mississippi river boat gamblers with pencil-thin moustaches and derringers hidden in their ruffled sleeves.

And for another glimpse of poker's illustrious yesteryears, just think of Paul Newman and Robert Redford in The Sting: A low-hanging table lamp illuminates cigar smoke rising from the ashtrays as a bunch of circa-1930's Chicago mobsters sit around a green felt table sharing smokes, jokes, and a bottle of bootlegged hootch, as cards are in the air.

These celluloid images, part myth and part reality, fuel thousands of Thursday night poker games held in homes, hotel rooms, and country clubs across America and around the world. It's not that we're a bunch of guys sitting around with shoulder holsters while a guy the size of a NFL linebacker watches the peep hole as he guards the door; it's that we're a bunch of guys (and women, too, in increasing numbers) in search of fun, friendship, humor — usually the politically incorrect kind — camaraderie, challenge, and, dare we utter the word, money. Money won, after all, is twice as sweet as money earned.

Poker is all these things and more. Though your authors are far too young to have played cards with Doc Holliday or Al Capone, we feel we know them well, if for no other reason than the myriad movies we've seen. After all, westerns and gangster flicks need poker scenes like you'd need an ace up your sleeve in the freewheeling games they depict. It's all part of the mystique and the myth.

Since the late 1980s, poker has undergone a renaissance of sorts — a greening, if you will. Like bowling and billiards before it, poker has moved out from under the seedier sides of its roots and it's flowering. In fact, it's in full bloom! If you want to play poker in a clean, safe environment these days, you're probably no more than a few hours' drive from a public card casino. And if that's too far, just sidle up to your computer and visit any of a number of online poker rooms, where you can play for real money right there in your jammies, from the comfort of your very own den.

Why You Need This Book

If you visit a card room — either the brick and mortar variety or one that's no more than a couple of mouse clicks away on your computer — you won't find all of those bizarre home games you and your cronies have conjured up, but you will find a variety of seven-card stud, Texas hold'em, and Omaha games on tap. And you'll find them at a variety of betting limits — there's something for everyone — so you can play within your means and have fun. If you play with skill and discipline, you might win a little, or even a lot, if the fates are with you.

If you've never played poker before, or even if you've played a lot of poker — particularly Texas hold'em, which is a kissing cousin of Omaha — you might wonder why you need a book about it. Why can't you just belly up to the table, plunk down your money, and give it a go?

After all, many players have learned in just that way. It's called the school of hard knocks, and the tuition can be costly. Moreover, there's no guarantee you'll ever graduate. But you can learn to play Omaha quite well from this book, and when you go to the table and put your hard-earned money into play, you'll have a greater knowledge base to draw on than you would if you simply flew by the seat of your pants with the hard knocks boys.

Poker's growing popularity has paralleled that of personal computers. A substantial amount of research has been done in recent years and some of those old concepts they're still teaching over at the school of hard knocks have been found wanting. As a consequence, players who don't keep their knowledge up to date by using a computer might just find themselves left behind. With that in mind, we've included some basic information on how to go about it.

But first you need to understand the game. This book explains the basics of Omaha/8 and provides a sound strategic approach so you can learn to play well in the shortest amount of time possible. And you'll be ahead of the pack by a country mile. When the table talk runs to poker books, you'll find that many of your opponents have never so much as picked up a poker book. Many, in fact, will boast of it. Yes, they're proud of their ignorance. Some of them disdain the new breed of computer literate, educated poker players.

While many self-taught players are remarkably skilled, most of them are not, and they've been making the same mistakes for years. And who's going to tell them? Certainly not their more savvy opponents, who are quite happy, thank you, to convert other players' ignorance into currency at the end of a poker session. After all, poker is a game of money played with cards, so if you find a leak in your opponent's game, you should exploit it for all it's worth. And why not? Don't forget, he'll be trying to do the same to you!

Awareness of a problem is the first step on the road to solving it, and until you're aware of the mistakes you're making at the poker table, you can't correct them. If you're new to Omaha/8, or even an experienced hand wanting to improve your skills, this book will provide a storehouse of knowledge and information that you can convert to usable know-how.

What We Assume About You

Although you've probably played some form of poker before deciding to take a shot at Omaha, we're gonna take it from the top by assuming you've never played poker before — not seven-card stud, not Texas hold'em, and not Omaha — and that you may not even know the difference between a flush and a straight. We start with the basics, so you're covered. Don't worry about a thing.

Maybe you've been playing poker since the time you climbed out of the crib, but for some reason you usually lose. You know the rules, but knowing how to win has somehow eluded you. Don't you worry either. This book will certainly help you. We present all the tips, strategies, tactics, and tricks you'll need to walk away from the poker table with money in your pocket.

Even if you're a real Omaha maven — an expert — you'll still benefit from what we have to offer. Some of our suggestions may surprise you, some may simply reinforce knowledge you've already acquired, and you may even find a few gems you've never thought of before.

How To Use This Book

This book is a reference as well as a tutorial, and you can read it in any fashion you wish. There's no need to read it from cover to cover to understand where we're coming from. If you know all the rules but want to find out more about proper starting hands, or about whether or not to continue on with your hand after the flop, jump right in there and start reading. If you want to learn the basics and save the advanced stuff for later, start at the beginning and wait until you feel ready to tackle the more advanced concepts. But if you really want to flatter us, go ahead and read the book from cover to cover. We promise you an enjoyable ride.

How This Book Is Organized

We've organized this book so that the discussion in each chapter is self-contained. Here's what each part covers:

Part 1: How To Play the Game

This section covers the nuts and bolts of how to play the game. If you've never played poker before, or you've had some experience playing poker but are new to Omaha, this is the place to start. You'll first learn hand rankings and how the mechanics of the game work. We'll also cover the need for patience, the importance of playing only good starting hands, and some tips on how to play in a casino. Finally, we'll mention points of poker etiquette you'll want to bring to the table with you.

Part 2: Advanced Strategy

Playing Omaha and winning at it involves much more than the luck of the draw, though you wouldn't know it by observing the way some of your opponents consistently play any four cards they're dealt. Here's where we dissect the game, showing you how to decide whether to play or fold your four starting cards, then how to play on the flop, then how to approach the last two betting rounds. You'll learn when to defend your blinds, and when to save money for a better opportunity by folding. We devote special attention to aces, since they're the most important cards in the game.

Part 3: Other Poker Skills

Poker is not played with cards alone, so knowing how to manage your cards is not the sole skill separating winners from also-rans. That's true in Omaha, and in every other form of poker you can name. So if you want to become a winning player, there's a bevy of skills you need to master. We teach you about bluffing, money management and record keeping, how to go about reading an opponent, playing poker online for play-money or real money, and we even show you where to go from here to learn more about poker. Finally, we provide some keys to success and some valuable tips to improve your Omaha game right now.

Where To Go From Here

It's your call. Check out the table of contents and see what catches your eye. Or choose a topic that interests you and give it a go. Or make believe this is like any other book. Pick it up, start on page one, and don't put it down until you finish it. You can even take it to work and read at your desk. No one will mind. Really. You can read it at the dinner table too. It's OK. Trust us. We've already talked to your boss and your spouse and they've granted permission. But just once. Just this time.

A Few Words of Thanks and Acknowledgement

This book, like most, builds on a foundation created by others. Many books and authors whose work we respect helped us produce the book you're now holding in front of you. These books and authors include: "Omaha Hi Low Poker" by Shane Smith, "High-Low-Split Poker For Advanced Players" by Ray Zee, "Omaha Hold'em Poker: The Action Game" by Bob Ciaffone, "Cappelletti on Omaha" by Mike Cappelletti, "Championship Omaha" by T.J. Cloutier and Tom McEvoy, and "Omaha High-Low: Playing to Win With the Odds" by Bill Boston.

We also take this opportunity to thank Linda Johnson, Mark Gregorich, Annie Duke, and Mike Caro for their ideas and their willingness to share strategic concepts and thoughts about the game of Omaha with us, as well as for their efforts in reading and reviewing this manuscript to make sure the ideas and concepts we present are correct, clearly stated and unambiguous. We'd also like to thank our publisher, Chuck Weinstock, at Con-JelCo for his many suggestions, and Kathy Watterson for a terrific job of editing and turning our mangled prose into a well-written gem of a book.

Part 1:

How to Play the Game

Chapter 1

History of Omaha Poker

A s with most poker games, the facts surrounding the birth of Omaha are somewhat murky, but we can tell you one thing with absolute certainty: The game was not invented in Omaha, Nebraska. Some things are deceiving. After all, lead pencils don't contain any lead; they're filled with graphite — and in any event, there are no truth-in-labeling laws where poker games are concerned.

It's a relatively new game too. In fact, it's so new that Doyle Brunson's classic *Super/System: A Course In Power Poker*, one of poker's seminal works, makes no reference to Omaha at all. David Sklansky's 1983 masterpiece, *Winning Poker* (now called *The Theory of Poker*) contains an appendix with rules of play for various games. Those games were: Five-Card Draw, Seven-Card Stud, Hold'em, Five-Card Stud, Lowball, Razz, and High-Low Split. The latter did not refer to Omaha. Back in 1983, the term "high-low split" referred to five-card draw, five-card stud, or seven-card stud games in which the best high hand and the best low hand split the pot, not to the game we know today as Omaha/8. Indeed, Omaha was not included in Sklansky's appendix at all. Moreover, each of the games listed in the appendix was defined in a glossary of poker terms that followed it. Once again, Omaha was among the missing.

So what happened? Did guys as astute as Brunson and Sklansky simply forget to include Omaha in their books? Not at all. The game simply hadn't arrived yet, and a glance at the appendix to Sklansky's *Winning Poker* showed us just how much things have changed in the poker world in but a few decades. Some of the games listed in that appendix are almost never played today, and others just occasionally. But Omaha, which was not even a blip on poker's radar screen back then, has become one of the most popular games played in casinos today.

But despite Omaha's lack of popularity in casinos thirty years ago, similar games were staples of home games for quite some time, and were known by a variety of names. There were versions in which players were dealt four private cards — just as they are in Omaha today — and others in which players received five cards. The five-card form of Omaha limits the number of participants to eight, and while that may not be a drawback for most home games, it's an important issue for casino poker, where nine-player or ten-player tables are standard for most games.

Omaha — the four-card version we know today — was introduced to Las Vegas casinos in 1982. It was an instant success and soon became a staple of tournament play, side action games during tournaments, and regular casino cash games. Because of its reputation for creating plenty of action, and because many aficionados were hard pressed to find a four-card starting hand they wouldn't play, Omaha was nicknamed "The Game of the Future."

Back when Texas hold'em was first coming into prominence, there were a couple forms of the game. The most popular variety — the game that's still played today and is currently the most popular form of poker in the world — allowed players to use any combination of their two personal cards and the five communal cards to form the best five-card poker hand.

Another version of hold'em, not nearly as popular and never played in casinos today, required a player to use both cards in his hand in combination with three of the five communal cards to form the best possible hand. That game was referred to as "Omaha," so when four-card hold'em was introduced in Las Vegas, it was called Omaha because the game required each player to use precisely two of his own cards in combination with three of the communal cards to form his hand.

Nevertheless, how that old version of Texas hold'em requiring players to use both hole cards came to be known as Omaha is still a mystery. You never know; it might just have been a rogue version of Texas hold'em played in a home game in someone's basement in Omaha, Nebraska, and when it was introduced elsewhere, that city's moniker just tagged along with the game. But there's no way to know for sure.

In a way we're lucky. Imagine if the game had been invented in Intercourse, Pennsylvania. Folks the world over would be staggering home at dawn, attempting to explain to their significant others how they lost all that money at intercourse. Losing at Omaha, while never pleasant, is probably less of a strain on familial relationships.

The name stuck. The game grew in popularity, and it's now known as Omaha whether one is playing Omaha/8 or Omaha high-only, and it's called Omaha wherever the game is played, be it Las Vegas or London, Amsterdam or Atlantic City, Finland or Foxwoods. Because most European casinos feature pot-limit betting for all forms of poker, Omaha high-only has become a staple in European cardrooms and casinos, while Omaha/8 — which is most often played with fixed betting limits — has continued to gain in popularity in North America.

With the growth of Internet poker, where players can play online in real time games against opponents all over the world for either play-money or real money — the choice is yours — you can play Omaha any time of day or night, regardless of where you live or how far you might be from a brick and mortar casino. If Omaha is the game of the future, that future appears to be now. The game has never been more popular. There's plenty of opportunity to play. And with the information you gain from this book, a little common sense, and a lot of discipline, you should find yourself able to hold your own in most games, and to beat all but the toughest of them. So step up to the table and say the magic words: "Deal me in."

Chapter 2

Playing Omaha For the First Time

Omaha poker, whether played as a pot-limit game for high only or as the "eight-or-better, high-low split variety" — the kind you'll find played in most American casinos — is a variation of Texas hold'em. In Omaha, as in Texas hold'em, five community cards are dealt face up in the center of the table and are combined with the private cards in each player's hand to form the best poker hand.

The games appear similar, and at first glance the differences seem small at best: Texas hold'em players are dealt two private cards and may use both, one, or even neither of them to form the best poker hand. But in Omaha each player is dealt four private cards and must use exactly two of them — you can't use more, nor can you use fewer than two — to form the best poker hand.

Those seemingly small differences in rules and procedures cascade so dramatically through the requirements for good play that even a skilled Texas hold'em player cannot make the transition to Omaha without significant forethought, major adjustments in strategy and tactics, and a real appreciation for the fact that while these games are structurally similar, they are very different beasts.

That's one of the reasons for this book. You just can't read a book on Texas hold'em and interpolate your actions into good Omaha play. The games are so different that separate books are needed. It's like the difference between driving a car and flying a small airplane. Both run on internal combustion engines and the engines aren't all that different in principle. But just because you've been driving a car all your life doesn't mean you're ready to step into that cockpit and take off. You need a new set of skills.

In Omaha/8, as in most split-pot games, there's no shortage of action, and lots of chips may be on the table. Some players vie for the best low hand, some for the best high one, and still others hope to scoop the entire pot. Omaha, whether it's eight-or-better, high-low split or played for high only, also creates action because each player is dealt four cards rather than the two that Texas hold'em players receive. Naturally, with four cards to choose from, many players have no trouble finding hands to play. In fact, many play most, or even all. But that's a rather slippery slope, and we hope you won't go there. At least, we hope you won't after reading this book.

Hand selection is one of an Omaha player's most critical skills. Because many players involve themselves in far too many hands, they create weaknesses for skilled players to exploit. You'll be able to exploit those weaknesses too. We'll show you how a little later in the book.

As a beginning Omaha player, you may get confused at times as you try to ferret out the best five-card poker hand among the five community cards on the center of the table and the four private cards in your hand. But don't worry. If you can play Texas hold'em, you can play Omaha too. It just takes some getting used to.

If You've Never Played Before

If you're playing Omaha high-only or Omaha/8 for the first time, but you've had some experience playing Texas hold'em, you can expect these differences:

- Omaha/8 is a split-pot game. That usually means you'll find more action: more players in each pot, more chips in the center of the table, more folks going all-in on big draws. This added action is one of the game's major attractions.

- Players must make their best five-card poker hands by using exactly two of their private cards and exactly three communal cards. In Texas hold'em, the best hand can be formed using two, one, or none of your private cards. If you're playing Texas hold'em and hold the ace of hearts in your hand while the board contains four additional hearts, you have a flush. But if all you hold is one heart among your four private Omaha cards, you have nothing at all. That's because you must play two cards — no more, no less — to make a valid

Omaha hand. To make a flush, you must hold two of the suit yourself.

- With four different starting cards to work with, you can form six different two-card combinations. That's so important, we'll say it again: With four private cards you have six times as many potential two-card starting hands as you do in Texas hold'em. As a result, winning Omaha hands tend to be quite a bit bigger than those in Texas hold'em. Suppose you've been dealt the following four cards: Ah-Ad-2h-3d. You can form the following two-card combinations from those four cards:

  1. A♥-2♥ (the two lowest cards in the deck, plus a chance to make the best possible flush in hearts),

  2. A♥-A♦ (a pair of aces, though aces alone are not nearly as strong as they are in Texas hold'em),

  3. A♥-3♦ (the second lowest two-card combination in the deck, which will be very important if a deuce appears on the board, thus "counterfeiting" your ace-deuce),

  4. A♦-3♦ (as above for A♥-3♦, this supplies counterfeit protection, plus the possibility of making the best possible flush in diamonds),

  5. 3♦-2♥ (counterfeit protection if an ace is dealt on the board. You'd love to see that happen, since not only would you still be drawing to the best possible low hand, but you'd also have a set of aces toward the high hand, giving you a chance to win both ends of the pot. That, in Omahaese, is called "scooping."),

  6. A♦-2♥ (again, the two lowest cards in the deck, and because you have two aces and a deuce in your possession, there's less chance that one or more opponents also hold an ace-deuce combination that would allow them to split the low end of the pot with you. When that happens, it's called "getting quartered," and it's generally not much fun.)

- Because you've got six potential starting hands to work with, straights and flushes are extremely common in Omaha. Two pair, often a winning hand in Texas hold'em, seldom wins in this game, and some of your bread and butter hold'em hands — like a pair of aces with a big side card — rarely, if ever, win. If you're playing Omaha/8, whenever three unpaired communal cards with a rank of eight or lower are on the board, someone probably has a low hand, meaning that the big pot you hoped to win has effectively been chopped in half.

Because beginning players often have difficulty determining the best Omaha hand, deal out a few hands and see how easy it is for you to identify the best high and best low hands. Here's a sample Omaha hand, with all the cards dealt:"

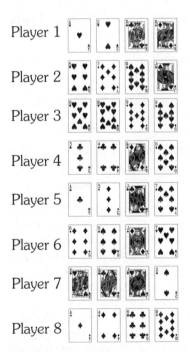

Common Cards

Player	Best High Hand	Best Low Hand
1	five-high straight	five-low (a wheel)
2	seven-high straight	seven-six low
3	set of nines	no low hand

4	nine-high flush	eight-seven low
5	ace-high flush	seven-five low
6	seven-high straight	seven-six low
7	no pair	no low hand
8	seven-high straight	six-five low

Player 1, who has the best possible low hand, will win the low end of the pot, while Player 5's ace-high flush will capture the high end. Player 8, with what's ordinarily a good low hand, figures to lose a lot of money here. Players 2 and Player 6 also figure to lose a few chips on this encounter. Each of them, along with Player 8, holds the best possible straight combination on the river. But the river card, a third club, made a flush possible.

If looking at all these Omaha hands seems confusing, you can take comfort in the fact that even professional casino dealers sometimes have trouble determining the best hands. Looking for high hands as well as low ones, especially with so many card combinations, can lead to brain lock. But once you get used to the game, it's like anything else you do repeatedly. With practice, you'll find yourself able to spot winning combinations in a hurry.

But there's good news in all this confusion too. With four cards in their hands, many players always manage to find something worth playing. These players are, of course, playing far too many weak hands — holdings that should be discarded rather than played. And you can take advantage of this loose play. Even a beginning Omaha/8 player can become a favorite in lower-limit games by simply playing better starting cards than most of his opponents play. Many players who have played Omaha/8 for years fail to realize that split-pot games are illusory in the sense that it appears as though one can play many more hands than in games where only the high hand wins. But winning Omaha players are more selective than their scattergun opponents. They enter pots only with hands that, on average, are superior to those their opponents play most of the time.

Before Putting On Your Poker Face

Omaha, like any other form of poker, is a house that requires a solid foundation. Only when that foundation is in place can you go ahead and build on it. When all the elements are solidly fixed to the structure, you can add flourishes and decorative touches. But you can't begin embellishing until the foundation is poured, the building is framed, and all other essential elements are securely in place. So we're gonna put first things first — where they belong — and provide a basic understanding of what you need before beginning to play.

One of the neat things about playing Omaha, or any other form of poker for that matter, is that you don't have to be one of the best in the world to earn money at it. If you learn to play Omaha at a level akin to that of a journeyman musician, you'll be good enough to win consistently. You'll have to reach that elusive world-class level to make a lot of money, but even good, work-a-day Omaha players can supplement their income by working to become the very best players they're capable of becoming. A modicum of work, study, practice, and analysis ought to be more than sufficient to ensure that you'll become a lifelong winning player.

Even if you've never played poker before — anytime, anywhere, for any limits, not even across the kitchen table with Uncle Billy and Aunt Edie — you can learn to play well. And we're going to show you how.

The Real Basics

The object of poker is to win money by capturing the pot, which contains bets made by players during the hand. Players bet because they believe they have the best hands, or to give the impression that their hands are very strong — thus convincing others to abandon their own hands by folding. Money saved is ultimately just as valuable as money won, so knowing when to release a hand that appears to be beaten is just as important as knowing when to bet.

In a casino, a typical Omaha game is composed of nine or ten players, and it's dealt by a professional dealer who is not an active participant in the game. The dealer wagers no money and gets no hand to play, but is simply there to run the game, deal the cards, and push the pots to the winning players. The deck is a standard, 52-card poker deck. There is no joker and there are no wild cards in play.

Chips

At home you can bet with pennies or peanuts, but real poker chips are used in all casinos. They're not those light, dime-store plastic ones, either; real poker chips have a substantial feel to them, and come in a variety of colors, with each color standing for a given denomination. In most Las Vegas casinos, the chips follow this traditional color pattern:

$1	White or blue
$5	Red
$25	Green
$100	Black
$500	Purple or Lavender

There are exceptions to this rule. For example, in Southern California — which has more poker games and card casinos than anywhere else in the world — dollar chips tend to be blue, five-dollar chips are usually yellow, and hundred-dollar chips are often white. If you're thinking of hosting a home game and want to get a good set of poker chips, there are stores that will supply them to you. If you're going to host a game with nine players, you'll probably want to buy a set of 750 chips in three or four colors. But if the chips are strictly for home game use, there's no need to have dollar denominations inscribed on them. You can just set the denominations at any values you wish, then change them as needed.

The Essentials

If you've never played poker before, you'll want to read this carefully. If you have played poker before, just not Omaha, you can zip right through to the end of this section. Here's where we show you the basics — the real beginners' stuff.

Poker is easily played, though a lifetime is often insufficient to master it. It's a game of money and of people, played with cards. Money is won by winning pots. A pot is the money, usually represented by chips, that has been wagered during the play of each hand (or round) of poker, from the first cards dealt until the showdown. (Don't get confused here, but a hand also refers to the cards in possession of a player.) Hands can be won in two ways:

- *At the showdown:* At the conclusion of all betting rounds, if two or more players are still active, they turn their hands face up and the best poker hand wins the pot. In a game like Omaha/8, which is a split-pot game, the best high hand and the best qualifying low hand — if there is one — divide the spoils.

- *Your opponents fold:* If all opponents relinquish their claims to the pot by discarding their cards rather than match your bet — because they believe, rightly or wrongly, that you hold the best hand — that's called folding. Whenever all of your opponents surrender the pot this way, it's yours.

In Omaha/8 the best high hand and the best low hand split the pot, provided someone makes a qualified low hand consisting of five unpaired cards with a rank of eight or below. The worst possible low hand is 8-7-6-5-4, while the best low hand — called a "wheel" or a "bicycle" — is 5-4-3-2-A. A wheel can be tied, in which case all players holding wheels split the low end of the pot, but it cannot be beaten. Because a wheel is also a five-high straight, it often stands a good chance of being the best high hand as well. If it is, it will scoop the pot.

While a high hand will always be made in a split-pot game, there won't necessarily be a low hand. And when there's no low hand, the best high hand wins the entire pot.

Omaha, whether it's a split-pot game or played for high only, requires blind bets to start each hand. In rotating fashion, one or two players are required to make a bet, or portion of a bet, before the hand is dealt. Because this requirement rotates around the table, each player pays his fair share. The game could be played with antes instead of blind bets, as is the convention in seven-card stud, but in flop games like Omaha and Texas hold'em, blind bets are the way it's done.

Each time a hand is dealt, players have an opportunity to call, fold, or raise the blind. On the second and subsequent rounds of betting, the first player to act may either check, which in essence is a bet of nothing, or he may wager. If he checks, the next player in turn may check or bet. Once a wager has been made, however, the next player to act may either fold his hand, call the bet by matching the amount of the wager, or raise. In most casinos, a bet and three or four raises are permitted for each betting round.

Any time a player decides to relinquish his interest in the pot, he can release his hand when it's his turn to act. Once a player folds, he's not required to place any more money in the pot. Of course, he can't win any, either. If a player bets or raises but no one calls, the hand is over. The pot goes to the last active player, the cards are collected and shuffled, and the next hand is dealt.

Poker really is that simple. Yet within poker's simplicity lies a wonderfully textured mosaic that is beguiling, fascinating, and, for many, a lifelong source of pleasure.

Hand Rankings

All forms of Omaha are played with a 52-card deck — there's no joker and no wild cards — made up of four suits: spades, hearts, diamonds, and clubs. Each suit is equal in value and there are thirteen ranks in each suit. An ace is the highest-ranking card, followed by the king, queen, jack, and ten through deuce, in descending order. In the split-pot variety of the game, the ace is also used as the lowest-ranking card for forming a low straight or a low hand. Therefore, in Omaha/8, an ace is actually two cards in one; it's simultaneously the highest-ranking and lowest-ranking card in the deck. Because of this unique dual attribute, an ace in your Omaha/8 hand gives you a decided advantage.

Although Omaha/8 and Omaha high-only are played with nine cards — the four private cards in your hand plus the five community cards dealt face up in the center of the table that belong to everyone — the best hand refers to the best five-card poker hand. Hand rankings are simply a function of probability. The more rare the hand, the more valuable it is, and the higher it's ranked.

Royal flush: A *royal flush* is simply an ace-high straight flush, and it's the best possible hand in poker. There are only four of them: A♠-K♠-Q♠-J♠-T♠; A♥-K♥-Q♥-J♥-T♥; A♦-K♦-Q♦-J♦-T♦; and A♣-K♣-Q♣-J♣-T♣.

Straight flush: This wonderful holding is comprised of five sequenced cards, all of the same suit, such as 8♦-7♦-6♦-5♦-4♦ or Q♣-J♣-T♣-9♣-8♣.

Four of a kind: Four-of-a-kind, or quads, is a five-card hand that contains all the cards of any one rank, plus one unrelated card, such as 9♠-9♥-9♦-9♣-3♥. The higher the rank, the better the hand. For example, four queens beats four deuces.

Full house: Three cards of any given rank along with a pair of another compose a full house. The rank of a full house is determined by the three-card grouping, not the pair. A hand like J♠-J♥-J♦-4♣-4♥ is referred to as "…jacks full of fours."

Flush: Any five cards of the same suit is a flush. The cards do not have to be sequenced; if they were, you'd have a straight flush. If there is more than one flush present, the winning hand is decided by the rank order of the highest hand. Thus an ace-high flush is better than one that is king-high.

Straight: Five sequenced cards, not of the same suit, is called a straight. If there's more than one straight present, the highest card in the sequence determines the winning hand. A nine-high straight beats a six-high straight.

Three-of-a-kind: Three cards of the same rank, along with two unrelated cards, is called three-of-a-kind. Sometimes you'll hear players refer to it as trips, or a set. If your best five-card hand is

K♦-K♥-K♣-2♠-4♥, you can refer to it as "...a set of kings," or "trip kings." It's all the same hand.

Two pair: Two cards of one rank, two cards of another, and one unrelated card comprise two pair. If more than one player has this holding, the higher ranked pair determines which two pair hand is superior. For example, aces and deuces beats kings and queens. But if two players each have two pair and each has the same high pair, then the rank of the second pair determines the winner. And if both hold the same two pair, the rank of the unrelated side card, or kicker, determines the winner. Finally, if both players have identical hands, they split the pot. In Omaha/8, if there's a low hand present, they'll split the high half of the pot.

One pair: One pair is two cards of one rank with three unrelated cards. If two players hold the same pair, then the value of the highest unrelated side card determines the winning hand.

No Pair: No pair is five unrelated cards, and the rank order of the unrelated cards determines the winner. For example, if Rick has A-K-8-5-3 and Stan has A-J-T-7-3, Rick wins because A-K is higher than A-J.

Low Hands: The best low hand composed of five unpaired cards, all with ranks of eight or lower, captures half of the pot when you're playing Omaha/8. A hand like 7♠-6♠-5♥-3♥-2♦ beats 8♠-5♦-4♦-2♣-A♣, but loses to 7♥-5♠-4♣-2♥-A♥. Figuring out the best low hand can take some practice, but if you always begin with the highest of the low cards and continue in descending order, you can't go wrong. Always remember, however: In Omaha/8 you must use precisely two cards from your hand with precisely three of the community cards on the board to form your best low hand.

Betting

If there were no betting, poker would be a game of luck and the best hand would always win. It would be pretty boring too, and about as exciting as flipping coins. Betting is the key to poker — remember, we told you that poker is a game of money played with cards — and maximizing wins with your good hands while minimizing losses when you're beaten is what poker is all about.

- In a fixed-limit game, the kind you'll find in most American casinos, bets and raises are made in predetermined amounts. In most Omaha games where the betting is fixed-limit, bets double on the third and fourth betting rounds. If you're playing a $4-$8 game, this means that the first two rounds of betting are based on four-dollar increments, while the last two rounds are based on eight-dollar increments.

- In spread-limit games, which are not nearly as common as the fixed-limit variety, bettors can wager any amount within given limits. If the limits are $2-$10, bets can be made at any amount of even dollar increments at any time, as long as raises are at least the equal of the bets that preceded them.

- If you play in Europe, you'll find that most Omaha games will be high only, and played pot-limit. While pot-limit poker is played in America, it's not nearly as common, particularly at lower betting limits, as fixed-limit games. If you find yourself in a pot-limit game, bets and raises are limited only by the amount of money in the pot at the time the wager is made. A player wishing to raise may count his call as part of the pot. So if the pot contains $20 and someone wagers $20, a raiser may match that $20 bet, thus making the total pot $60, and raise another $60. When the raiser is done, he will have tossed $80 into the pot, making the total $120.

- In no-limit, a player may bet or raise any amount of chips in front of him at any time.

Most of the time you should bet your playable hands, particularly when you think you have the best hand. After all, you want to drive out players who might end up beating you if they can draw for free. Unless you're holding a monstrously huge hand, the best play is usually to bet. Hopefully, your bet will discourage opponents from calling and catching cards that might beat you. With really big hands, however, hold back and give your opponents a chance to improve somewhat. That way, they'll be committed to their hands so you can take even more money from them.

On the other hand, there are times when you're not in the lead, but have a drawing hand and want to see the next card as inexpensively as possible. That's the time to check and hope your opponent checks too. If he does, he's given you nearly infinite odds to chase him down and beat him. If it costs you nothing to try and improve your hand, why not stick around? When there's no cost involved, no longshot is too long to play.

All of this applies as long as there are more cards to come, while hands have some potential for improvement. Once all the cards have been dealt, betting won't win you the pot simply because your opponent won't pay to look at another card. There is no other card, and the winning hand has already been dealt.

If you bet on the end, bet when you think you'll have the best hand if you are called. That's important. If you bet and your opponent has not improved his draw, he'll fold and your bet on the river won't garner an additional cent. But if he calls, he must have some sort of hand. So you should refrain from betting unless you believe your hand will be the best most of the time it's called.

If you check and your opponent bets, he could have a good hand or he might be bluffing. If you've got a good hand, you'll call him, or even raise if your hand is huge. In any event, whenever you win that pot, you'll have won at least one additional bet because your check induced your opponent to bet. Had your bet caused him to fold, you wouldn't have gathered in that last wager.

Scooping

Although Omaha/8 is a split-pot game, the objective is not to chop the pot and gladly share it with the opponent. The objective is to scoop the pot. That means pushing hands that can make both the best high and the best low, rather than getting trapped by calling along in situations where you figure to win just half the pot — and then only if you get lucky. That's not to say you should never play hands that can win in only one direction. After all, you might flop the best possible flush, a full house, or even four-of-a-kind in a hand with a bunch of opponents. Even if you split the pot with a low hand under these circumstances you're going to make money.

But most of the time you won't be lucky enough to flop a good hand. Much of the time you won't flop a real hand at all. You'll be drawing instead. Maybe it's a draw to the best possible straight or flush, or maybe you've flopped a big set and believe you need the board to pair so you'll beat the inevitable flush or straight that always seems to get there whenever you're in the pot.

When that happens, consider your pot odds. See how they stack up with the odds against making your hand, so you can decide whether to continue playing. Although you don't have the best hand at this juncture, there's a silver lining in that cloud, and here it is: If you fail to make your hand and don't improve, you're certainly not going to call a bet on the river. Since you're going to save that last bet on the river whenever you miss your hand, you're actually getting slightly better pot odds than any player with a made hand who is planning to bet on the river.

If you're playing Omaha high-only, these are simple issues, and they're the same ones you faced playing Texas hold'em. After all, if the pot is offering four dollars for each dollar you're required to wager, and the odds against making your hand are only 2-to-1, you're going to chase every time. But what if you're playing Omaha/8 and figure to win only half the pot if you do make your hand?

Suppose you can rake in a $500 pot for calling a $100 wager. That's a net profit of $400 (a total pot of five hundred dollars minus the $100 you invested by calling) and it's a good call if the odds against making your hand are only 2-to-1 or 3-to-1. But what if you're in an Omaha/8 game and figure to win only half the pot? When that happens, the dealer will push $250 dollars in your direction if you make the hand you're hoping for.

While the size of your win was just cut in half, the odds against making your hand remained the same. The cost to draw for half the pot was still $100, which was identical to the cost of drawing for the entire thing. Now your profit on that hand has been reduced from $400 to $150 (you'll receive a total of $250 but your investment was still $100, so your net profit now is only $150).

The odds have changed dramatically, since you've changed one side of the equation but not the other. Your profit has gone down dramatically, yet your costs have stayed the same. You'll see numerous instances in Omaha/8 where opponents are drawing for half the pot but the payoff doesn't even come close to offsetting the odds against making their hands. In the long run, plays like these bleed a player's bankroll away. Remember this when it's costly to draw to a low that might not get there and you've nothing at all for high.

In Omaha/8, scooping is the main strategic objective. While you won't scoop all that often, it's important to play hands that can scoop. And, of course, anytime you can play a hand offering a sure win of half the pot along with an opportunity — regardless of how long the odds may be against it — of winning the other half too, you've got a terrific situation, since you have a lock on one side of the pot and you're "freerolling" for the other half. Whenever you can draw to half the pot at no cost, you are, in essence, getting infinite odds. You just can't lose on bets like that!

Later on in the book we'll talk about how important it is to bet and raise at every opportunity whenever you've got a cinch high hand and there are two low cards on the board. You should make it as costly as possible for low draws to stick around trying to beat you. You're better off if they all fold right then and there so you're assured of capturing the entire pot, even though it's smaller than it would be if the low draws continued to play.

Raising either knocks them out or charges them the maximum price possible to stick around in hopes of capturing half the pot. But the time to do all that betting and raising is before the river card is dealt. Once that last card is out, none of the low draws will call your bet if they haven't made the hand they were hoping for.

Scooping is the name of the game in Omaha/8. We can't emphasize that enough. In fact, if all you retain from reading this book is the fact that Omaha/8 is a game of scoops and not a game of split pots, you'll have learned a very valuable lesson. Consequently, any strategy or tactical ploy that improves your chance of scooping is a good one, but anything you do that allows someone to draw for the low half of the pot inexpensively when you've locked up the high side is a poor play.

Discipline and Structure

Some poker players, like prodigies in many other fields, really do have a genius for the game, a talent that can't really be defined and usually has to be seen to be believed. After all, Mozart was composing symphonies by the time he was six or seven, and every couple of years you can pick up People Magazine and read a story about some 14-year-old who's about to graduate from Yale.

Don't take it personally, but we're assuming — at least where poker is concerned — that this isn't you. It isn't us, either. But even in the absence of genius, poker is a learnable skill, and it can be taught. Inherent ability helps, and although some innate talent is needed, you really don't need all that much. You don't have to be Mozart to play music, Picasso to paint, or Michael Jordan to play basketball.

What is needed is a solid plan for learning the game and the discipline to stick to it. Poker can be a gut-wrenching game. After you've lost a few stacks of chips to players who had the worst hands all the way but caught miracle cards to beat you at the very end, it's easy to lose all discipline and begin playing as poorly as your opponents.

We can tell you about discipline and why it's so critically important to winning poker, but only you can exercise it. When you're at the table, you're the one in charge of decisions. If you make them as someone who's lost all discipline, on tilt and over the edge emotionally from losing a few hands you were favored to win, there's nothing anyone can do about it except you. In poker, as in life itself, you're the master of your fate.

Some pundits are fond of saying that poker builds character. We're not so sure of that, but we're absolutely certain that poker reveals character. All the strategic knowledge in the world doesn't guarantee success. It's a precursor to success, since you certainly can't succeed without a surfeit of know-how. But personal characteristics are equally important.

Success at poker, as in most things, demands a certain quality of character. Players lacking self-discipline will seldom win consistently. A player who simply lacks the will to fold poor starting hands can never overcome that flaw, regardless of how much knowledge he may have. Without discipline, knowledge is merely unrealized potential, and that's simply another road to ruin.

Selective and Aggressive Play

Selective and aggressive play is what separates winning players from consistent losers. It's not the only thing, mind you — the poker toolbox is wide and varied — but there's not a single consistently winning player who doesn't practice this philosophy.

Unlike casino table games such as craps, roulette, and baccarat, where the odds are fixed and set so the house always has an edge, in poker the odds shift as cards are dealt off the deck. Winning players know when they have the best of it, and they're skilled at getting more money in the pot when conditions warrant it. By the same token, they're extremely reluctant to commit chips to the pot when the odds don't favor that kind of action.

For now, it's enough to know that you must be both aggressive and selective to win. Aggression and selectivity generally don't walk hand in hand, so it's important to realize when to come in with guns blazing and when to realize that discretion is the better part of valor. If you're too aggressive, particularly when your cards don't warrant it, your opponents will wait until they have better hands than yours, allow you to do their betting for them, then raise on later rounds to collect double bets when they have the best of it and you don't.If this sounds vague and abstract to you right now, have patience. Much of this book's content is designed to first show you how to identify situations where you have, or are likely to have, the best of it, then teach you how to manipulate those situations to your advantage.

If you're too passive, you won't win a sufficient amount of money on your good hands to overcome both your blind bets and those hands you lose to opponents during the course of play. Don't forget, aggressive players have two ways to win a hand: A bet or a raise might cause an opponent to fold a hand that would have wound up winning the pot had the hand been played to its conclusion.

On the other hand, passive play, such as checking and calling when a hand really warrants betting or raising, will take the pot only when the hands are shown down. While the advantages of aggressive play are obvious to most players, the equally important need for selectivity requires much consideration.

If you play every hand and also passively call every bet or raise as long as you have any hope whatsoever of winning a pot, you'll win every pot you're capable of winning. That's the good news. But playing in this manner will make you a long-term losing player in any poker game. That's the bad news. Remember, the objective of the game is to win money, not pots. Poker, as we'll continue to point out throughout this book, is a game of money played with cards; it's not a game of pots played with money.

According to poker expert Mike Caro, "In poker, you don't get paid to win pots. You get paid to make the right decisions." When you're playing Omaha, you'll have many more opportunities to make decisions than in some other poker games. You tend to play deeper into a hand than in hold'em or seven-card stud, so you'll have more information to evaluate. As a result, making consistently good decisions, especially early on in each hand before getting in too deep, is what separates winning players from contributors.

If you're playing correctly, you'll fold all weak starting hands. They're not worth your investment. But you should take command of the pot with your best hands. Every good player does this. There's no mystery to it. Poker is all about minimizing losses with weak hands, while maximizing money won with good ones.

If you're neither selective nor aggressive in your play, the best you could hope for as the cards tend to break closer and closer to even in the long run, would be a lifetime of breaking even. But even that actually translates into a lifelong loss, since you also have to overcome the cost of the rake or time charges. After all, the casino has to be paid for providing the game, the dealers, the cards, the chips, and the tables. Poker is like any other for-profit venture; you have to overcome your cost of doing business in order to make money. In Omaha, the way to do this is to play a selective, aggressive game.

Chapter 3

The Elements of Strategy

The Nature of the Game

We'll never know for sure, but it seems likely that Omaha was invented by hold'em players wanting better action. They figured that by giving each participant four starting cards instead of two, there'd be more combinations and bigger hands, leading to hotly contested pots with more participants. Also, with four cards to start with, players would be tempted to play many more hands. Whoever they were, those innovators were right on a couple of counts.

Hands tend to be bigger in Omaha, and there's certainly more action, because many participants find something worth playing in almost every hand they're dealt. After all, even the weakest Texas hold'em players have learned that hands like 9-3, 7-2, and a raft of others just can't be played profitably, and they've learned to release them. But you'll still find plenty of Omaha players happily entering pots with hands like K-Q-8-8, T-7-4-2, and a host of similar awful combinations.

Don't make their mistake of playing too many hands; it's the most common mistake recreational Omaha players make. You might be a great poker player at every later stage of the game, but if you aren't selective about choosing your starting hands carefully, you're doomed to failure. After all, only one hand can win the pot — or in the case of Omaha/8, two of them: a high hand and a low one. And you know what? Despite all the carping you'll hear at the table from people who figured to win the pot until the dreaded last card took it away from them, the best hand going in is more likely than not to be the best hand coming out. There are some exceptions to this, like when you've got a wraparound straight draw with 20 outs that's favored over hands currently better than yours, but we'll get to that later. For now, just remember this: Most of the time, best in equals best out.

The implications of this simple little statement are profound. It means you should throw away all but your better starting hands, and the sooner you do so, the better off you'll be. You'll be saving all the money you'd otherwise lose by making weak calls with bad hands.

Here's a fact little known to chronic losers: The more cards you're dealt in a specified poker game, the stricter your requirements must be for entering the pot with your starting hand. For example, it's a lot easier to find two-card combinations in Texas hold'em that work together well enough to be played before the flop than it is to find four coordinated starting cards that you can profitably play in Omaha. That's particularly true in Omaha/8. Nevertheless, time and time again you'll see clueless players entering pots with two big cards and two small ones, even if there's no synchronicity whatsoever between them. This folly will soon be yours to exploit.

We'll get into the details of hand selection later on in this book, and we'll provide guidelines to ensure that your starting hands are playable and profitable. But for now, realize you'll soon be able to profit from the fundamental error most of your opponents make: They simply enter too many pots with too many weak hands. So by playing fewer hands, and playing your good hands strongly, you'll have a significant, profitable edge.

Most winning players don't call many raises, even though they're the very players who are doing the raising a good deal of the time. How can that be? There are a couple of reasons:

Raising gives the aggressive player two ways to win: He may either have or improve to the best hand and win in a showdown, or his raise may cause the other players to release their hands. With a call, you're usually hoping to improve your hand so that it might win in a showdown. But if you raise, you could win the pot now, with nary another card to be dealt.

Raising also enables one to seize control of the hand and dictate the pace of play. If you've raised the flop, you might get to see the turn card for free, or you can go ahead and bet if you like your hand if all opponents check to you. If you raise the flop, you might get someone with a mediocre low draw to release his hand, and that might just enable you to scoop the pot later on.

So winning players make the most of the advantages gained by raising. But although they do a goodly share of raising themselves, they're careful about calling raises.

Remember: Whenever someone raises, he's announcing to the table that he's got a good hand. While a raise may be based on a bluff and nothing more, or just predicated on a strong draw, most of the time it signifies a good hand. So why would you call a likely premium hand with one not strong enough to beat most "good hands?"

As a general rule, unless you're on a draw for a low hand, straight, or flush, you ought to be betting or raising unless you've decided to fold.

The Flop Has to Fit Your Hand

In most forms of poker, your hand can be good right from the get-go. If you're a Texas hold'em player, you already know how strong a pocket pair of kings or aces can be. Those are hands that can win the pot even if they don't improve at all.

But that's not the case in Omaha/8. While it's always nice to have a pair of aces in your hand, don't count on winning anything with them in this game without some help. And where you get most of your help — if you get it — is on the flop. After all, you will have seen seven ninths, or seventy-seven percent, of your hand by the flop. There are only two more cards to come, so if you're not well on your way to making a hand you can be proud of, you should give up on the flop, regardless of how pretty your cards may have looked prior to that.

A critical skill in your development as an Omaha player involves examining the hand you're playing to determine the key card or cards you want on the flop. If you catch well, and the flop helps you, carefully consider what you want to do next. Maybe you'll decide to come out betting. Perhaps you'll check, with the intention of raising if an opponent bets into you. You'll have to make those decisions in the heat of battle, so think ahead as much as you can.

But if the flop misses your hand and fails to deliver the key cards you need, you should check and fold. You need a solid reason to continue playing once you've seen the flop, but very little reason to fold. Suppose you hold K-K-2-3. You're looking for an ace or a king. If you hold 6-4-3-2, you're looking for an ace, a five, and any other low card to flop. Hand/flop assessment is a relatively easy skill to master, but it's an important one. You should practice it with every hand you're dealt.

Flops that hit the bulls-eye on your wish list are easy to play, as are flops that miss your hand completely. You bet or raise at will on the former, fold on the latter. No mystery there. Then are those flops that help you, but only partway. Yes, we're referring to draws.

Much of the time you find the flop favorable, it will be because it provides you with one or more good draws rather than a made hand. But this can be a good thing. Premium hands offering a draw to the nuts have it all over hands that are lesser in value. If you've begun with A-2-3-K in your hand and two other low cards appear on the flop, you have a draw to the nut low with protection against being counterfeited if the board pairs one of your low cards. This is an excellent draw, and one usually worth pursuing.

Consider the difference between that hand and one like 7-6-4-2. It doesn't look so bad, does it? All that's missing from making this a top-notch hand is an ace in place of the seven. Many of your opponents will go ahead and play such a hand. But the absence of an ace will usually prove costly. What happens if both players make a low hand? The player with the nut low can and should be aggressive with it, particularly if he has a draw at the high end of the pot too. Meanwhile, the player without the ace in her hand is always forced to wonder whether she'll lose the low end of the pot to an A-2, and she may be playing without much hope for a high hand, either.

This kind of situation comes up frequently. Each player looks at his or her hand, notices one or more draws, and decides to play on. But the player holding the ace in his hand is more likely to make the nut (best possible) low hand than his ace-less opponent. If he completes his low, he can then bet or raise with the assurance that he has the winning low hand, while his rival is always left to wonder how her hand stacks up against the competition.

In addition, if the player with the ace has another card of the same suit to go along with it, he might even flop a nut flush draw to go along with the nut low draw. Now he has draws to the best hand in both directions and can put enormous pressure on his opponent through aggressive play. His opponent doesn't have this luxury. She's forced to either fold or just passively check and call, never sure until the showdown whether she'll win a portion of the pot or not. This twilight zone of uncertainty surrounding second-best (or worse) hands, a place that wreaks havoc on bankrolls, is exactly where you don't want to be in a split-pot game.

So in Omaha/8 you should be drawing to best possible hands — "the nuts" — most of the time. If you're drawing to less, it's frequently not worth your time and money to pursue the hand. That's particularly true for the low end of the pot, since someone often has the nut low at the river.

Look at it this way: If the board doesn't pair and a flush is the best possible hand, a king-high or queen-high flush will wind up winning the high end of the pot much more frequently than an A-3 or A-4 will win the low half. They are all the second and third best hands in the designated direction, but a nut low is much more likely to be present than a nut flush. Anyone holding an A-2 is likely to see the flop and then pursue the hand to the river as long as a low draw is available and hasn't been counterfeited. But not everyone holding a suited ace will see the flop — good players usually do so only when their two flush cards coordinate well with the other two cards in their hand.

A great hold'em hand does not a good omaha hand make

One of the major differences between Omaha/8 and Texas hold'em is that many good to excellent Texas hold'em hands are just drawing hands in Omaha/8. Not only that, but unless they're accompanied by a couple excellent low cards, many of hold'em's premium big pairs, like J-J through K-K, or even A-A, are but costly trap hands in Omaha/8. And any players new to Omaha don't even recognize that such large-pair hands are draws; in trying to apply what they've learned from hold'em, they see them as made hands.

Here's an example. Suppose you've flopped a set of queens and the board is Q-10-6-4-3. If you were playing hold'em, you'd be jumping for joy, and for good reason. Even though one of your opponents may have made a straight, it's pretty unlikely since the cards to complete that straight aren't often played in hold'em games.

But in Omaha/8 this is anything but a good hand. Even if that set of queens holds up, it will probably win only half the pot, since in all likelihood there will be a qualifying low hand when the river brings that third low card. Moreover, that same trey makes possible a seven-high straight, and the very cards that complete that straight are those favored by Omaha/8 players.

So to win the high half of the pot, a set of queens (or jacks or kings or even aces) frequently needs to grow into four-of-a-kind or a full house. Playing a set too optimistically is one of the first big traps encountered by players making the transition from Texas hold'em to Omaha/8. A set is a very strong hand in most hold'em games, and when it holds up, it wins the entire pot. But a set in Omaha/8 may be shooting at only half the pot, and often needs to improve to a full house or better in order to win at all. If all this seems strange to you because you're coming from hold'em to Omaha, just remember this: A big-pair premium hand in Texas hold'em is but a drawing hand that may win only half the pot in Omaha/8.

Play it Straight

The more opponents you encounter in a pot, the more straight-forward they're going to play — and so should you. In early position, with a large number of opponents yet to act, a bettor almost always has what he represents. The reason for this is self-evident: It's simply much more difficult to bluff five players than to scare off a single opponent. So with five opponents, and each player holding four cards that can be used to form six different two-card combinations, the flop is almost certainly going to be favorable to someone. So play straightforward poker against a large field of adversaries.

In fact, you should continue to play straightforward poker until you're a consistently winning player. Then, and only then, should you consider mixing up your play by occasionally trying for a check-raise, attempting a well-timed bluff against one or two opponents, and making other creative plays. But if you take our advice, you'll be playing straightforward poker most of the time.

When Good Hands Go Bad

If you've been playing Texas hold'em for any length of time, you're probably aware that some hold'em hands that start out strong generally remain strong — no matter which cards jump up on the flop. A pair of aces is certainly a hand in that category.

If you've been dealt the eye-popping pair, you're going to have a strong hand unless the flop announces possible trouble like three suited cards unmatched by one your aces, or three sequenced cards such as Q-J-10 that are right in the playing zone, or range of cards sought by most players to help their hands. But even with a scary flop, your aces may hold up if there's no appreciable action. After all, your opponents won't always have every straight or flush made possible by the board's alignment of cards. In hold'em, what's strong going in is very often strong going out, regardless of what comes on the flop.

But in Omaha/8, as you'll learn, regardless of how strong your starting cards may look, the flop is critical. Many a premium starting hand is ruined by an uncongenial flop. Let's look at a hand like A♣-A♠-2♠-3♣. They just don't get better than that in this game, and they don't come around too often, either. You've got a big pair toward high, with the possibility of flopping highest set; a three-card draw to the best possible low offering some counterfeit protection; and both your aces are suited so you can make the nut flush if the board manages to come up with three spades or three clubs.

But wait, you've just seen the flop and it's J♥-J♦-10♦, and you don't have a red card in your hand. Now there's a bet and several calls, and maybe even a raise. What should you do? That's easy. Fold. Sure, you've got two pair, aces and jacks. So what? This isn't Texas hold'em where two pair is usually a good hand and frequently a winner.

This is Omaha, and with nine cards to make a five-card hand, each opponent has a better chance to beat your two pair than he would in Texas hold'em, where he's limited to choosing the best five-card hand out of seven. Against a bunch of opponents, aces up is very unlikely to hold up as best hand. So you had A-A-3-2 double-suited. Better say goodbye to the pot, and do so quickly. Your possibilities for a low hand are dead. If there's a flush draw afoot, it's not in one of your suits, so your chances of making a flush are dead, too. Any seven, eight, nine, queen, or king may give someone a straight. (So could an ace, but you'd love that, since you'd have a huge full house.) Already, someone probably has made trips, at least, and a full house is also a good possibility. You'll make a larger full house if you stay past the flop and another ace falls, but drawing to two outs is a sure path to the poorhouse. So do yourself a favor and fold on this flop.

To paraphrase a country song, "Your good hand's gonna go bad." And bad it's gone. So we'll paraphrase another honky-tonk classic while we're at it: "Take these cards and shove 'em." Just bite the bullet and do it. Sticking around hoping for a miracle card is for losers. At this point, no matter how pretty those cards may have looked before the flop, they're history. The only sane thing to do is fold.

Yet there's a positive spin to all of this. In Omaha, you can see quite clearly when a flop has brought your hand to death's door. But in a Texas hold'em game, you can't be sure. Does your opponent have trip jacks, two pair, a big straight or flush draw, or is he bluffing with absolutely nothing at all? It's hard to tell. But in Omaha you can take it to the bank that your hand is doomed against several opponents unless the flop really fits. Throw it away now, with no regrets, no remorse, no second-guessing. It's just a good hand gone bad. That's all.

Controlling Your Emotions

If you're a recreational poker player who visits a casino or plays in a home game one or two days a week, there'll come a time when you'll get extremely frustrated following the tight but aggressive style of play we recommend.

After all, you came to play, not to throw away hand after hand. Playing the way we recommend is easy when you're receiving a relatively normal distribution of cards. Usually, you'll find enough decent starting hands to ensure that you'll enjoy your stay at the poker table. And when the deck is "...running over you," as poker players like to say, most of your hands will be playable — and you'll win your share of pots.

But you'll have days at the table when you're dealt miserably unplayable hands one right after another. When that happens, you'll find yourself throwing hands away for hours on end without a respite. Sometimes it will seem like the only hands you get to play are when you're in the blind — and then only if the pot isn't raised by one of your opponents.

Right around then, you'll face the enormous temptation to lower your starting standards. Many hands you'd routinely throw away when you're dealt a normal distribution of starting hands will begin to look better and better as your run of miserable cards goes on. This is when it's more important than ever to adhere to the standards we've given you, and not give in simply because playing is more fun than throwing away all those weak hands.

Playing is more fun. We know that. That's why you came to the cardroom. You certainly didn't come to throw away hands and watch your opponents duke it out for the money in the pot. But that's exactly what you'll have to do much of the time.

In essence, the choice is simple. You can begin softening up your starting standards and have a lot more fun playing, though the fun is likely to be reduced by the amount of money you'll probably lose, or you can adhere to the starting standards we provide later in this book, hold onto your money, and enter pots only when you have cards that warrant an investment.   It's your choice. But we've learned that winning more money — though playing fewer hands when the cards just aren't cooperating — is much more fun than squandering a bankroll on poor hands that figure to win pots only through sheer luck.

Omaha Poker Is a Game of Patience

All poker games require patience. Players who play too many hands — and you'll find quite a few Omaha/8 players, particularly in games with lower betting limits, who play virtually every hand — can never win money in the long run. Asking for patience on your part is nothing more than emphasizing the "be selective" part of our "Be selective, be aggressive" mantra.

Because you have four starting cards in your hand, representing six unique two-card combinations, you should play hands in which all four are coordinated in some meaningful way. Many of your opponents will be playing hands that include danglers, misfit cards that add little to a hand. Suppose you've been dealt Q-J-T-3. The three ten-pointers are components of a playable hand, but the trey is almost useless. You've got a three-legged stool with a dangler. Now, three legs might suffice if you were milking a cow, but they're not good enough to milk money from an Omaha pot.

When a card like that orphan trey fails to work in concert with any of the other cards in your hand, it's much as if you were playing only three cards against four for your opponent. Guess what? With four cards in his hand he has six potential starting combinations, presuming those cards all work in concert with one another. But by starting with only three effective cards, you've whittled yourself down to just three potential starting combinations. By sitting on a three-legged stool instead of a four-legged chair, you've cut your starting combinations in half.

Think of that classic scene from the first Indiana Jones movie, the one where Jones' adversary takes out a sword, brandishes it menacingly, then swings it through the air a few times. Finally he charges Indy, who shrugs, casually withdraws a pistol from his holster, and shoots the swordsman before he can even get into thrusting range. When your opponent's four starting cards are coordinated but you choose to play only three coordinated cards plus a dangler, he'll have the same kind of edge.

Yes, sometimes you can play danglers and get away with it. But those occasions are in pots that haven't been raised, when you're either on or next to the button, and your other three cards are really strong. But that's it. And while you're learning the game, if you simply refrain from playing danglers altogether, you won't be missing out on much.

Patience in Omaha/8 means becoming a bit of an extremist. You'll play hands at both the big and small edges of the spectrum, but if you're playing correctly you'll throw away hands in the middle range. Imagine Omaha/8 as though it were a game with the sevens, eights, and nines removed from the deck, and that you'll play only cards dealt from that smaller but vastly improved pool. If you can hold that image in your mind, you'll do OK in the long run.

Patience also requires that you avoid hands that look good but usually spell trouble. Suppose you're dealt a hand like 9-9-8-8 double-suited. Two-pair hands always look pretty, particularly when double-suited, and you don't get them often, but this hand will kill you in Omaha/8. If you make a set of eights, there's already a low card (an eight) on the board, which increases the likelihood that someone will make a low hand and take away half the pot. And if you flop a nine on a board of only high cards, you run the risk of running into a bigger set, a straight, or a big wrap-around straight draw. Moreover, a higher flush can beat you if you happen to hit one of your suits along with your set. This can be a very costly trap hand: Consider yourself warned.

Play patiently, and don't play hands that include the dreaded seven, eight, or nine. While you'll win some of the time with those cards — actually, you'll win some of the time with any cards — in the long run you'll bleed to death at the table. Be selective, be patient, and, in Omaha/8, throw those problematic mid-range cards away.

Check Your Ego at the Door

This may seem to counter some of what we've already told you, but, trust us, it really doesn't. Some of your opponents will be playing a lot more hands than we're recommending to you. In low-limit games, some players play each and every hand they're dealt, as though it were required of them. If so, they'll win a relatively large number of pots. But remember, poker is about winning money, not pots.

The loose players will almost certainly win more pots than you do. And in so doing, they'll occasionally beat you out of pots you figured to win. In most cases, you'll have the better starting hand, and you may be ahead on the flop and the turn as well, only to find yourself run down at the river when your opponent catches a miracle card.

Even after you've read this book, learned its concepts, and applied your new knowledge, you still may become frustrated when a poor player with inferior cards beats you out of a pot that had your name all over it until the very end. It's a slap to your ego, but you'll have to learn to deal with it. In poker — particularly in a game like Omaha/8 where players enter pots with all sorts of raggedy hands — you'll lose to long shot draws some of the time. As a result, you'll need to check your ego at the door.

Your opponents are taking by far the worst of it by entering pots with poor hands, but every now and then they'll win hands they really shouldn't have played. Even the worst dogs from the deck win every once in a while. If a few of your premium hands lose to lucky underdogs, don't get upset and allow the lost pots to throw you off your game.

If you do go on tilt this way, you'll find yourself playing down to your opponents' level, or even playing below it. Face it. Poor players will draw out on you; it's the nature of poker. If they never got lucky, they'd simply cease coming to the casino. Then you'd be facing only adversaries who really know how to play, and how would you like them apples?

Poker is a game in which skill always wins out, but only in the long run. In the short run, even the best of the very best will have days when nothing at all goes right. Poker is full of short-term luck, though in the long run, when all the variance in cards and fortune is bled out of the equation, the good players will beat the poor ones. This is what makes poker such an attractive game. Even really weak players win some of the time, and they occasionally experience some pretty extended runs of good luck. That's what keeps them coming back time and time again.

It's not that way in other sports. You're not going to beat Tiger Woods over 72 holes even on his worst days; you won't get the better of Michael Jordan in a game of one-on-one; nor would you stand much of a chance going mano-a-mano against Lennox Lewis. And if you were to play chess against Kasparov, you'd be toast. But you can beat up a table full of great poker players in the short run, even though they figure to carve you up over the long haul. So if you have an edge — and you will if you pay attention to the information in this book and integrate it into your Omaha game — don't throw it away simply because your ego has temporarily gotten the better of you.

Most poker players have egos. Big ones, in fact. But the better players keep their egos in check and out of the game. If it helps, think of your ego as a gun. You've just ridden into town and Wyatt Earp sidles up to you saying that you'll have to check your firearm at the Marshal's office until you're ready to get out of Dodge. Unless you're very, very good or your judgment is very, very poor, that's exactly what you'll do. And while you're at it, ask Wyatt if you can check your ego too. That'll give you a much better chance when you sit down to a poker game with his good buddy and sidekick, Doc Holliday.

Poker Is a Long-Running Game

If you want to think of poker as something like a sporting event, imagine a baseball game with about 3,000 innings instead of nine. If that were the case, you wouldn't be too concerned if your team was outscored 11-0 over the course of any nine-inning stretch, as long as it performed well enough to win in the long run.

That's what Omaha and every other form of poker is about. It's a very long game. So if you made the very best decisions you could at the table today but lost money nevertheless, there's no need to worry about it, or berate yourself, or think about what you might have done differently. Any time there's a turn of a card involved, you have a game with an element of luck, and in the case of poker it takes a pretty long time for that luck factor to filter out. But over the long run, solid play translates into solid profits. Only then can someone look at his results and state with some degree of certainty that his achievement is the result of skill and skill alone.

All you can do in the short run is to be very selective about the games you decide to play in, and then make the very best decisions you can. If the cards fall your way, you'll win because you were lucky and made good decisions. If the cards are neutral, you'll win because you made better decisions than your opponents. If the cards fall against you, you'll lose because short-term luck overcame the quality of choices you made at the table — and there's nothing you can do about that.

Nevertheless, that's no reason to skip reviewing the decisions you made during each session. Try to isolate any mistakes you made, then apply what you've learned from them. Learning to become a better poker player requires a cyclical process of reading and studying the game, playing poker to put the concepts you've read about into practice at the table, and then reviewing your actions to determine where you might have erred and how you might correct those mistakes the next time out.

If you aspire to become a winning player, realize that all you have control over is the quality of decisions you make at the poker table. Many of your opponents will blame and even berate the dealer for a run of bad cards. Some bemoan their fate, complaining that they, of all people in the universe, have the worst luck of all. That's nonsense. You know it and we know it. And they probably know it too. But for many players, it's easier to place the blame anywhere but squarely on their own shoulders, where it rightfully belongs.

Such players are probably too focused on short-term results. They want to make every session a winning one. It's one thing to want to win every time out. No one likes losing at poker. We certainly don't. It's a blow to the bankroll and to our egos and pride. But better players realize that no one wins all the time, and they've also learned that poker is really a 3,000-inning ball game. What happens today is not nearly as important as the score at the end of the year, or the year after that.

We can harp on the need for the long-term view until the cows come home, but understanding that need intellectually and putting it into practice are two entirely different things. Emotions often get in the way, causing players to play too loosely and too aggressively when on tilt, or to play when tired in an effort to get even. All too often, a small loss snowballs into a nightmare session because a player has temporarily forsaken the long-range view. While it's essential to realize that a lifetime of poker is but one very long game, consistent application of that realization is even more essential, and far more difficult. You know that now. But from this moment on, all you need do is put the long-term view into practice each and every time you play.

This attitude is totally within your control. We can't make it happen for you. No one else can. You're the only one who can achieve it. Because maintaining the right attitude and discipline is solely within your power, it's simultaneously the easiest and most difficult thing you'll need to accomplish to become a winning Omaha player. Once you learn the skills and techniques to become a good Omaha player and have some experience under your belt, you'll have a couple of legs up on most of your opponents. (If you don't, you might want to find an easier game.) But it's the discipline to realize that Omaha is a long-running game that often separates winning players from those who know just as much about the game but fail to maintain discipline and a sense of perspective at the table.

If it helps, you might want to imagine that you're playing on our money and that we're standing behind you and watching everything you do at the table. We'll continue to pay you to play poker as long as you make good decisions, but we'll sack you immediately if your discipline and decision-making falter. We don't care whether you win today, this week, or even this month. Play well and you stay on the payroll. Play poorly and you're out of a job. How's that? Do we have a deal?

It sounds like it's easy to do, but it's not. There's a lot of emotion in poker, and you'll probably have to work long and hard to keep your emotions, ego, and pride from pulling you off course. But the choice is yours. You can do it if you want to. Anyone can.

Chapter 4

Poker Etiquette and Rules of the Road

Poker rules and etiquette help speed the game along and keep it orderly, not to mention more enjoyable, so poker etiquette is as much a part of the game as the cards themselves. In fact, when you play Omaha in a casino for the first time, poker etiquette is likely to take as much getting used to as the game itself.

It's unfortunate but true that you'll find a few players willfully flaunting all of poker's unwritten rules, as well as some of the written ones. But these players are regarded by their peers as boorish at best, "angle-shooters" at worst, and they won't make many friends among their opponents. You wouldn't emulate boorish behavior away from the poker table, so don't take your cues from the bad apples. Forget about them. They're jerks — grown adults who ought to know better, but for some reason have not only chosen to be ignorant, but to act proud of that ignorance to boot.

Act In Turn

Each player should act in turn as play proceeds clockwise around the table. If someone bets and you plan to fold, please wait until it's your turn to act. Acting out of turn can give a big advantage to one of your opponents. If he knows you're planning to fold your hand, it makes it easier for him to bluff, and that's unfair to the rest of the players. In poker, as in most of life, it's considered polite to wait your turn.

Keep Your Cards In Plain Sight

In order to maintain the integrity of the game, players should keep their cards on the table during a hand. The best way to look at the cards you've been dealt is to shield them with your hands, then lift a corner of each card to peek at it. It's customary to leave your cards on the table after looking at them, and to then place a chip — or a small lucky charm — on top of them.

This alerts the dealer that your hand is still in play. If you need to look at your cards again during the play of the hand, that's OK, just take another peek. But you should train yourself to look at your cards only once and remember them while a hand is being contested. That gives you more time to study your opponents, and gives your opponents far less time to scrutinize you.

Discussing Hands In Play

Discussing your hand with others, even if you've tossed your cards into the muck and are no longer involved in the hand, may provide information that would give another player unfair advantage. If you want to discuss a hand with a neighbor, wait until the hand is concluded. During WW II folks would say, "Loose lips sink ships," and they still can sink poker hands.

Turn Your Hand Face Up At The Showdown

If you're not sure whether you have the best hand or not, turn your cards face up at the showdown and allow the dealer to read your hand. If there is doubt or debate, even if the hand is over, casino security cameras can review the hands that were shown down in order to determine the winner.

Once cards have been turned over at the showdown, it's considered good form to point out a hand that the dealer may have overlooked. Omaha hands can be confusing, so if you see a winning hand that the dealer overlooked, go ahead and mention it. Because "cards speak" in casino poker, it's considered proper to point out the best hands, and not permit a pot to be awarded to the wrong player simply because the dealer overlooked a winning hand.

One interesting though inexplicable phenomenon at the Omaha table is that many players don't turn their hands face-up at a hand's conclusion, preferring instead to read the board and turn a hand face up only if it's a better hand — high or low — than the other exposed hands. Players occasionally misread their hands — yes, sometimes even experts do this — and when that happens a winning hand can be tossed in the muck. Unless you're purposefully trying to disguise your play and don't want others to get a read on it, please turn your cards face up at the showdown and let the dealer and other players read your hand.

To make it easier for the dealer and your opponents to read your hand, put the two cards of your winning hand together, slightly separated from your two inconsequential cards. This is good poker etiquette and will help keep the dealer from misreading your hand and mucking a winner. If that unfortunate event should befall you, you'll need a floor decision, confirmation from other players, and perhaps a review of the hand on the casino's security tapes before you can get the pot or the portion of it you've rightfully earned.

Table Stakes

"Table Stakes" means that you can't add chips or money to the amount in front of you during the play of the hand. If you run out of money during a hand, you're said to be all-in, and you can contest only the portion of the pot that your bets cover. If there are active opponents who still have chips in front of them, they'll be betting into a "side pot" that you have no investment in. But you'll be eligible for the main pot, and once the hand is over, you can reach into your wallet and buy as many more chips as you'd like.

Toking

We're not just blowing smoke, but "toking" the dealer — poker parlance for tipping — is customary when you win a pot. Tokes constitute a significant part of a dealer's income. The size of the pot and the game's betting limits generally determine the amount of the toke. If you're new to the game, take your toking cue from other players at the table.

Playing In a Casino

Casino poker differs from poker at home, and there are many reasons to play in a public cardroom. First, and probably foremost, is that there's always a game. You'll generally have a choice of games, and most of them are available twenty-four hours a day, seven days a week.

Then there's the safety factor. Casinos are safe. They provide professional dealers, floor supervisors, and video security to ensure that games are run squarely. Because people walk around with large sums of money, there are more security guards than you'd find in most banks. Parking lots are brightly lit and well patrolled. Player banks, safety deposit boxes, check cashing, casino credit, and ATM machines eliminate the need to walk around with large amounts of cash.

Moreover, there's never any pressure to stay. Nobody minds if you quit the game because someone else is usually waiting for your seat. You do, however, have to pay to play. It costs more to play in a casino than in a home game, where all you have to do is split the cost of food and drinks.

Five Good Reasons to Play Omaha in a Casino

If you've never played Omaha in a casino, and you're thinking about giving it a shot, here are some reasons why it's a good idea:	• There's no pressure to stay. You can play when and where you please, for as long as you like.

If you've never played Omaha in a casino, and you're thinking about giving it a shot, here are some reasons why it's a good idea:

• There's usually a game, or even a choice of games, any time you want to play — day or night. And every game is on the up and up.

• Casinos are safe. They provide video security, well-lit parking lots, security guards, and safe deposit boxes and players' banks that eliminate the need to walk around with large sums of money.

• There's no pressure to stay. You can play when and where you please, for as long as you like.

• There's a social aspect to even the toughest of games: Rich, poor, young, old, students, business execs, housewives, people of every race, color, and creed — everyone plays poker.

• By playing in regular games, you can become a skilled player and you have a hobby that pays. Most hobbies cost money, but many people earn money playing poker. You can too.

Avoid Making A String-Raise

Calling a bet, then reaching back for more chips and announcing a raise, is called a string-raise, and it's not permitted. If you do this, one of your opponents will probably shout "String-raise!" The dealer will then inform you that a string-raise just occurred, and you'll have to take your raise back and simply call. The rule against a string-raise prevents players from first reading the reactions of opponents to the movement of chips, then deciding to raise if they think they've got the best of it.

Raising Made Simple

If you want to raise, it's easy. Just say, "Raise." Then you can go back to your stack and count out the proper amount of chips. If you'd prefer to let your action announce your intention, you must put the correct amount of chips into the pot in just one unambiguous motion.

Don't Splash the Pot

Don't "splash the pot" by tossing chips into the center of the table where they're likely to mingle with those already in the pot. Instead, stack your chips neatly on the table about eighteen inches in front of you. The dealer will pull them into the pot when the action has been completed on that round of betting.

Some casinos have added "betting circles" to the green felt. A betting circle is an oval line that mirrors the contours of the table and is stenciled on the felt about twelve inches in front of each player. Once you move your chips across that line, it's a bet. When you're playing at a table that has a betting circle, just place your bets and raises either right on or just inside the line of the betting circle directly in front of you. There they will stand visibly alone, well apart from both the pot and any other bets and raises from that betting round. Adhering to these guidelines will avoid confusion and the arguments that inevitably ensue, and make for a faster paced, well-run game.

If you've never played in a casino before, tell the dealer so he can help you through the mechanics of the game. After a few sessions, you'll feel comfortable and you'll be familiar with the majority of playing procedures. Then you'll not only feel like a regular, you'll be one.

Protect Your Hand

In a casino, you're always responsible for your hand. If you're a boxing fan, you know that the referee always tells the fighters to protect themselves at all times. It's the last and most important admonition given each fighter before the match begins. Poker is similar. Protect your hand at all times. That means ensuring that the dealer doesn't inadvertently sweep it into the muck, and that cards folded by other players don't foul your hand by mixing with your own cards. The best way to prevent these mishaps is to place a chip or other small object atop your cards.

Also, shield your hand from the eyes of other players. Many players don't realize that they inadvertently expose their cards almost every time they look at them. Practice with a buddy until you can look at your cards quickly and easily without revealing them to someone sitting next to you. While the dealer and the rules are there to make things fair and to protect all the players, you are your own first and last line of defense.

If you toss your hand toward the muck and it's thereby *fouled* by touching the discards, it can't win. If you don't know whether or not you hold the winning hand — and when you first begin to play Omaha, there will be times when you won't be sure how your hand stacks up at the showdown — simply turn it face up and let the dealer read your hand. Remember that although cards speak, they can't speak at all if their faces aren't showing. Dealers are only human and sometimes make mistakes. If you think yours is the best hand, turn your cards face up and announce it. Place it halfway between your chips and the pot, and hold on to it firmly on the edges with your fingers while the dealer determines the outcome to your satisfaction. Only then should you release your hand.

Time Out

Anytime you're unsure of anything, your best course of action is to call "Time!" This freezes the action and allows your questions to be resolved before you have to act. But please don't abuse this privilege, particularly if you're in a game where the players are charged by the half-hour. It's not as cardinal a sin in a raked game, but players usually want fast, efficiently run poker, with as few interruptions as possible.

Decks And Dealing

Dealers — and decks — are generally rotated every half-hour. In addition, some players are prone to holler, "Deck change," because they're unhappy with their run of cards. This is silly, because the cards don't know whether you're winning or not, and even if they did, why would they care? Neither of your authors, who have more than 60 years of playing experience between them, recalls asking for a deck change for any reason other than to replace a clearly damaged card. You shouldn't ask for deck changes either, because all it does is slow down the game. Besides, decks are generally rotated when there's a dealer change.

Shuffling And Dealing

Shuffling procedures are much more rigorous in a casino or public cardroom than they are in home games with amateur dealers. The idea is to ensure as random a deal as possible. Home game players are usually unfamiliar with the mechanics of a good shuffle and most lack the manual dexterity to perform one.

Well-trained casino dealers assemble the deck so that the cards face the players, frequently scrambling the cards on the table beforehand. Next comes a four-step procedure of shuffle, shuffle, riffle, and shuffle. Finally, the dealer cuts the deck and deals. It's efficient, quick, and no cards are flashed in the process.

The ability to shuffle thoroughly and deal effectively is a skill. The fact that someone has been playing poker for years doesn't make him or her a good or even barely adequate dealer. Your authors are both experienced players, but you wouldn't want anyone with our inadequate skill level shuffling the cards and pitching them to you. Trust us; neither would we.

How To Get In A Game

When you enter a cardroom, you may see a white board full of players' initials. These initials are listed under available games. For example, if you walk into a large casino you might find seven players ahead of you waiting for a $2-$4 Omaha game. Just give your initials to the board attendant and indicate the games you want to be listed for. You might say: "My initials are ABC. Please put me up for the $2-$4, $3-$6, and $4-$8 Omaha high-low split games."

It's no more complicated than taking a number at Ben and Jerry's. Your initials go up on the board for each game you request, and you're called as seats become available. If the board for a particular game is so long that the club can start another, the attendant will announce that game, calling players in the order listed. When you hear your initials, go to the table and grab a vacant seat. You're in the game.

Some cardrooms don't use a board. Just give your initials or first name to the attendant and state the games and limits you want to play. In small cardrooms, where there are only one or two tables, ask the dealer if a seat is available or if there is a waiting list for the game.

Buying Chips

When you first sit in the game, either the floorperson or the dealer will ask you how much you want in chips. Give him your money and you'll get your chips. Large casinos have chip attendants. One of them will take your money while making an announcement to the table like, "Seat 5 (or whatever seat you occupy) is playing $200 behind." That means you bought in for $200, and the casino is in the process of fetching your chips. You can play that hand, even though your chips haven't arrived yet. The dealer will either lend you some chips or just keep count of how much you owe the pot. Meanwhile, your chips will probably arrive before that first hand is played to its conclusion.

What Will Your Opponents Be Like?

The kinds of players sitting at your table will vary depending on the betting limits you play. In low-limit games, you'll be playing mostly against recreational players.

Recreational players love to play poker, and they play for the fun of it. It's simply a hobby, and no matter how much they lose, it's less expensive than keeping horses, restoring classic automobiles, or a hundred other money-eating pastimes. If you integrate the lessons in this book into your game, you'll soon be superior to the vast majority of recreational players because most of them — regardless of how many years they've been playing poker — will have neither your knowledge base nor the know-how to use and apply it.

Everyday regulars are a cut above casual recreational players, and come in a wide variety of shapes and sizes. They include retirees, housewives, students, people with no fixed job hours, dealers who are playing before or after their shift, and almost anyone else you can imagine. Some regulars have independent sources of income and often play in big games. Some regulars play well. Others don't, but they do play on a regular basis and have probably learned something about the game, if only by osmosis. You, on the other hand, will know more about Omaha than they do by the time you finish this book. Nevertheless, you're still in spring training and will need some time to adjust to this entirely new environment. So give the edge to the regulars, but only for a month or so. Once you round into playing shape, you figure to have the best of it by virtue of your knowledge and discipline.

Professionals and semi-professionals can be found in most of the larger games, but if you're playing in low-limit games — at betting limits below $10-$20 — you're unlikely to find pros in your game. Although the games are generally easier at lower betting limits, a professional poker player just can't earn a living in a $2-$4 or $4-$8 game. In these lower limit games, you'll be competing with regulars and recreational players, not professionals. But when you graduate to the higher limits you can expect to encounter some players who earn all or part of their living playing poker.

A proposition player, or prop, plays on his or her own money but receives a salary from the house to help start or "prop up" certain games. You'll typically find props late at night when the club is trying to keep games going, or early in the morning when it's trying to start them for the day.

A prop's life can be tough. Playing in short-handed games, or games struggling to get off the ground, isn't always a bed of roses. The minute a live player wants his seat, the house pulls the prop from it — often when the game is just starting to bear fruit. Props typically play better than most regulars, but not as well as top players. Their defining characteristic is that they tend to be conservative.

There's no reason to feel outgunned at the thought of a prop in your game. Since the casino pays the prop, players often believe the prop has a big advantage. But that's just not true. Props play on their own money, and as long as they're reliable and maintain their playing bankrolls, the house cares not one whit whether they win or lose. I suspect that, given a choice, any cardroom would prefer to employ a weak player as a prop rather than a good one, simply because a weaker player will be a bigger draw.

In fact, the ideal prop would be a poor player with a winning personality, the face and figure of Marilyn Monroe, and an unlimited bankroll. But the first time you encounter a prop, you're more likely to see a semi-retired, pale, and personable fellow with a slight paunch who loves poker, plays a tight, controlled game, and hates losing money. He may win a little or — less often, a lot — but he's unlikely to lose much.

The first few times you play in a casino, the speed of the games may startle you. And you may think that the players there play better than your home game cronies. But after becoming familiar with the environment, you'll find that your skill level is right up there with that of your opponents, if not beyond it. Most of your casino adversaries are not students of the game. Many are recreational players who just want to have fun. Even most of the regulars, who run the gamut of skill levels, seldom bother to study the game. Though many of them have been playing in cardrooms for years, they simply repeat and reinforce the same errors they've been making for decades.

Therefore, don't worry too much about the skill level of your opponents when you first begin playing in a public cardroom. By studying and playing the game you should soon catch the field. Mind you, if you live in an area where poker has only recently been legalized, you probably don't have any catching up to do at all. You can start ahead of the crowd and never look back. Think of yourself as a wire-to-wire winner. Your opponents may improve slowly, simply through osmosis. But through frequent play and study, you'll be improving at a much more rapid rate.

Part 2:

Advanced Strategy

Chapter 5

Outs 'n' Odds

Omaha, like every form of poker, is bounded by mathematical parameters governing how often you'll make the
hands you draw to, and how often your made hands will
hold up against those drawing to bigger hands than yours. The
certainty with which these theoretical mathematical expectancies
— or probabilities — will occur depends on how long a view we
take. During one session, you might make every draw and have
a big win as a result. On another day the force might not be with
you at all, while all your opponents get lucky and catch the cards
they need to beat you on the river.

A Little Probability, Please

But over the long haul, the laws of probability tell us that your
results ought to come pretty close to mirroring mathematical
expectation. In other words, if you play properly, and make the
right decisions, in Omaha — as in other forms of poker and in
life itself — you figure to be rewarded in proportion to the quality
of decisions and choices you make.

One of the major differences between Omaha and Texas
hold'em is that more information is available to you in Omaha,
and while that may make it a bit easier to reach a decision in a
game of Omaha/8, the impact of a wrong decision is likely to be
more costly. Because of the large number of possible hands to
be formed from the five community cards and the four cards in
each player's hand, it's critical to be able to size up how well
your hand stacks up against hands your opponents might be
playing.

If you're chasing the low end of the pot with a deuce and a trey
in your hand, don't be shocked if one of your opponents shows
up with ace-trey, and another with ace-deuce. After all, you were
chasing with the third best possible low, not the best one, and
that's not the way to win at this game. Likewise, if you've made

the best possible flush but the board contains a pair, you shouldn't be surprised to see one of your opponents turn up a full house, or even four-of-a-kind. While that happens in Texas hold'em, it doesn't happen often enough to substantially diminish the value of a flush. Omaha is different. Better accept this right now: Once the board pairs in Omaha, your straight or flush is very likely to cost you money.

There's no need for dismay, however, since a silver lining can be found in this dark cloud. That silver lining lies in knowing what your chances are of winning the pot, then manipulating the size of that pot by betting and raising accordingly. But you can't do that without knowing at least a little something about your chances of succeeding. And that means — dare we say it? — knowing just a little about probability and statistics.

Flush With Success

Here's an example. Suppose the turn card gives you the best possible flush, no cards are paired on the board, your opponent has flopped a set, and there's one more card to come. If you assume that you'll win if the board doesn't pair, but that you'll lose to a full house or quads if it does, you can count your outs with certainty.

At this point there are 40 unknown cards. Ten of them will pair the board and allow your opponent to win the pot. Yet 30 of those unknown cards will not pair the board and you'll be the one raking in the chips. In the long run, you figure to win this kind of confrontation three times out of four.

When you have the best of it and figure to win a given hand most of the time, your best strategy is to build the pot before the river. While that last river card will determine the winner, it will also constrain the betting. The time to get more money in the pot is when there's still good reason for anyone with a drawing hand — and a set is a drawing hand in Omaha, particularly when there are three suited cards on board — to stick around and pay you off, chasing that draw for a win.

While the winning hand in Omaha is frequently determined on the river, it's the preparation for the river that determines the size of the pot. Winning at Omaha requires the skilled player to manipulate the size of the pot to the best of his ability. But when? And how? To do this successfully means getting more money in the pot and driving it with the best hand. It also means playing on the cheap when you don't. Because the nuts are so common in Omaha, made hands that are the nuts and quality draws to the best hand can drive the betting in a way that non-nut hands never can.

Straightening Things Out

If you've been playing Texas hold'em and are now learning to play Omaha, the potential of straight draws is one area where the difference between the games is incredibly dramatic. In fact, some Omaha straight draws are so powerful that they're mathematically favored over made hands in many situations.

In hold'em, if you have Q-J in your hand and the board is 10-9-4, you've flopped an open-ended straight draw, and either a king or an eight will complete your hand. Since there are four kings and four eights, you have eight outs. But in Omaha, a straight draw with only eight outs is dwarfed by many other straight draw possibilities. Take a look at these:

Suppose you hold 9-8-7-6 and the flop is 10-5-4. Here are the cards that will complete your straight: 4 threes, 3 sixes, 3 sevens, 3 eights. That's thirteen outs. But wait. It gets better than that:

Perhaps you hold 8-6-4-2 and the flop is Q-7-5. You can complete your straight with any of 4 nines, 3 eights, 3 sixes, 3 fours, and 4 threes. Now you've got 17 outs. But there's more.

Let's say you're holding 10-8-6-5 and the flop is 9-7-4. Now you can make a straight with any one of these cards: 4 Jacks, 3 tens, 3 eights, 3 sixes, 3 fives, and 4 threes. That's a total of 20 outs. How good are 20 outs? If you flop a draw with 20 outs, you'll complete your straight by the river an astonishing 70 percent of the time! That makes you a big favorite over any smaller made hand.

But here's a note of caution before you get too carried away: Having a large number of outs, whether it's 13, 17, or 20, doesn't necessarily mean you'll win the hand. It's possible that a card completing your straight draw might result in a bigger straight for an opponent. For example, with the 20-out straight draw given above, not all outs yield the nut straight for the given board. And other things can go wrong: If the straight card you need puts three cards of one suit on board, chances that an opponent has made a flush are now a real possibility. And if you make your straight but the board pairs in the process, you might be looking at a full house or better.

You can make the nut straight in Omaha/8 and still win only half the pot, but in Omaha high-only, the nut straight wins all the marbles as long as the board doesn't pair, and a flush card doesn't appear on the river. (Of course, in Omaha/8, if there's only one low card — or none — by the turn, the hand will play for high only, with no low possible, and the wraparound straight draw will prove as powerful here as in Omaha high-only.)As you can see from all this, there's a big difference between "outs to your hand," and "outs to the nuts." Outs to the nuts are far more important, particularly when you've got a one-way hand and figure to win only half the pot at best. In Omaha high-only, these big wraparound straight draws are often much more potent than they are in Omaha/8. That's because in Omaha/8 the card that makes your straight might also provide the nut low to another player, effectively cutting your pot in half.

Let's look at another example: Suppose you've got A-8-7-2 of mixed suits and the board is 6-5-3. You've flopped the best possible low, and any card except an ace or deuce will protect your low hand. You'd love to see a four or a nine, because either would give you a straight and a terrific chance to scoop the pot. But even if you get lucky and make a straight on the turn, a seven on the river might just make someone a bigger straight and cost you half the pot.

These kinds of things happen all the time in Omaha, but in this case, there is something you can do about it. If you flop the nut low and make the highest possible straight on the turn, you're essentially free rolling in at least one direction. In this situation, you must bet or raise all you can, getting every possible dollar into the pot. The idea is to charge your opponents handsomely for the right to stick around hoping to get lucky.

Now let's put some of this information about straight draws into perspective. It's easier to grasp that way.

- Just like in a war, you're much better off when you can surround your enemy. The number of possible straights is higher if you have the flop surrounded by possessing the cards not only immediately above but immediately below the flop. In one example given earlier, we had 9-8-7-6 when the board showed 10-5-4. We didn't have the board surrounded, and had a 13-out straight.

- If you have 9-8-5-4 and the flop is 7-6-2, you have a wrap-around straight draw going into the turn, with 4 tens, 3 nines, 3 eights, 3 fives, 3 fours, and 4 threes available to complete your straight, for a total of 20 outs. Wraps, particularly when you're playing Omaha high-only — where you won't have to split the pot with a low hand if you make your straight draw — are incredibly good gambling opportunities. Not only are you an odds-on favorite to complete your straight, but if your opponent has two pair or a set, you stand a good chance of getting a lot of money into a pot you're favored to win.

- All else being equal, you're much better off if your straight draw contains cards higher in rank than those of the flop. While it won't increase your number of outs, you figure to have the nut straight when you hit one. In the example above, where you have 9-8-5-4 and the flop is 7-6-2, if an eight comes, you'll complete your straight, but there's always a chance that one of your opponents will make a bigger straight with a 10-9 in his hand, and that will cost you some chips.

- Another advantage of having bigger cards in your hand than the cards on the board is that you might make one straight along with a draw to an even bigger one. If that's the case, and an opponent has the same straight you do on the turn, you might get lucky and make a bigger one on the river. You are, as poker players like to say, "free rolling" on him. If you're playing Omaha high-only, you'll either win the pot or split it, while your opponent will either split it or lose it entirely. That's a no-lose situation for you; whenever it comes up, it's a nice position to be in.

- The gap between cards is important in calculating the number of outs you have. With a gap of two or more ranks, the board will not support a 20-out wraparound straight. If there's a gap of two ranks in the board cards (let's say you have 9-7-6-3 and the board is 8-5-2) you're holding a 13-out draw, and will make your straight with any of 3 nines, 3 sevens, 3 sixes, and 4 fours.

Getting Counterfeited

Let's say Chris holds A-2-9-10. The flop is 3-7-8 of mixed suits, so he's flopped the nut low. In addition, he's flopped an open-ended straight draw; a six or a jack on either the turn or river will give him the nut straight, allowing him to scoop the pot unless the board pairs or the turn and river bring runner-runner cards of one of the three flop suits.

There's quite a bit of action on the flop. It appears that someone has flopped a set, and two loose players are probably drawing for second-nut or third-nut low. Or perhaps one of them has made two pair or has a lower straight draw.

Lo and behold, the turn brings a king of the fourth suit, and the river delivers a delightful little six. Chris scoops the pot, raking in a nice mound of chips.

In this example, things worked out pretty nicely for our hero. He had a naked ace-deuce and it held up for the best low, giving him half the pot with a shot at scooping if he got lucky and made a straight on the turn or river. And that's exactly what happened. His nut low held up and he made his straight, giving him a scoop.

But what if he hadn't been so lucky? What if an ace or deuce had fallen on the turn, and he'd held two face cards instead of the 9-10? Suppose his hand had been A-Q-Q-2 instead. How would his hand have fared then?

The answer is, not well at all. A pair of queens, or even a pair of aces, is the best high hand in Omaha/8, so that side of the pot almost certainly won't be pushed to Chris. As for the low side of the pot, Chris almost certainly lost that as well. With either an ace or deuce on the turn, his nut low has been counterfeited — rendered virtually worthless.

Getting counterfeited, as Omaha players say, means a card hits the board that duplicates and destroys your low hand. For example, as in the situation described above, although you may flop the nut low when you have an A-2 in your hand, an ace or a deuce will jump up on the turn or river about twenty-five percent of the time. That's why holding acey-deucy without a backup card is a dicey proposition at times. After all, if the flop is 6-5-3 and a deuce appears on the turn, the best low hand is now A-4. The deuce and trey were both counterfeited by the board, which read 6-5-3-2 on the turn.

Remember, you must use exactly two of your hole cards to make the best hand — no more, no less. You must also use three of the board cards. That means that once an ace or deuce is on the board, someone else can use it to make a better low hand than yours. Cruel though it may seem, an opponent drawing to third best low may gather in the low side of the pot even though you had the nut low all the way until the deuce appeared on the river. That's poker. That's Omaha/8.

That's why a low draw with protection is so important. If Chris had held four low cards like A-4-3-2 when he flopped his low hand, he couldn't have been counterfeited. With A-4-3-2 and the same flop, he'd have made the nut low regardless of what cards fell on the turn or river. But premium low hands like A-4-3-2 that provide top-flight counterfeit protection are rare. And when you do get them, the flop may greet you with three painted faces or a pair of nines or tens with an odd card. Just accept such disappointments as part of the game.

Drawn and Quartered

When you have a low hand, even the nut low hand, you won't win your side of the pot outright all the time. It's not uncommon for two players to be dealt A-2, and when that happens, you'll wind up getting "quartered," which means splitting half of the pot. Though this isn't what you hope for when you're going low, things could be worse — your hand is still good, just not exclusive. It's always better to be quartered than to be counterfeited and lose the low altogether.

A low hand is never as secure as you might think, so a little protection is always a good thing to have. In fact, if you're dealt A-2-3-x and flop the nut low, hope for an ace or deuce to fall on the next card. Any opponent holding a naked acey-deucy combination will be counterfeited, giving you a better chance of winning the entire low side of the pot. In addition, the card that counterfeits your opponent's low might just be the card that turns your holdings into a low straight or wheel that can win the high as well as the low, allowing you to scoop the pot.

You'll never know for sure if you're on the road to being quartered, but if there's a low on the board, plenty of action, and lots of players in the pot, you can be fairly sure someone else has an A-2, too. Identical low hands are far more common than high ones. After all, if two players have flushes, one will outrank the other. Only straights and, rarely, full houses can wind up in a dead heat. It's therefore much more common for low hands to be quartered than to see the high side chopped up. Every experienced Omaha player knows this, so the player with the nut high will be betting and raising at every opportunity to get as much money into the pot as possible.

On the other hand, raising it up with the nut low only is the mark of the inexperienced player. (That's putting it kindly. Pros refer to such players as fish.) If one of your opponents has A-2 and is right in there betting and raising, he probably has the nut low plus a draw for the best high hand, or else he's playing incorrectly.

Even with the nut low hand on the flop or the turn, your hand may be vulnerable. You may be quartered, or what's worse, counterfeited if an ace or deuce jumps out of the deck on the turn or river. When that happens, you'll have gone from having what was the best hand in your direction to being ignominiously counterfeited and getting nothing back for all the bets and raises you've called on your road to ruin.

A word to the wise: If you have an inkling that war is about to break out, and you've got no protection for your nut low, you're walking a tightrope and working without a net. Playing a naked ace-deuce is a lot like walking through a rough neighborhood to make a big cash deposit at the bank. You might make it, but then again, you might not. It's a lot nicer to have some protection, like a trey to go along with that ace-deuce. Then it's more like walking to the bank with Tony Soprano and some of his boys who are there to make sure nothing untoward happens to you along the way. Omaha can be frightening at times.

Basic Arithmetic For Omaha Players

A little probability is worth knowing if you want to become a better poker player. But before your eyes glaze over and you tune out this section entirely, hear us out. We're going to show you how to convert outs into the percentage chances of making the hand you're shooting for, and while we're at it, we'll show you how to convert percentages into the odds against making your hand.

The math is really simple. All you need to know is basic arithmetic — the kind of stuff you learned in seventh grade. But if you're math-phobic, don't despair. You can just skip to the end of this section and find all the calculations neatly wrapped up in a chart for you. By skipping this section, you won't learn how to figure them yourself, but you'll have the answers available. You can commit them to memory quite easily.

Let's begin by calculating the odds against making a flush when you hold two suited cards, and two cards of your suit appear on the flop. This is a common situation in Omaha. Let's say you're holding

along with two other irrelevant cards and the flop is

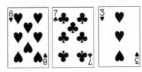

Since there are thirteen cards of each suit in a deck, and you've accounted for four of them, only nine of the remaining 45 cards can be hearts. Why are there 45 remaining cards? We began with a deck of 52 cards. The four cards in your hand are known to you, as are the three cards that appeared on the flop. That's a total of seven known cards, which, when subtracted from 52, leaves 45 unknown cards.

It's easier to calculate the number of ways to miss your flush. Subtract the misses from the universe of possibilities, and the result will be our answer.

On the flop there are 45 unknown cards. Since only nine of them are hearts, the remaining 36 will not help you. If you miss your flush on the turn, there are now only 44 unknown cards. Since nine of them are hearts, 35 others won't help you. Let's multiply fractions. That's easy. Multiply the numerator (the number on top) of the first fraction by the numerator of the second, then perform the same calculation for the denominators (the bottom numbers on the fractions). The result: $36/45 \times 35/44$ equals $1260/1980$.

If you subtract the number of misses (1260) from the total number of possible events (1980), you're left with 720 combinations that result in a flush. Now divide 720 by 1980. The answer is 0.363 (or 36.3 percent). If you flop a four-flush, you'll make your flush by the river slightly more than 36 percent of the time.

Would you like to convert that percentage into odds? Here's how to go about it: Subtract 36 percent from 100 percent, and divide that by 36 percent $(100 - 36 = 64; 64 / 36 = 1.77)$. The odds against completing your flush are 1.77-to-1. So if the pot figures to pay 2-to-1 or more on your investment, your flush draw will be profitable in the long run — regardless of whether you make the flush right now.

But before you get too fired up over how strong flush draws are, remember this: To win, you must often have the best possible flush, since a smaller flush can be beaten by a larger one. And if the board pairs on the turn or the river, your flush might not be good regardless of how big it is. Let's assume that you're drawing to the nut flush. For purposes of this exercise, we'll ignore those situations where you have a smaller flush draw along with a draw to the best low hand, which is certainly worth playing even if you lose the high end of the pot. You might not win this hand, but as long as you make this play, you'll have the best of it in the long run.

Since you have no control over what cards are dealt, you should focus on making plays with positive expectations. That's what "having the best of it" is all about. It's also why players can never win over any extended period at craps, roulette, baccarat, or any of the other pit games, with the exception of blackjack.

Every professional poker player, and every skilled amateur who wins steadily at the game, takes the best of it most of the time. Winners separate from the rest of the pack through this simple fact: Winning players take as much of the gamble out of poker as they possibly can.

Now that we've looked at a simple flush draw, let's take a look at the myriad straight draws abounding in Omaha games. First we'll examine the odds against making a straight when you flop an open-ended straight draw — the same kind of eight-out straight draw you're likely to flop in a Texas hold'em game.

This is very similar to the flush problem. If you can solve this problem effortlessly, you're well on your way to a passing grade in Omaha arithmetic, and you're far ahead of any opponent who neither understands, nor wants to perform these calculations. But just in case you're having trouble, here's how to go about it:

If you hold 9♦8♦ along with two other irrelevant cards, and the flop is A♣7♠6♥, you've flopped an open-ended straight draw. Either a ten or a five completes your straight. Since there are four of each, any of eight cards completes your hand.

Once again, we're going to multiply fractions. In this case you'll miss your straight 37 times out of 45 on the turn, and 36 times out of 44 on the river. When you multiply 37/45 x 36/44, you'll find that you'll miss your straight 1332 times out of 1980 attempts. By subtracting the number of misses from the universe of possibilities (1980 - 1332), you find that you'll make a straight 648 times for every 1980 times you flop an open-ended straight draw.

By dividing 1980 into 648, you'll find that you'll complete your straight 32.7 percent of the time — which equates to odds of 2.06-to-1 against making your hand.

Another common calculation involves flopping a set or better when you have a pair among your hole cards. In this case, you want to determine how many possible choices of three cards can be taken from a universe of 48 cards. Why 48, instead of 52? Well, 48 represents the universe of unknown cards. The four cards in your hand aren't included in this universe because they can't possibly appear simultaneously in your hand and on the flop.

Your opponents also have four cards each, but since you don't know the specific cards they're holding, you must assume that any of the 48 unknown cards are equally likely to appear on the flop. Of course, if you happened to get a peek at one of an opponent's cards, then the universe would be reduced to 47 — since you'd also know with complete certainty that the card you saw in your opponent's hand can't make it to the flop either.

Setting up the problem involves dividing the product of (48 x 47 x 46) by (1 x 2 x 3). If you don't cancel out to simplify the calculations, you'll wind up dividing 103,776 by 6. It's that easy. There are 17,296 possible flops — and it's a handy number to know.

Now that you know there are precisely 17,296 possible flops, here's how to go about figuring your chances of flopping a set. If you calculate the number of ways you might flop a set when starting with a pair among your four hole cards, you can compare that number with the 17,296 combinations representing the universe of possible flops. It's that easy.

It's actually easier to calculate the number of ways to miss making a set. Let's try that. If, for example, you hold 8♦8♣ in your hand, there are two other cards in the deck that will form at least a set from a universe of 48 unknown cards — excluding the rather remote possibility that the flop itself is a set. If the flop is 9♣9♠9♥, any opponent holding a bigger pocket pair now has a bigger full house, and if someone happens to hold 9♦, he's made quads and you're drawing dead!

So for all practical purposes, if the 8♥ and 8♠ are the only two cards that will make at least a set, then 46 of the remaining 48 cards will miss. If the first card up on the flop is neither the 8♥ nor the 8♠, then 45 of the remaining 47 cards will also miss, and if the second card brings no help, that third and final flop card will not be the 8♥ or 8♠ 44 times out of the 46 remaining unknown cards.

Your next step is simple. Just multiply the fractions, as follows (46/48 x 45/47 x 44/46). When you multiply the numerators (top numbers) you get 91,080, and when the denominators are multiplied the answer is 103,776.

What does this all mean? It means you won't flop a set or better 91,080 out of 103,776 times. Subtracting 91,080 misses from the universe of 103,776 leaves you left with 12,696 hits. Now you know that flopping a set or better figures to occur 12,696 times out of 103,776.

But 12,696/103,776 is a large, unwieldy fraction. To reduce it, divide the numerator and denominator by 12,696. When you do, you'll find yourself left with 1/8.1. If you divide 1 by 8 (or 12,696 by 103,776), you get 0.1223. Expressed as a percentage, you'll flop a set or better 12.2 percent of the time that you hold a pair in your hand. If you do flop a set, you'll have seven outs to improve on the turn (you can catch the last remaining card of your rank to give you quads, or you can make a full house by pairing either of the two other board cards — and there are three of each of those ranks that will accomplish that for you.) Going from the turn to the river improves things a bit, since you now have an additional board card that might pair. Now ten outs will improve your hand from the turn to the river.

There. Wasn't that easy? Because you've worked your way through these calculations and now understand the relationship between outs, odds, and percentages, we're going to reward you with a handy little chart that sums it all up for you.

By now you've probably reached the conclusion that odds, outs, and probabilities are all ways of saying essentially the same thing, and are nothing more than variations on a theme. While we don't want to needlessly complicate things, it's important to

Outs, Odds, and Percentages

Outs	Percentage chance of making your hand by the river	Odds against making your hand by the river
4	17%	4.8-to-1
5	21	3.8-to-1
6	25	3.0-to-1
7	29	2.4-to-1
8	33	2.0-to-1
9	36	1.8-to-1
10	40	1.5-to-1
11	43	1.3-to-1
12	47	1.1-to-1
13	50	1.0-to-1
14	53	0.9-to-1
15	56	0.8-to-1
16	59	0.7-to-1
17	62	0.6-to-1
18	65	0.5-to-1
19	67	0.5-to-1
20	70	0.4-to-1

realize that each way of expressing the relationship between the chances of making and missing your hand has its own uses.

Odds give you the bad news first. When you have eight outs on the flop, the odds tell you that you're a two-to-one underdog. In other words, you'll fail to make your hand twice for each time you do make it. Odds are useful because it's easy to compare the odds against making your hand to the money odds offered by the pot. By comparing the odds against improving your hand to the dollar odds offered by the pot, you can make rational decisions about whether to fold, call, raise, or reraise.

Otherwise, you're simply looking at odds in a vacuum. Is a 2-to-1 underdog a good deal, or is it something to be avoided like the plague? It depends. If the pot is offering $60 on a $20 call and you're only a 2-to-1 underdog, that's a good deal because the pot odds of 3-to-1 exceed the odds against making your hand. If you repeat this situation over and over again, you'll have the best of it whenever you call a bet in this situation. But if the pot were only offering $20 on a $20 call, you'd be better off folding.

Our chart points out that once you reach 14 or more outs, the odds are no longer against you. In fact, with 14 outs or more you're an odds-on favorite to make your hand. When you're an odds-on favorite, it somehow seems easier to look at percentages rather than odds. While the picture is quite clear and very understandable when you're a 2-to-1 dog, it's much easier to understand that you have approximately a 70 percent chance of making your hand, rather than couching it as odds of 0.4-to-1.

Percentages are useful in other ways, too, such as when you want to combine the probabilities of independent events. You can't do this by multiplying the odds against each event happening, but you can multiply percentages. And outs are useful in the basic poker calculation: How many cards are there that will help me?

Here are some percentages you'll need to know whenever you're drawing for the low end of the pot in an Omaha/8 game:

- If you hold A-2 and two unpaired low cards flop that don't counterfeit your hand, you have a 59 percent chance of making a low hand, and a 49 percent chance of making the nut low.

- If you hold A-2-3 and two unpaired low cards flop that don't counterfeit your hand, you'll make a low hand 72 percent of the time, and 69 percent of the time you'll make the nut low.

These odds are pretty good, no matter how you look at it. But notice that if you happen to have a trey in your hand to accompany your acey-deucy, not only do the odds of making your low increase substantially, but you'll find yourself rooting for an ace or deuce to fall once you've made your low hand. If that happens, any opponent drawing to a naked A-2 will find himself unceremoniously counterfeited, while you'll still be in the catbird seat. And that, of course, is where you want to be in Omaha/8.

Chapter 6

Getting Down to the Nitty-Gritty

U p to this point we've filled your head with concepts, advice about general strategy, and mathematical parameters of the game. We've shown you how to calculate the odds you'll need to make common decisions — the kind that come up all the time in Omaha games. But we've been overarching in our view, painting with a broad brush, and we did that for a purpose: to put the game into a perspective that allows you to get the overall picture, and to provide a framework for you to think about as you analyze your play. But there comes a time when one must cut to the chase, and this is it. In the next few chapters, we're going to get right down to the nub of the game by providing specific advice you can use to quickly improve your play.

While your authors are dead set on developing your own analytic capabilities so that you can quickly and effectively react to changing situations as they occur during the play of a hand, we're going to give you very specific advice about how to play in certain situations, and also provide a set of starting hands you can use in any Omaha game. We hope your play improves to the point that you can creatively and profitably deviate from these standards on occasion, but for those readers who are Omaha newbies, and for those who may have some experience at the game but have never studied it before, we suggest you stick to the recommendations we provide until you know them cold. After all, if you were learning to play the saxophone, you'd spend a long time playing scales and playing tunes exactly as written before thinking you were as good as Charlie Parker and able to improvise and play jazz with the best of them.

People play Omaha for a variety of reasons, and as you begin to understand this, you'll see that profitable opportunities abound in this game, perhaps more so than in any other popular form of poker. Some play Omaha because it gives them an opportunity to exercise the mind. After all, there are more variables in Omaha because there are more cards. There are more decisions

75

to make in the game, particularly if you're playing Omaha/8, and you have to assess your chances of winning the high side of the pot, the low end of it, or scooping all of it.

With hold'em as popular as it is, play in that game, at least, has improved. If you have a table full of Omaha players, it's a pretty good bet that most have had extensive experience playing hold'em and have a pretty good sense of that game. At the higher limits, such as $15-$30; $20-$40, this is particularly true. Fortunately for you, that skill at hold'em hasn't always transferred well to Omaha.

You'll find outstanding hold'em players even at the $4-$8 level. If you were to rate players on a scale from one to ten, the average score at a hold'em table would probably exceed that of an Omaha game at similar betting limits. So if you really learn to play Omaha well, you'll find yourself with a distinct advantage because your competition is likely to be much softer than in hold'em games. Moreover, most Omaha players seem to think they know the game cold. Just ask them. Why is this so? Perhaps it's because they're simply unaware of what they don't know. And awareness is the first step to learning. After you've studied the game, you'll have a big edge over those who are blind to their own deficiencies.

Having said all that, the *biggest* reason people play Omaha gives you significant opportunity to win money at it. Many, many players prefer Omaha because it gives them an opportunity — or an excuse, if you will — for playing more hands. If you're skeptical, try this little experiment and see for yourself: Just stand behind a hold'em player — anyone who looks like he knows what he's doing will suffice — and out of 30 hands dealt, count how many he plays. Now watch a similar Omaha game and count the number of hands typically played there. We're betting that the Omaha players will wind up playing more hands than the hold'em players — many more, in some cases.

Ask a poker player why he or she plays and you'll usually hear something about winning money. But that's really not the truth. Most people *just like to play*. They love the action. They crave the competition. They like the mental gymnastics associated with poker, whether those gymnastics are mathematical, psychological, or some combination of both. And since they love the adrenalin rush of warfare, the struggle for each and every pot, they hate to fold a hand and sit on the sidelines. Because they're enthralled with the excitement of the game, the more opportunities they have to actually *play* the game, rather than just watch, the greater the thrill.

In hold'em, you're initially dealt one two-card combination. In Omaha your four starting cards yield six two-card combinations. Even if your cards aren't related, you can always get lucky with all those combos and make two pair or even a full house. That's why people play Omaha: they want to play more hands. And this is your opportunity come calling: your chance as an educated, savvy, and disciplined Omaha player to take profitable advantage of this situation.

Since your competition is looking for any excuse to play a hand, you should look for reasons to fold marginal hands and ways to capitalize on your good ones. The idea is to win more money with your best hands while losing less on those doomed to be second or third best. And most importantly, you want to put yourself in a position to scoop pots whenever you can.

For winners, Omaha is a game of scoops, not a game of splits. We've said that before and we'll keep repeating this mantra until it's ingrained into your head and into your playing style as well. Consistent Omaha losers are usually happy to split a pot, thinking that proves they're doing something right. And their egos seem to be bigger than those of their hold'em counterparts too. Those who play Omaha/8 on a regular basis tend to believe they're much better than they actually are. Hold'em players just seem to have a better sense of their own skill level. You should take full advantage of this distinction. As you develop the skills discussed in this book, you'll not only play better than the competition, but also be better able to evaluate, modify, correct, and improve your own play.

You'll learn to rate and evaluate your play against the principles given in this book, even as you learn to deviate from them. If you're playing too many hands, if you aren't making the profitable plays we suggest, or, as Mike Caro so eloquently puts it, you're suffering from "fancy play syndrome," you'll spot what you're doing wrong and be able to make necessary corrections in your game. You'll be able to evaluate your play on a far more objective basis. Then if you lose, it won't be that you got unlucky — at least not most of the time. Remember: It wasn't that you were always getting *rivered*. It was that you put yourself in a position to get unlucky, and the cards broke even.

So if one of your authors were to ask you why you play Omaha, your answer shouldn't be, "...so I can play more hands." Just between us, your answer should be that as a savvy reader of this book, you have a distinct advantage in Omaha against most opponents because you can recognize profitable opportunities easily and quickly, while avoiding common traps that bleed a bankroll. As a diligent student of the game, you're far more aware now of what it takes to win consistently. Or, to put it more concisely, you've learned to think when you play.

Chapter 7

Starting Hand Selection

O f all the decisions you make playing Omaha/8, the most important is whether to play or fold before the flop after you look at your four face-down cards. Starting hand selection is crucial to your success in this game. Not only is the decision important because every other tactical choice during the play of the hand stems from your initial decision to fold or play, but it's a decision you'll encounter on each and every hand. There's no getting away from it; you'll have to be right about playing or passing the vast majority of the time to become a winning Omaha player.

A wise choice depends on your position, the number of opponents and their skill level, the betting limits, and the qualities of your specific four-card hand. In this chapter, we provide a framework to help you develop a feel for the rhythm or texture of the game as you watch opponents and learn their style of play. We also supply guidelines to help you evaluate those all-important first four cards in your starting hand.

The list of starting hands we suggest is intended to allow some flexibility for game texture while providing reasonable guidelines for most games. If you're a break-even player who can't seem to win, our analysis of starting hands will help you become a winning player. If you're a losing player, our recommendations should bring you to a break-even point, or even turn you into a winning player.

If you're already a consistently winning player, you probably know these guidelines already. But even winning players get into ruts from time to time where they lose session after session. This list will get you back into rhythm and back where you'll feel more comfortable, into the flow of your winning ways.

Though we give no absolutes about hands to play or hands to fold since there are so many variables to consider, our advice to shun hands containing middle-range cards comes about as close to an absolute as we can manage. We talk about that very important mid-range "blacklist" in more detail later in this chapter. In the meantime, let's look at some general guidelines.

In Omaha, your four starting cards should work in concert with one another.

Let's call them "A," "B," "C," and "D." Card "A" plays with "B." "A" also plays with "C." And "A" plays with "D," too. "B" plays with "C." And "B" plays with "D." Card "C" also plays with card "D." If you add up the number of possibilities, you'll find six two-card combinations. And ideally, all these combos should be happy ones, not mismatches. Your cards should work in unison like a good team of oarsmen pulling together.

Compare that situation to hold'em, where you're dealt only two cards. Ask yourself this: How many two-card combinations can I make with two starting cards in hold'em? The answer is simple. It's one hand, and one only. While there are 1,326 two-card combinations in hold'em, with two cards you can make just a single two-card starting hand. Remember: In Omaha there are six, and you want all six to pull together. This is a crucial difference from hold'em, but one that all too many players, especially those coming from a hold'em background, disregard at their peril.

There are cardrooms where you'll find five-card Omaha/8. With five private cards you can make ten two-card combinations instead of six. If you're beginning to get the impression that four-card Omaha is a game where you should either have the nuts or be drawing to the nuts most of the time, in five-card Omaha it's an absolute imperative. If you don't have the nuts or a draw to it, you have an unplayable hand and must fold. In five-card Omaha you should play even fewer starting hands than in the four-card variety. But that's not what most people do. Most people play more, and skilled Omaha/8 players know how to exploit that tendency by springing traps on such opponents in a five-card game.

The same thing happens in four-card Omaha/8: Savvy players know exactly how to glean extra bets from those applying hold'em's two-card thinking to a four-card game. If you suspect you're on the wrong end of this equation, don't despair. Just read on.

If one of your cards doesn't relate to the other three, your possibilities for forming a winning hand have been reduced.

Suppose you have three coordinated cards but one oddball card that doesn't fit — a hand such as: king, queen, jack, and, oops, an offsuit deuce. That deuce just doesn't coordinate at all with your other three cards. It's called a dangler, and danglers are the kiss of death in Omaha starting hands. Top players muck most hands containing danglers. You should too.

We can safely ignore the obvious exception that occurs if you wind up making a full house when there are two kings and a deuce on the board. But other than miracles like these where you have an absolutely perfect fit by making a full house involving your dangler, that orphan just won't play. Even worse, if lightning does strike to bring the flop of your dreams, you may run into a costly brick wall because your full house isn't the whole story. It's only the good news. The bad news is that whenever an opponent also makes kings full, his hand will always be higher than yours. Why not avoid trouble? Our advice is to avoid playing hands with danglers, or *three-legged dogs*, as they're sometimes called.

If you insist on playing a dangler, your hand contains four cards, but only three of them will play most of the time. Since three versus four represents long odds, you'll have to learn to avoid such situations to become a good Omaha player.

Recommended Starting Hands

Here is our recommended list of hands to play. Remember, this list is designed for beginning players, or for experienced players trying to get into the rhythm and flow of the game. It can also be used as a discipline-builder for any player who thinks he or she may be playing too many hands, or as a baseline of solid play for anyone who has been running badly. Moreover, it's a good list of hands to play in the first 30 or 45 minutes of a poker session simply because you won't play too many hands. This, in turn, allows you to see what kinds of hands your adversaries are playing. All right. Are you all ready? Here's the list:

- Play any hand with ace-deuce in it.

- Play any hand containing ace-trey, as long as the ace is suited to any of your other starting cards. If you have the ace of spades, one of your other three cards has to be a spade. It doesn't need to be the trey of spades. Any spade will do.

- Play any ace-trey when your other two cards are ten-point cards. Ten-point cards are tens, jacks, queens, and kings. So if you have ace-trey and your ace isn't suited, but your other two cards are ten-point cards — K-Q, K-J, K-T, Q-J, Q-T, J-T, K-K, Q-Q, J-J, or T-T — go ahead and play. If your trey is suited with any of your other cards, so much the better. And if your hand is *double-suited*, that's better yet. For example, if you have A♠-Q♦-T♠-3♦, that's much better than having A-Q-T-3 with four different suits. Nevertheless, any ace-trey accompanied by two ten-point cards is playable.

- Play any ace plus two prime cards. Prime cards are aces, deuces, treys, fours and fives. You can play an ace with any two other prime cards. So you could have A-5-3, A-5-4, and even A-5-5, because those paired fives are prime cards. Logic, however, should tell you that A-5-5 is a pretty weak hand. Unpaired prime cards are what you're really looking for because that gives you three wheel cards, and if one of them should be counterfeited — when one of the community cards matches it, thus reducing or destroying its value — you still have two other low cards that play.

- Play any suited ace if two of your other three cards are ten-point cards. You may play a suited ace if two other cards in your hand total 20. So you can play A-K-T-7, A-Q-J-8, or A-J-10-9 with any card suited to your ace, but remember that these are weak hands that shouldn't be played from early position.

- Play any four prime cards, even four prime cards without an ace, as long as there has been no raise in front of you. The best hand in this situation would be 5-4-3-2 double-suited. The worst would be 5-5-4-4 of mixed suits. When playing four prime cards without a raise in front of you, the closer you are to the button, the more valuable the hand becomes. If you are in first position, immediately to the left of the blinds, you probably shouldn't play this hand, even though it meets our suggested requirements. But if you want to play it, make sure you're in a very loose, passive game with plenty of callers before the flop and very little raising. As you move closer to the button and the pot hasn't been raised, four prime cards become more and more playable.

Many players look for any excuse to play a hand; they're not on the lookout for reasons to fold. You, on the other hand, must relentlessly strive to release marginal hands. In this somewhat constricted playing mode, it's in your better interests to scuttle likely underdogs. Take time to think before you play borderline hands — even though they're on the list — and use logic as well as judgment.

So far, every hand we've recommended has had an ace, with the exception of four prime cards without an ace. But here's another hand cluster you can play:

- Play any hand totaling 40 points or more *as long as it doesn't contain three-of-a-kind and the lowest ranking card is ten or above.* Aces count as eleven points. Deuces through nines are taken at face value, while tens and picture cards are ten-point cards. Hands containing eights or nines do not qualify under this provision, although they may qualify under the suited ace categories listed earlier, or if they contain an A-2. Note: Hands like K-Q-J-T or Q-Q-J-T play very well when lots of players have come in before you.

Remember, most people play hands with aces in them. If a lot of people have entered the pot in front of you, it's an indication that they have low cards, since most Omaha/8 players favor hands filled with low cards. If you look at the starting hand guidelines we've just given, low hands predominate there too. But this very bias toward low hands in Omaha/8 is what makes the 40-point high hands so very playable. With lots of callers in front of you, most of the low cards are probably out, so the deck figures to be rich in high cards.

In every deck there are 20 high cards. These are the 11-point and 10-point cards: aces, kings, queens, jacks, and tens. There are also 32 cards of ranks deuce through nine. If you eliminate the nines because they can't be used to make a low hand, there are 28 remaining low cards (32 if you count aces as low cards) to go along with 20 high cards and four worthless nines.

Think this through with us. If five players have already come into the pot, and the blinds haven't had an opportunity to act, that's an indication that most players are holding low cards. So if you're holding high cards, your hand is very valuable. We like to raise in such situations, even without an ace, because the chance of hitting a flop that fits is quite good. If the flop misses, it's a very easy hand to get away from, but if you do hit a big hand, you stand a very good chance of scooping the entire pot.

Moreover, from the button or the cutoff seat (the seat immediately to the right of the button), whenever there are already four or more players in the pot and it's been raised, we like to make it three bets with these 40-point hands. When someone raises, it's as though he's telling us that he has an ace with either another ace or with other low cards. Three of the aces have probably been accounted for in situations like this one; and if somebody cold-calls that raise, all four aces are probably out.

Under these circumstances, a high hand is very live to scoop a big pot. With so many low cards out already, there may not be a low hand. In any event, a 40-pointer is worth a raise — or even a reraise — and if the flop misses it entirely, you'll never be in jeopardy because the hand is very easy to release when confronted with a low flop.

That concludes the hands we recommend. But you can't play every one of the hands on our list in every position. Hands like 5-5-4-4, A-x-5-4, A-x-5-5, and A-K-T-8 with a suited ace shouldn't be played in early position. If you play them in late position, be cautious.

The hands covered by our guidelines are not the only hands you can ever play, but if you're learning the game, there's safety in knowing you won't be seduced into playing too many hands. If you really enjoy playing Omaha/8 but have been losing far too frequently, this structure will make you a break-even player, presuming, of course, that other bad habits aren't bleeding your money away.

If you've been a winning player in the past, but you're now in a trough, mired in one of poker's inevitable losing streaks, following our suggested guidelines for starting hands will help you get back into a winning mode. First, you'll be playing fewer hands, avoiding many that would have wound up second-best. Second, you'll be watching more, learning more about your opponents in the process. Finally, you'll seldom find yourself trapped in confusing, problematic, and potentially costly hands.

If you follow our suggestions, you'll, as poker players say, "...always know where you're at." Releasing hands that don't catch part of the flop will be easier, and less costly too. And when you do play, the quality of your hands will be of a higher quality than those you've been playing. Since most people play Omaha because it offers an easy rationale for playing more hands, our recommendations will allow you to take advantage of that propensity and profit from it.

Fit or Fold

Just about every book on poker contains the suggestion that where a flop is concerned, it's best to "fit or fold." "Flop" games include Omaha, Pineapple, Crazy Pineapple, and hold'em. In all of them, the fit or fold principle is relatively simple to apply: If your cards don't fit the flop, just release your hand. Regardless of how many cards you start with, once the flop is dealt, your hand needs to coordinate with it.

For example, if in an Omaha/8 game you hold A-A-3-2, with both aces suited — a hand most players consider the very best Omaha/8 starting hand — but the flop brings K-Q-J in the two suits you lack, your precious gems are fool's gold. They're worthless; and while they may be difficult to throw away, that's precisely what you'll have to do with them.

If you can't release a hand that's harmed — or simply not helped — by the flop, no matter how potent it looked just moments before those three communal cards were turned face-up on the table, you have a major leak in discipline that you'll have to repair to turn your game around. While it's not hard to remember, it's often tough to act on. "Fit or fold," that wonderful phrase coined by poker author Dana Smith, is the byword to avoid hemorrhaging away money in any poker game. Omaha is no exception.

Although we began this chapter by stating we'd give no absolutes specifying hands that should be played or folded, we'll close it with a short advisory warning we hope you'll heed:

- The worst hand to play might be 9-9-8-8 double-suited because it *looks* playable but generally leads one down that old primrose path. If you never play this hand — and don't worry, you won't be dealt this particular combination very often — you won't be missing a thing, and your bankroll figures to be better off for it.

- The biggest trap hand in Omaha/8 is probably 6-5-4-3 double-suited. Although you'll win occasionally with this hand, you'll lose with it much more often. In the long run, your losses will far exceed your wins. It's one of those "win a little, lose a lot" hands. You usually can't be too aggressive when you make a hand with this holding, and when you lose — flush over flush is a good example — you'll probably be hammered by someone holding the nuts. This is the worst of both worlds, a place you don't want to be in poker.

Maybe this advice sounds a little like Mom telling you to take your jacket and look both ways when crossing the street, but where Omaha/8 starting hands are concerned, you're better off safe than sorry. So start slowly. Err on the side of caution, at least for the first 45 minutes after you sit down to play, and stick with our recommendations. They won't lead you astray. You'll seldom find yourself in a complex or confusing situation when you see the flop, and any downtime can be well spent getting a fix on your opponents. You might even win some money in the process. We certainly hope so!

Chapter 8

Playing the Flop

I f the flop doesn't fit your hand at all, that's an easy fold. On the other hand, if it's a marriage made in heaven, with nuts and nut draws in both directions, that's a no-brainer, too; you're river-bound. Seems straightforward enough, doesn't it? But sometimes the fit of flop to hand is only partial, or it's deceptively congenial and fraught with danger. These situations require more thought. In this chapter, we look at various types of flops and how to handle them in terms of their relative compatibility with your hand.

When Three Low Cards Flop

Depending on your holdings, three low cards can be a cause for jubilation or just silent recognition that it's time to throw your hand away. When three low cards flop, someone surely holds a low hand already, and it's very likely the nut low hand. If that someone isn't you, you'll be fighting for only the half of the pot if you stay.

Since Omaha is a game of scoops, not a game of splits, whenever three low cards flop, you'll have some important decisions to make regarding how to play the hand — if, in fact, you plan to play it at all. These decisions are based on whether you have the nut low, or a draw to the nut low, in addition to a high hand. Of course, many players do stay after a three-baby flop with nothing but a draw to the second or third best low hand, or just a very weak high hand. If this is something you do, and you don't plug that leak in your game right now, you'll never be a winning Omaha player.

Here's a guideline you should take to heart if you want to play winning Omaha/8: Without the nut low or a hand offering a draw to it, you should have a very strong high or a draw to the nut high to continue past a flop of three low cards, and even then it's not an automatic green light, but something to be carefully weighed.

Let's say you've flopped a draw to the best possible flush because two cards of your suit are present on the flop. Or, instead, you've flopped top set, the nut straight, or a draw to the nut straight without the possibility of making a low hand. In such cases, you have difficult decisions to make:

Let's start with something fairly clear cut: *If you flop a straight draw or the nut straight with no low draw whatsoever, you must be willing to get away from your hand.*

This is a tough concept to grapple with, and many players have a very hard time applying it. We ourselves understand just how difficult it can be to release the best hand once you've seen the flop. When three low cards flop, you've no choice but to assume that someone already has a low hand, and you're relegated to winning only half of the pot at best or possibly losing all of it. The sad truth of this conundrum is that you might wind up losing all of it more often than you'll win half of it — and you'll seldom, if ever, scoop the pot. So straight draws are candidates for the scrap heap when three babies flop. So, unfortunately, are straights themselves — even nut straights. A nut straight without other possibilities, like a low draw or flush draw, should be thrown away in this situation.

But if against a flop of three low cards you have the nut flush draw or you've flopped top set — not middle set and certainly not bottom set because anything less than top set may easily become a costly trap — you have a decision to make, and it's not an easy one. Your decision should depend on the amount of money in the pot, the number of active players, and how much it's likely to cost to see the turn. If someone bets, you're facing a decision. With no low, you can win half the pot at most. Should you call?

Here you need to ask yourself: How many players remain to act after me, and if any of them call, how much money is likely to be in the pot? You'll have to determine how much money will be in the pot and whether it will be worthwhile to go for your draw if one, two, or three players call. "If I make that draw," you should ask yourself, "how much money will I win if my hand wins half of the pot?"

Though it may not be easy, you'll have to do the math and think before you act. Your authors are far more comfortable drawing to the nut flush than they are chasing a full house, because you'll always know whether you have the best possible hand when you make the nut flush. But if you make a full house, it's frequently vulnerable to a bigger one. Here's one of our cardinal rules of Omaha/8: In addition to Omaha/8 being a game of scoops, not splits, it's also a game of flushes, and not a game of straights or, for that matter, full houses. So feel free to draw for the nut flush but please take our advice and refrain from drawing to second, third, or lesser flushes in this situation.

You'll have to apply some judgment about drawing to improve top set when the flop brings three low cards. Notice we say top set. Please don't play bottom set here, or middle set, for that matter, as you may well wind up with second-best hand even if you make a full house. We recognize that it's very, very difficult — and it may well prove psychologically impossible — to release top set on the flop, even in the face of three low cards. While folding is the right play much of the time under these circumstances, it's very tough to do. We know this from experience. It's not easy for us to muck top set, either.

Our psychological poker programming leads us to this default action: "I've got to take a card off." But make sure you give in to temptation only when there's a pile of money in the pot and a lot of players in the hand. If you're heads-up, or confronting only two other players, just tell yourself, "No," and fold.

Consider this example: You've flopped top set but the flop has three low cards. There's a bet and a call and now it's your turn to act. Many players make an automatic call here, and wouldn't dream of folding. Believe it or not, you won't miss a thing by passing this one by. In fact, over time, you'll save money by folding in this situation. You may not want to face these facts, but face them you should: If you proceed, you're chasing half the pot, and you're in trouble because your hand isn't complete yet. In fact, if you don't hit a full house on the turn or river, an opponent's straight or flush is almost a certainty. If the board is unpaired, there are very few boards that won't contain a possible straight or flush or both. While that doesn't mean your opponent will always make a bigger hand than your set, it does mean you can't be too aggressive with it, even if it does wind up capturing half of the pot.

None of this, however, is set in stone, and the nature of the flop itself is often a determining factor in whether you should play or fold. If you flop a set of eights and the board is 8-7-2, you can play because there's no chance of a straight at this point. On the other hand, if you flop a set of fives and the board reads 5-4-3, you're probably in serious trouble. Discretion is the better part of valor and if you throw such hands away, you'll find yourself many dollars ahead of the game in the long run. Remember: A bet saved spends just as well as a bet won.

To recapitulate: When there are three low cards on the flop, play draws to the nut flush and top set very carefully, *if* you play them at all. Base each such decision on the number of active players, the amount of money in the pot, and the amount that figures to be in the pot if you make your hand.

Some players refer to the amount of money you figure to win if you make your hand and are paid off by the opposition as "implied odds." Since you'll never know for sure how many — if any — of your opponents will pay you off when you make your hand, try to estimate this amount as realistically as you can. It doesn't help at all to be overly optimistic if your optimism has no foundation in logic or reality. When it's based on blind faith, hope, and unbridled optimism, all self deception can do is cost you money in the long run.

The ability to make and carry out correct decisions when three low cards flop is often what separates big winners from marginal winners and losers. When three babies flop, you'll frequently see opponents chasing flush draws, drawing to full houses, and even going to the river with just two pair. Amazingly, all of this activity flies in face of the fact that someone has probably made the nut low or something close to it.

But it's not all gloom and doom when three low cards flop. Sometimes three low cards on the flop have "scoop" written all over them. The easiest way to scoop occurs when you have ace-trey and a deuce flops along with two other low cards, and you also have the nut flush draw or top set or a wheel draw. Even if you make the second or third best flush, or can draw to the middle or bottom set, you now have the best low hand plus the possibility of a scoop.

More problematic are cases where your low is second best or less rather than the nut low, but you also have good high hand possibilities. Although you still have flexibility and scoop potential, much more judgment is required. It's a tough hand to release, but you'll have to get away from it if someone bets and there's a raise and a re-raise before you get a chance to act. It should then be easy for you to throw your hand away, although this situation doesn't happen very often. But notice we say that it *should* be easy to fold such hands. The problem is that it's easy to say but harder to do.

If you're like many players, you'll find yourself playing that hand even though it gets tricky when you're holding the second, third, fourth, or fifth best low hand along with high options. It's a judgment call as to whether you ought to take a card off. The further away from the nut low you find yourself, the easier it should be for you to throw your hand away when three low cards flop and you have high possibilities accompanying a marginal low hand.

On the other hand, the closer you are to the best possible high hand, the less likely you'll be to release your hand. If you're holding the third, fourth, or fifth nut low along with bottom set, it's a much easier hand to release than it would be if you held top set. With a marginal low and a draw to the second or third best flush, it becomes more difficult to get away from your hand.

The further your hand is from the nut flush and the further away you are from the nut low, the easier it is to release your hand. The corollary to this is that the closer you are to the nut flush and nut low, the more difficult it is to fold. But to be a winning player, you must release your hand when the situation dictates.

Nevertheless, when you do decide to play with a two-directional problem hand, be aggressive. Let's say there's a bet and players behind you who have yet to act, and you've got the second, third, or fourth best low hand along with a draw to a good (but not great) high hand — such as middle or low set, or a flush draw that won't be the best possible flush even if you make it.

If you play here, you must play aggressively to force opponents with long-shot draws to fold. It's imperative to get them out of the pot, so if you don't think your aggressive play will succeed in doing so, you're better off passing up on the hand altogether. But if you can manage to play the pot heads-up with the player who came out betting, you're gambling on the fact that your opponent has only the nut low, which may yet be counterfeited, and that any high hand possibilities he has aren't the equal of yours.

If your adversary winds up counterfeiting his or her low on an ensuing betting round, you'll scoop the pot with a hand that was anything but stellar quality. To be a winning player, you need to put yourself in such positions frequently, and you can't do that by playing passively. Play aggressively, particularly if your opponents play well enough to get away from troublesome hands.

OK, you may be wondering if you should try this maneuver in loose low-limit games. Isn't it possible that a raise against an original bettor may only lure more players into the pot rather than drive them out?

Yes, unfortunately, aggressive action may backfire on you in the smallest games. In lower limit games, players are reluctant to release marginal hands. In loose games, a hand such as the scooper just described may not even be playable because a raise probably won't eliminate players who have yet to act.

Therefore, your play in low-limit Omaha/8 should be quite straightforward. In these games, when three low cards flop, you're better off having the nut low along with high possibilities that will enable you to scoop the pot. You don't particularly want to get quartered, and you don't want half the pot, either, although you'll take it if you have no other choice. While you won't throw a nut low hand away, it's far better to have high possibilities to go along with it.

Sometimes even the best low hand won't be any good. Suppose a tight, early position player raised before the flop, and the flop hits the top of the low end with something like 7-6-5 rainbow — we'll assume there's no flush draw possible — and you're holding a hand like A-K-T-2. If the player who raised before the flop now comes out betting, and is raised, your best play is to consider folding your hand. You have no high hand and no protection in case your low hand is counterfeited, so you figure to win either one-quarter or even one-sixth of the pot — and you might lose it all if an ace or deuce comes on the turn or river. We realize this is a hard hand to let go of, and that you're probably not going to do it until you've been burned a few times, but it's frequently the correct play.

Flopping Flush Draws

As a general rule, if two flush cards flop, your only flush draw should be to the nuts, unless you have at least *two* other draws — such as a draw to the best or second best low hand, or a draw to a straight — to accompany your primary drawing hand. If a flush comes on the turn or river, you can be fairly confident that either the nut flush or the second best flush is out there. However, a "runner-runner" flush makes any flush draw a playable hand, and you can bet or call on the river with any flush that happens to come in via the backdoor.

In addition, when two flush cards flop and one of them is an ace, smaller flush draws become playable. Most of your opponents will play any suited ace, but will play other suited cards only as "extra" combinations and not as their primary hand. So if an ace and another card of the same suit fall, there's considerably less chance that an opponent holds two similarly suited cards, since he'd be holding them "accidentally," and not as a primary holding.

Note this word to the wise about flush draws against a paired flop: Playing a flush draw when the flop is paired is a real chip-burner unless you have a piece of the pair or a full house. A flush draw with a paired board is a check-and-fold situation unless you have the nut flush draw along with the first or second nut low draw. Don't say we didn't warn you!

Flopping A Flush

• When you flop a flush and three low cards are on board, you should bet or raise with all nut flushes. Second or third nut flushes *with the nut low* should also be bet or raised. But if your second or third nut flush only has the second or third nut low to accompany it, you'll have to rein in your aggression. In this situation, just check and call, and release your hand if there's a bet and a raise before it's your turn to act. We recognize that sometimes this means throwing away a hand that would have won half the pot, but this play will save money in the long run.

• When one or two low cards accompany a flush, you should bet the second nut flush but check all other flushes — except for the nut flush, which, of course, you'll bet or raise. You can check or call if you're holding any other flush, as long as you have the first or second nut low draw or a draw to a full house. But any other hand should be discarded if there's a bet or raise in front of you.

Flopping Straight Draws

More money is probably won or saved in Omaha/8 as a result of decisions related to flopped straights and straight draws, than is won or saved due to any other situation. In fact, one major difference separating expert players from all others lies in how experts play straights and straight draws on the flop.

You can flop straight draws with at least eight outs under a variety of conditions. An eight-out straight draw is either open at both ends, or a double belly-buster — a term poker players use to describe a straight draw comprising five cards with two "holes," such that any of eight cards can make it into a straight. It really doesn't matter if a straight draw is a double belly-buster or open-ended, since eight outs are eight outs, regardless of how you slice them.

Your straight draw may come with no low cards on the flop, or with one, two, or even three of them. The flop providing your draw may have two or even three suited cards, allowing a possible flush to threaten your straight if you make it. You can also flop a straight draw that includes both low and suited cards. We're about to examine each of these combinations:

Straight draws and low cards

Let's talk about low cards first. In all of the examples that follow, we're going to assume that the board contains unpaired cards of different suits.

- If three low cards flop and you don't have the nut low or second nut low to accompany your straight draw, don't play.

- If two low cards flop, you should draw to the nut straight, as long as the straight you make won't produce a low hand, too. But you can draw to a straight that will also make a low hand *if* you have the best, second best, or third best nut low draw to go along with your straight. The only hand of this type that should be played aggressively when two low cards flop is the nut straight draw with a nut low draw. All others should be just checked and called so you can determine what action to take on the turn.

- If one low card flops and you have the nut straight draw with at least eight outs, you should bet if first to act, and call if someone bets into you. If you have more than eight outs, you have a hand Omaha players call a "wrap." A wrap occurs whenever your four downcards contain several consecutive cards that can combine with three board cards to form five consecutive cards, so that a large number of turn or river cards can give you a straight. For example, if your downcards are 6-5-4-A and the flop is K-8-7, you can make a straight on the turn or river with any of 13 cards: any six, five, four (three of each rank remain), or any of the four remaining nines. You'll find wraps with 13, 17, and even 20 outs. Let's take an example where the flop is K-J-2 and you have A-Q-T-3. Here you have 13 cards that will complete your straight and all of them make the nut straight. When you flop big draws like these, you should bet if you're first to act and raise if an opponent bets first. If you have the nut straight draw as well as top pair, bet if first to act or raise if an opponent bets into you. If an opponent bets into you, there's a good chance you're behind at the moment, but it's critical that you raise to eliminate secondary draws by opponents who have yet to act. Betting or raising tends to eliminate players who might call one bet with a "runner-runner" draw and perhaps beat you by getting lucky on both the turn and the river.

- With no low cards flopping, it's always possible that someone might have made a straight, so the only time you should play a straight draw is either when you have at least seven outs to the nut straight, or you're holding secondary straight draws with additional outs — such as top two pair, or the top or second-best set. Secondary straight draws with bottom two pair or bottom set should be mucked, and those accompanied by top and bottom two pair should be played cautiously.

Straight draws and suited cards

Let's consider straight draws where the board is suited. For purposes of this analysis, we'll assume that low hand issues aren't applicable.

- When the flop yields three cards of one suit, your straight is probably worthless and ought to be thrown away — no exceptions.

- When the flop contains two of a suit, you must have a draw to the nut straight with at least eight outs, or seven outs if you have top pair along with your draw. Your draw must be played cautiously, in a check-and-call manner, and if there's a bet and raise in front of you, your hand should be discarded. If there's a bet and call, you have our permission to keep playing, but please, be cautious.

- If you flop a straight draw and the board contains two low cards and two cards of the same suit, unless your draw is to the best or second best low hand as well as to the nut straight, just throw your hand away and wait for a better opportunity to risk your money. If all you have is a draw to the nut low and nothing else, you'll have to assess each situation individually and act accordingly.

Straight draws when the flop is paired

Our advice here is simple. Don't play them unless you also have a draw to a full house. If you're drawing to a full house, your straight draw is merely an insurance policy; if no one makes a full house, you can get lucky and back into the winning hand by completing your straight.

Flopping Straights

The following situations assume that the flop contains cards of three different suits, so that no flush draws are possible:

Flopping a straight with low cards on the board

- When three low cards flop and you have the nut straight, the hand should be played very defensively unless you have the nut low or second-nut low. It's a check-and-call situation when three or fewer opponents are contesting the pot. If you're up against four or more opponents, save yourself some money and release your hand, because the most you can accomplish is to win half the pot and you might wind up losing it all. If you had your druthers, of course, you'd like to flop the nut straight along with the first, second, or third best low hand and a redraw to a higher straight. A backdoor draw to the nut flush or a full house to go along with all that doesn't hurt, either. If you haven't made the first or second best low hand in addition to your straight, fold your hand. If you have only a straight and no low, the hand should also be folded.

- When two low cards flop, you should check and call with your straight, simply because a bet or raise won't eliminate any nut low draws. You're better off seeing the turn on the cheap before deciding on your course of action. On the other hand, if you flop the nut straight with a draw to the first or second nut low, you should bet if first to act and raise if someone bets before it's your turn to act.

- When only one low card flops, bet your straight if first to act and raise if it's bet into you — regardless of whether you have a redraw to a low, a flush, or any other hand.

- When no low cards flop, bet if first to act, call if bet into, and raise if you have a redraw to a higher straight or a full house. Our advice to you is simple and straightforward: When you flop the nut straight and no low cards are on board, never raise without a redraw. When you flop the *second best* straight, you need at least a six-out draw to the best straight or a full house draw to justify calling. If you're first to act, or if it's checked to you, bet only if you're last to act, and be prepared to throw your hand away if you're check-raised.

Flopping the nut straight with flush cards on the board

- With three flush cards on the flop, throw your nut straight away unless you have top or middle set or the nut low draw along with it. The value of your straight in this situation is virtually worthless; only the presence of other draws should keep you in this pot.

- With two flush cards on the flop, just check and call. Wait to see what the turn brings unless you have the nut low, or a draw to the nut low, to accompany your made straight. If you do, bet if you're first to act, or raise if someone bets into you.

Flopping middle straights

A middle straight is any straight other than a Broadway, which is poker jargon for A-K-Q-J-T, the highest possible straight. Flopping middle straights can be a money-eater in Omaha/8. The problem with this hand is that it very rarely holds up, even when it's the best hand on the flop.

If you flop a middle straight that's not the nut straight, you're in even greater jeopardy. The most dangerous flops for your hand contain two suited cards and/or two low cards, or, worse yet, three low cards plus two suited cards. An example is if the flop is 8d-7d-6c and you have T-9 in your hand. Although you've flopped the nut straight, there's already a low made.

When you see this type of flop, simply assume that someone already has a low hand and that the best you can hope to win is half the pot. This is a hand that cries out for conservative play. Anyone with a good low draw or a low hand that's already made won't fold if you bet, and neither will anyone with a flush draw. You're in a very dicey pickle. At best, you figure to win half the pot, and you can't even be sure of that. You have no claims on the low end of the pot, either. You might not even have the best straight, and if someone makes a flush, you're even more likely to lose the entire pot. Our advice is to get to the river as inexpensively as possible, and don't be afraid to release this hand if there's a bet and a raise in front of you.

If a third suited card falls on the turn or river, there's a pretty good chance someone will make a flush. In addition, there's ample opportunity on the last two cards for the board to pair. If it does, you can easily lose to a full house. You can see that middle straights are extremely vulnerable, since you can easily lose to a higher straight, a flush, a full house, or even quads. So play middle straights cautiously. Without opportunities to make a bigger hand or a low hand, you should play warily, and if there's already a made low on the flop, you won't miss much by folding.

But let's be realistic. If you flop the nut middle straight and there's neither a low hand nor a made flush, you probably won't throw this hand away. But indulge us, please, and refrain from betting the flop. Check instead, and see what happens on the turn.

If, on the turn, you still have the nut straight and the chance to scoop the pot, go ahead and bet so as not to give a free card to flush draws and low draws. But if a low card appears on the turn and a player who had previously checked to you now bets into you, just call. Don't raise. If someone has the nut flush draw or a set, your raise won't eliminate him. You'd just be putting more money into a pot you stand a good chance of losing.

To put it bluntly, you'll be money ahead in the long run if you release your hand each time you flop a nut straight that's not a Broadway when the flop contains two suited cards and two low cards. Yes, we know: It's easier said than done. But at least we've warned you. Play middle straights, if you must, but play them very, very cautiously.

High Hand Scoops

Starting hands with only high potential are best played from Seats 7, 8, and 9 — or from Seats 1 and 2 without a raise — and preferably with a bunch of players already in the pot before you act.

High hands with no low options need to be played in a very particular way. If you're in a multi-way pot, you can generally assume that most of the players are playing low cards. The deck, as a result, figures to be rich in high cards. So if you have a high hand, the flop might provide just what you need to scoop the entire pot. Here are some guidelines for playing your high-only hand:

- Once you've decided to play a hand that only has high potential, play in a straightforward manner. If you have the best hand, go ahead and bet. If someone bets before it's your turn to act, fire a raise into the pot.

- Don't get fancy. Don't slow-play big high hands, especially when one low card flops. The downside of any deceptive play resides in its potential for luring low draws into the pot only to watch the opposition catch two running low cards, or two running flush cards, or both, to snatch half the pot — or even all of it — out from under your nose.

If you really feel like getting tricky, do it when no low cards flop, when you know only high hands can contest this particular pot. But if one low card flops, you need to bet or raise — thereby announcing to your opponents that you do, in fact, have a high hand, and a good one too — because low hands can't be allowed to pick up backdoor draws that could enable them to snatch half the pot.

If you make the best possible high hand on the turn while two low cards are on the board, you must raise if an opponent bets into you. This isn't optional; it's mandatory. After all, you have the best hand right now and must discourage low draws from trying to capture half the pot.

The best way to discourage low draws is to make it expensive for them to draw and get lucky. If all your opponents check, you must bet. Please don't slow-play your hand under any circumstances. Usually, all that does is give every player with a low draw a free ticket to get lucky. High hands must force opponents on low draws to pay handsomely for the right to chase down half the pot. Never give a player with a low draw a chance to get lucky on the turn.

Playing Middle Cards

Middle cards, as you might expect, are the six, seven, eight, and nine, and they represent Trouble with a capital "T." Although these four cards will be discussed here as a group, draw imaginary circles around the six and the nine.

While the six is considered a middle card, it's not nearly as bad as the seven, eight, or nine. Nines are the low water mark — the worst of the worst in the deck in Omaha. Nines can't be played for low, since this is Omaha/8, not Omaha/9. Moreover, nines are seldom involved in the nut straight. If you want to see this for yourself, just hang around an Omaha/8 game and watch the winning hands when they're turned up. You won't see many nines.

You can play nines in Omaha high-only, but you should virtually never play them in Omaha/8. When you see a hand full of nines and other middle cards, visualize a big red stop sign over your chips. Then put on the brakes and stop yourself from calling. Middle cards tend to put you in positions where you either win half the pot or lose it all, and they almost never allow you to scoop the pot.

With middling cards, think of yourself as approaching a dangerous intersection, where dangers come at you from all directions. Even with middle cards on the board and in your hand, there are always higher straights, higher flushes, and higher full houses, as well as low possibilities. If you're holding 9-8-7-6 in your hand and the flop is 9-8-7, you have two pair and a straight draw.

"So what's wrong with that," you ask? For starters, your straight won't be the nuts if you complete your draw, and if someone makes a low, you'll win only half the pot. But things can get even worse: If high cards come on the turn and river, they'll be bigger than yours and one of your opponents will probably make a bigger straight. In fact, the only cards that can do you any good in this situation are an eight or a nine on the turn or river.

Our bottom line, straight from the top: When you find a fistful of middle-range cards, just release your hand. Let'em go. Now. All too many Omaha/8 players pick up a hand like 8-8-7-6 or 9-9-8-7 and stay to see the flop because their cards are connected and contain a pair. They're going to make straights or full houses, or so they believe. But while they can make the nut straight or top set on the flop, there's probably a low hand afoot, too.

Remember that most Omaha/8 players look for excuses to play hands. They're prisoners of hope, while you ought to know better. Hands full of middle-range cards should be released before they do what they usually do — cost you money and eat into your bankroll. With middle-range hands, you figure to either lose a lot of money or win a tiny amount. That's a bad bargain, no matter how you slice it. Professional poker players call these "trap hands," hands they avoid like the plague.

Even middle cards with an ace and a deuce accompanying them need to be carefully played. While you can certainly play a hand like A-8-7-2, realize it will be all but worthless if an ace or deuce comes on the flop. If that happens, your nut low draw will be counterfeited, and that happens more often than you might realize. That's why a hand with three good low cards is so much more valuable than a hand with just A-2 toward low. In addition, if you hold a naked ace-deuce, you'll have to toss your hand away much of the time when the flop contains fewer than two low cards.

If you hold an ace and a deuce in your hand, one or the other or both will be counterfeited on the flop approximately one-third of the time. In such situations, an unwary player who also holds middle cards can easily be relegated to playing a junk low hand, or a junk low draw. So remember that these vulnerable acey-deucey-middly-middly hands need to be played carefully. Winning Omaha/8 hands contain aces much of the time; in fact, more winning hands have aces than any other card. Losing hands, as you might expect, often contain sevens, eights, and nines. This should tell you to be very wary of middle-range cards.

Remember our circled cards? We circled the nine, and described it in a word: "worthless." We circled the six because it becomes an emergency backup card toward low when you have an ace and a deuce in your hand. It's far more valuable than a seven; if your emergency low card is a seven or, worse, an eight, you'll probably be beaten by a better low.

Once in a blue moon, a nine becomes a key card for you, and that's almost always when you make a full house that allows you to scoop the pot. But that's a real rarity. A nine in your hand usually signifies a losing hand. It's a real handicap. The six is extremely useful as a third or fourth low card, because whenever you make a wheel you'll often make a six-high straight too. A six in your hand becomes a critical card when 5-4-3 is on the board. A straight to the six with a wheel will usually scoop the pot or allow you to take at least three-quarters of it. But an ace-deuce-seven usually won't scoop at all. And if you toss a nine into that mix instead of a six or seven, you've got real trouble. Nines are cards you hate to see in your hand. You can play them with three good cards such as ace-deuce-trey when the nine is your straggly fourth card. Yes, it's a dangler but you can play the hand because of your other three cards.

When you see hands turned face-up at the showdowns, you'll see nines — and very often eights — in the losing hands, while you'll see aces in the hands of the winners. You'll rarely see middle-range cards in a winning hand. And when you do, it's because there's a straight opportunity on the board. But that's hardly reason for celebration. On the infrequent occasions when they do make a lucky straight, middle-range hands usually win only half the pot — and they frequently lose it all. Take our advice: Avoid these trouble hands most of the time.

One Expert's Advice

If all this advice is beginning to confuse you, Omaha/8 expert Mark Gregorich offers a few questions you might ask yourself when deciding what to do on the flop:

• Am I playing for all of the pot or only half of it?

• What are the pot odds, and how do they relate to the number of outs I have?

- What are the implied odds if I make my hand?

- If I hit my hand, is there a logical bettor on my left or right? (If you have a pretty good idea about who might come out betting, you can decide whether to bet or try for a check-raise.)

- If I bet, can the pot be raised behind me, and how likely is it that someone will indeed raise if I bet?

- How do my remaining opponents play?

- Will I get paid off if I hit my hand?

- Have I thought things through before acting?

While you obviously won't be able to take this list of questions to the table and spend time thinking deeply about each issue, if you study this list and begin to ask yourself these questions each time you're involved in a hand, you'll soon find that the questions — and the answers — will become second nature to you. Once that happens, you'll be resolving these issues on autopilot, and you'll be well on your way to becoming a highly skilled Omaha/8 player.

There's so much detailed information in this chapter that we've summarized it in the chart that follows. It might not make it any easier to commit this material to memory, but at least all the information about playing the flop is in one convenient place:

This chart presumes that all straight draws are open-ended with at least eight outs, or wraps with an even greater number of outs.

Hand	Flop	Requirement & Playing Strategy
Straight draw	3 low cards	Fold, unless you have first or second nut low.
Straight draw	2 low cards	Draw to any nut straight that won't yield a low hand; and any straight if you have the nut, second, or third best low draw.
Straight draw	1 low card	Bet nut straight draw if first to act, otherwise call.
Wrap straight draw	1 low card	Bet or raise with 13,17, or 20-out wrap hands.
Straight draw	0 low cards	Play if you have at least 7 outs to the nut straight, or you're holding additional outs, e.g., top set.
Straight draw	3 suited cards	Fold.
Straight draw	2 suited cards	Draw to the nut straight with 8 outs, or 7 outs if you also have top pair or better.
Straight draw	2 low and 2 suited cards	Draw only to nut straight and nut or second nut low.
Straight draw	Paired board	Draw only if you also have a full house draw.
Straight	3 low cards	Check and call nut straight unless you've a good low.
Straight	2 low cards	Check and call, reassess based on turn card.
Straight	1 low card	Bet, but raise with nut straight.
Straight	0 low cards	Bet or call; raise with redraws to bigger hands.
Straight	3 suited cards	Fold, unless you also have top set, middle set or the nut low draw.
Straight	2 suited cards	Check and call.
Nut flush draw	3 low cards	Draw with 3 or more opponents; with fewer than 3 opponents, draw for the flush with any low hand.
Nut flush draw	2 low cards	Draw.
Other flush draws	2 low cards	Fold. You need at least two other draws, such as best or second best low, or a straight draw.
Other flush draws	Suited ace on board	Play with multiple draws, or with the fifth best flush draw or better.
Any flush draw	Paired board	Check-and-fold unless you've got a piece of the pair.
Flush	3 low cards	Bet/raise with nut flush; bet/raise second nut flush. with nut low; check and call with "second-second."
Flush	2 low cards	Bet nut and second nut flush; check and call all other flushes if you have first or second nut low draw.
Top set	3 low cards	Draw or fold.
Bottom or middle set	3 low cards	Fold.
Low Draw	3 low cards	If one of your low cards is counterfeited, you can only play with a nut low draw and high draw.
Low Draw	2 low cards	Draw to nuts, or to second low with another prime card or second nut low with high draw.
Low Draw	1 low card	Play only with set, two pair, or nut flush draw.
Nut low, no high hand	3 low cards	Bet, or call cautiously with nut low and no high hand.
Nut low, high hand or high draw	3 low cards	Bet or raise.
Second low, no high	3 low cards	Check and fold.
Second low, high draw	3 low cards	Check and call.
Second low, high hand	3 low cards	Bet or raise.

The following chart summarizes the likelihood of making a low hand under various conditions.

Number of Different Low Cards Dealt to You	Pre-flop Chances of Making a Low Hand	Chances of Making a Low Hand if Two New Low Cards Flop	Chances of Making a Low Hand if One New Low Card Flops
4	49%	70%	24%
3	40%	72%	26%
2	24%	59%	16%

Chapter 9

Playing Aces

Pocket Aces: Omaha/8's Most Overrated Hand

A pocket pair of aces is Omaha/8's most overrated hand. Most Omaha/8 players were hold'em players first, so when they look at their cards and see A-A, their inclination is to play that hand, regardless of what their other two cards might be. They want to play any pair of aces from any position, no matter how many other players have already entered the pot or how many have yet to act.

Rather than jump for joy, tread carefully whenever you see aces in your hand. Your antenna ought to go up whenever you're dealt A-A in an Omaha/8 game, and you should dive right into your evaluation and analysis mode. The first step is to examine your other two cards and determine how well they dance with your aces. If they're prime cards, you've got a good hand. Go ahead and play. But if they're not prime cards? The answer depends on a variety of factors. So read on: We're about to give you some guidelines.

If you've been dealt A-A-5-5, you have the weakest possible prime cards to accompany your aces. Still, if both fives happen to be suited to your aces, your hand is a lot more valuable than if they're not. Obviously, if even one of your aces is suited, it's far better than not being suited at all. A rainbow cluster of unsuited cards, even with two aces, is far from a premium hand in Omaha. You won't miss much if you pass on such a hand, especially in early position.

That's just one example. There are many other cards you can have to go along with A-A. You could have A-A and just one prime card. Or A-A and one low card that's not a prime card, such as a six, seven, or eight, plus a face card. Another possibility is A-A with two low cards that aren't prime cards. And for an entirely different type of hand, you could have A-A with two other high cards, whether paired or not.

With A-A, Omaha heaven lies in having at least one and preferably both aces suited, and to prime cards. But if neither ace is suited, two prime cards are still terrific hand components. Then again, if your aces are neither accompanied by prime cards nor suited, you should hope for two other unpaired big cards rather than another big pair — you'll have a better chance of making the nut straight.

A pair of aces, for example, with K-Q, K-J, or J-T is far more valuable than that same pair of aces with two tens or a pair of face cards. Why? Because the power of your hand lies in the two aces, not the other two cards. Unless you flop a set with your subsidiary pair, which makes your pair of aces irrelevant, that secondary pair adds no value to your hand.

Some Cases of Aces

- When the overwhelmingly predominant asset of your hand is a pair of aces — meaning you don't like your other two cards very much, if at all — you should play *only* if somebody has raised in front of you and no one else has called. You're then in position to make it three bets so you can play heads-up, hoping to scoop the pot with your aces.

- When your aces have other quality cards to accompany them, your options are significantly broader, particularly if your other two cards are suited to your big guns. The closer your hand is to the ideal hand of A-A-3-2 double-suited, the more offensive and aggressive your play should become.

- A-A-9-2 is the only "dangler" hand involving a pair of aces that's playable. While you might find yourself attracted to A-A-9-3, thinking it's almost as good, it's a hand that can lead you into a trap, for you'll need to play with an eye towards mucking your hand if you suspect you're up against a nut low. Naturally, it's a bit more playable if one or both of the aces are suited. If that's the case, you'll know whether you have a flush draw or simply two irrelevant suited cards once you see the flop. *Special case: Shorthanded, aces-with-trey hands become raising hands.* Your goal then is to play your A-A-3-x against one or two opponents, because hands like these play well shorthanded.

- Other dangler hands, such as A-A-9-4 and A-A-9-5, are almost always unplayable. (The one exception, as we explained above, is when you can get heads-up against a raiser by making it three bets.) Just take our advice: Pass up these temptation hands and await better things.

Aces Up, Bankroll Down?

If you're playing A-A for high because you remember how powerful aces are in hold'em, you're probably hoping to make either aces-up or a set. Either can pose considerable risk to your chip stack.

If you make aces-up with your aces, we hope you'll do so on the flop, then be aggressive and have nobody call you, for this hand is fraught with peril in Omaha/8. Any pair on the board is likely to make three-of-a-kind for someone else.

Aces-up is a very strong hand if you're heads-up, but a toss-up or worse — especially if the board is paired — against two, three, or four opponents. And if there are five or more opponents sparring over a paired board, surrender this hand before it costs you dearly.

The Big-Gun Set You May Regret

When you don't have accompanying low cards, you're playing a pair of aces in hopes of making a high hand. Ideally, you'd like to flop top set. Just keep in mind that whenever an ace flops, that's one low card available for opponents to use in forming a low hand.

Also, if you're holding two aces and another ace flops, your hand is not nearly the mortal lock it is when you flop a set of aces in hold'em. For one thing, your hand isn't complete. You'll have to improve to a full house or better if you don't want to worry about all those nasty straights and flushes that appear with great regularity in Omaha/8. For another thing, an ace on the board gives your opponents at least a backdoor draw to a low hand. While a set of nines, tens, jacks, queens, or kings isn't as good as a set of aces, it does reduce the possibility of a low hand, and may preclude it entirely.

Straights are another big threat. If two other unpaired high cards should fall on the flop along with an ace, watch out — someone is likely to have the nut straight or a big wraparound draw to it. In this situation, your set of aces becomes a potentially costly second-best hand, and must be played defensively. And even if no one has a straight on the flop, another high card on the turn makes it far more likely that someone has completed one.

But a low card on the turn doesn't help you, either. It creates low draws, and, very possibly, small straight and/or wheel draws to boot. You'll then find yourself attacked from all sides, since there will be something on board for everyone, with some players going high, some going low, and others hoping to scoop. The betting on the turn is likely to be capped. If the board doesn't pair on the river to make you a full house, you'll lose a bundle on this hand.

It's also a potential trap hand — another of those situations where you figure to win a little or lose a lot. This is a classic defensive hand; it's not one that's offense-minded. So play the hand defensively. If somebody raises and you make it three bets, that's a defensive play. It may look offensive on the face of it, but when you assess the situation, you're trying to play the pot heads-up and have your aces survive to scoop the pot for you. A-A is a hand that needs to be played defensively, and often not played at all, unless the other two cards in your hand support your aces.

In Conclusion

Our message is simple: Please don't fall in love with an unassisted A-A. In general, it's folly to play this hand without good complementary cards when you're in a family pot. When a lot of people have entered the pot in front of you, you should assume that one or both of the two remaining aces are gone. Without quality prime cards or suited cards to go with your ultimate pair, you're playing mostly to make aces-up, and you'll usually lose even if you make your hand.

What's worse, you may be tempted to call just because of the size of the pot. When a lot of players are contesting the hand, one of them will probably match the community pair on the board. Nevertheless, with all those chips in the middle of the table, you'll probably wind up calling and losing at the showdown.

Remember that an ace on the board is also a low card for your opponents. Be wary if other low cards appear. If two low cards flop, at least one of your opponents will be drawing to a low hand. If another low card appears on the turn or river, you can usually win half the pot at best.

This is a classic defensive hand. So play it defensively. Note: If somebody raises and you make it three bets, that's a defensive play. It may look offensive on the face of it, but when you assess the situation, you're just trying to play the pot heads-up and have your aces survive to scoop the pot.

The lesson is simple: A-A without accompanying coordinated cards is a very marginal hand. It's also a potential trap hand — one of those situations where you figure to win a little or lose a lot.

Although AA is a very pretty and seductive hand, and you remember how absolutely dominating it can be at the hold'em table, you'll have to learn to ditch it like the dog it often is in Omaha/8.

Chapter 10

Playing the Blinds

Playing the Small Blind

Most players in the small blind call if the pot hasn't been raised, and that's usually the correct play. Virtually every situation provides pot odds that make it correct for the player in the small blind to call — *if* the pot hasn't been raised. Nevertheless, some top pros will only call that half-bet in the small blind with a hand that's good enough to call a full bet from the button. There are two schools of thought on this, but no clear-cut answer.

If no one enters the pot other than the big blind, you'll need to decide whether you will chop the *blinds*. This is allowed, but not mandatory, when only the small and big blinds remain in the hand before the flop. If the blinds agree to chop, each player takes his or her blind bet back and a new hand is dealt, with the button passing to the left as usual. The majority of players in flop games, such as Omaha and hold'em, chop the blinds when the table is either full or close to it. Nevertheless, when you join the game you should ask your neighbors if they prefer to chop the blinds or play.

You can have a different chopping agreement with each opponent, or the entire table can decide one way or the other. But remember: Once you've agreed to chop, it's considered rude to change your mind without prior discussion. If you look down and see AA, and you've already agreed to chop, don't be a jerk. Toss 'em away with a smile.

One last thing about chopping: It's not allowed in tournaments. You'll just have to duke it out with the big blind.

If there's one caller in addition to the big blind, there will be two bets in the pot, and all you'll have to do is add one additional betting unit. With more players, your pot odds significantly increase and that makes calling the correct play. However, the more players in the pot, the greater the chances are that you will have to show the nuts at the hand's conclusion to win. In almost every situation involving three or more players, you should call from the small blind whenever the pot has not been raised. Although that's an easy decision to make, deciding to continue once you see the flop is a much more complicated issue.

To continue past the flop, the flop needs to fit your hand, or you'll have to fold. When you're in the small blind, you'll be first to act on each betting round, which puts you in the worst possible position. Moreover, you have only one unit invested in this pot, since your original small blind bet is simply an obligation that you and each of your opponents have to the game. Don't count that forced bet as part of your investment in the pot.

Since you've voluntarily contributed only one betting unit to the pot, you have an opportunity to catch a perfectly fitting flop at a bargain basement price. If it's not a perfect fit, and all your opponents check on the flop, you'll have another opportunity on the turn.

But in a typical low-limit game, with lots of loose players, the flop is sure to hit somebody, so you'll rarely be able to see the turn card for free. If there's a bet, you'll need an almost tailor-made fit to continue in the hand. Many players are tempted to throw good money after bad because they just hate to give up on a pot. They wind up chasing mediocre or bad hands as a result. Remember: Money saved spends just as well as money won, so invest your money only in good hands that also work in tandem with the flop.

Although we've said most hands are worth calling to see the flop from the small blind as long as the pot hasn't been raised, there are exceptions. Hands not playable, even from the small blind, are those where you have three-of-a-kind in your hand, or hands loaded with troublesome middle cards, like 9-8-8-2. However, from the small blind you can play three aces with a deuce, or three deuces with an ace. Those are the only exceptions.

The subtlety of our suggestion lies not in the recommendation to play most small blind hands in unraised pots, because if things go badly we can hear you say, "Well, in the book it said

I'm supposed to play that hand." What we're saying is that in the long run, the small blind provides an opportunity where the pot odds are almost always in your favor.

But keep this in mind: When you play from the small blind, you'll have the disadvantage of acting first after the flop. So you'll probably have to play the hand conservatively, if you decide to play at all. Playing a hand from the small blind is a longshot and the flop should fit your hand perfectly to make it worth your while.

Calling a raise in the small blind: Deciding whether to call a raise in the small blind is a somewhat easier decision than whether to call a raise from early position, because you've seen what all of your opponents have done before the flop and you have more information at your disposal. If you're fourth to act, for example, and your opponent in Seat 3 has raised, your decision to play or fold would be the same as deciding whether to play that same hand from the small blind.

In fact, you can lower your requirements for calling a pre-flop raise from the small blind by a notch, because there are some strategic advantages to playing in that position. Since you'll be perceived as having a random hand — even though you've called a raise — players won't give you as much credit for having a good hand as they would if you just called a raise cold from late position. Most players believe that people call more liberally from the blind. While that's true, the blind doesn't *always* have a weak hand.

After all, a random hand can be a strong one too. Nevertheless, calling a raised pot in the small blind does require a quality starting hand. And there's a strategic advantage when you do call. You'll know you have a better hand, but your opponents won't think so. As a result, you can be "crafty." You can check-raise — sometimes on the flop, often on the turn — when you really hit your hand. So don't be afraid to call a raise from the small blind if you would call a raise with the same hand from early position.

When to raise in the small blind: Raising or re-raising a pot from the small blind provides opponents with a tremendous amount of information. Since you're in the worst possible position because you'll be first to act on each succeeding betting round, raising tells the world that you have an extremely good hand — one that will play in any before-the-flop situation.

You've made it easier for players to put you on a premium hand. This is somewhat like playing with your cards face up. That's not necessarily a bad thing, though, because if your hand is extremely powerful, you'd prefer to have more money in the pot. Why not put your opponents to a decision about whether or not to call your raise?

The *only* reasons to raise or re-raise from the small blind are to get more money in the pot and to knock out the big blind and play heads-up against one other opponent. Nevertheless, with the possible exception of the big blind, you're not going to raise other players out of the hand once they've already invested one bet in the pot. But when many players are already in the pot, you can assume most of them are holding low cards — or at least you can if it's a game where your opponents are playing reasonably well, and not playing "any four cards." As a result, you may not want to raise if many players are already in and you're holding a high quality low hand.

On the other hand, if you have one of those big hands — the kind that's full of face cards — and a lot of players are already in the pot, go ahead and raise. The flop is likely to be rich in big cards and you're probably going to scoop if you make a big hand.

There's a fine line here, and the trick to walking it is to weigh the value of getting more money in the pot pre-flop against the value of crafty play that comes from being able to check-raise if you hit your hand on the flop when the deck is rich in high cards. *As a general rule, we don't recommend raising from the small blind.* The exception is when you hold A-A along with two prime cards, single-suited or double-suited, against three to five players.

In all other situations, there is probably more value to be found by quietly calling, hiding the quality of your hand, and not allowing opponents to deduce your holdings. Lying in the weeds this way will give you more options on subsequent betting rounds. Besides, it's nice to have an unbounded set of options once everyone else has acted. Checking and watching, particularly on the flop, provides just that sort of opportunity. You can take that opportunity to consider what you want to do on the turn to either win the most money or lose the least.

Playing the Big Blind

If you're in the big blind and no one has raised the pot, you have an option to raise, or to just check and see the flop at no additional cost. All too many players give this decision little thought. With premium hands, they raise. With average or worse hands, they check. This autopilot style decision is a costly leak in their game — don't let it be yours. Here are some things to think about when considering a raise from the big blind:

Raising from the big blind is different from raising from the small blind. Raising from the small blind signifies an extremely strong hand, or a play to eliminate the big blind and contest the pot heads-up. But a raise from the big blind generally suggests a typical raising hand, though a rather strong one since the raise is coming from a very early betting position.

Very conservative players who seldom raise give away a great deal of information when they choose to raise from the big blind. When a conservative player raises from the big blind, it's tantamount to announcing that he or she holds a powerhouse hand. Opponents will naturally credit such players with strong hands when they raise from such an early position. So if you fall into that "very conservative" category, consider simply calling from the big blind to disguise the true strength of your hand, then do your raising on later rounds when the betting limits double.

As a general rule, raise from the big blind strictly to get more money in the pot. Players with one bet already in the pot will call a raise almost without exception, so a raise intended to eliminate such opponents will fail miserably. But when a number of players have invested one bet already, a raise from the big blind will get more money into the pot. If it's your heart's desire to build a mound of bets by taking your option to raise, you'll succeed admirably.

The decision to raise from the big blind should be based on the number of players already in the pot. A large number of active opponents who play reasonably good starting hands suggests that low hands predominate and that the deck is probably rich in high cards, while a pot contested by only a few players indicates a more random distribution of cards. It's important to remember, when deciding whether to raise or quietly call, that raising from the big blind offers no positional advantage. Your opportunity to be deceptive is taken away the very instant you raise from the big blind. At the risk of repeating ourselves: *It's important to emphasize that you should raise from the big blind specifically to get more money in the pot. That's it. That's the only reason.* Raising from the big blind is similar to raising in late position when your goal is to get more money in the pot, not to eliminate players.

We recommend that you raise from the big blind more frequently than from the small blind. Your raises from the small blind should be relatively rare, and made mostly in cases where you hold a top-flight hand against a table full of clueless players who won't make better decisions because you've raised.

While you should raise somewhat more often from the big blind than from the small blind, you shouldn't do it just because it costs less. Avoid raising from the big blind simply because you already have one small bet in the pot. Even though the raise won't cost as much as it ordinarily would, it should be based on your cards, your position, the number of players in the hand, and the type of hands they normally play.

Your play from either blind on the flop, turn, and river should be the same as from Seats 3, 4, or 5. That means fairly straightforward play. Every now and then a top quality hand will afford an opportunity to check-raise the flop, or to check and call with the intention of betting or check-raising the turn. But for the most part, it's best to play straightforward poker from early position, especially from the blinds.

Betting on the come from the big blind is normally not advisable, since checking and calling with big drawing hands usually wins more money. If you bet in early position and someone raises, you'll probably lose players behind the raiser and wind up playing heads-up. With a drawing hand, that's just not a good place to be in this game. With a big draw, you want lots of players in the pot. Checking and calling provides strategic flexibility; you can try for a check-raise on the turn, or just lead out with a bet if you make your hand.

But note this exception: You can bet when you have a draw to the nut flush if one low card has flopped and the pot odds justify your wager. This is a case where having a backdoor draw to a low hand in addition to a draw to the nut flush increases your opportunities to win all or half of the pot, and betting is usually a better course of action than checking and calling.

Suppose you have A♥-Q♦-4♣-3♥ and the flop is K♥-J♠-5♥. You have a draw to the nut flush, a backdoor low draw, and a gut-shot straight draw to boot. By betting, you might knock out any opponent holding a backdoor low draw with no high possibilities. After all, if an opponent is holding A-2 along with two unrelated cards, he'll have to hope for a "runner-runner" low to give him half the pot. If your bet on the flop eliminates him, you won't have to worry about some miraculous fall of cards snatching half the pot out from under your nose.

A pair of aces without good supporting side cards isn't worth a raise from either blind. Yet many players raise from the blinds with such skeletal hands. We consider this to be one of the biggest errors in Omaha/8. A pair of aces is simply nowhere near the powerhouse it is in hold'em, yet many Omaha/8 players haven't learned this. If you can remember that even sets are drawing hands in Omaha/8, you'll be able to place that pair of aces in proper perspective: It's not a raising hand without help from the other two cards.

Chapter 11

Playing When They Kill The Pot

Kill Pots

Although it sounds like something that harkens back to poker's Wild West origins, "killing the pot" is done with chips, not a Colt .44. In most public cardrooms, a new feature, called a "kill," has been added to Omaha games. Here's how it works: Whenever a player scoops a pot containing a predetermined amount of money, he's required to post a special blind bet on the next hand. That blind bet is called a "kill," and it's in addition to the two normal blinds.

A player who just scooped a pot large enough to meet the kill requirement is said to have "killed the pot" for the following hand by posting this additional blind. To designate the player who killed the pot, the dealer often places a special button, called, reasonably enough, a "kill button," in front of the appropriate player.

The amount of the kill changes depending upon the game. You'll find full-kill, half-kill, or even one-third kill games, depending on where you play. The effect of the kill is to change the stakes for the next hand. If you're playing $4-$8 Omaha/8 with a full kill and scoop the pot, you're required to post an eight-dollar blind bet for the next hand, even if you've just paid your two usual blinds. For as long as the kill remains in effect — and it will stay in effect as long as you or someone else continues to scoop pots meeting or exceeding the predetermined dollar threshold — you'll be playing $8-$16 instead of your usual $4-$8 stakes. Alternatively, if the game is played with a half kill rather than a full kill, the stakes rise to $6-$12 every time someone scoops a pot meeting the threshold size.

A one-third kill is rare. It's usually found in games like $15-$30, where the rotating blinds are $10 and $15. The kill in such games is usually $20. For a kill pot, the game escalates to betting limits of $20-$40. You'll also find a one-third kill in $75-

$150 games, where the standard blinds are $50 and $75. Here the kill becomes $100 and a kill pot is played at $100-$200 betting limits.

At limits of $20-$40 and below, the determination of whether or not the next pot is to be killed is based on the size of the scooped pot. In general, it takes a pot ten times the small blind to trigger a kill. In a $4-$8 game, a player needs to scoop a pot of $40 or more to reach the kill threshold. However, an uncalled bet on the river doesn't count toward that threshold. In a $10-$20 game, the minimum scoop for a kill is generally $100; in a $15-$30 game, the minimum is $150; and in a $20-$40 game, the threshold is usually $200.

Order of play: Each individual cardroom determines the order in which the "killer" acts before the flop. In some rooms the killer acts in turn pre-flop, while in others he acts last, after all action has taken place in front of him. Since the kill is a "live blind," the killer may raise when it's his turn to act.

But if there's a raise before the killer has acted, the killer must choose to fold, call the raise, or reraise when it's his *usual* turn to act. If all this seems confusing, be sure to inquire about the killer's options and order of play before you begin playing in any game with a kill. Specific kill pot rules vary with various cardrooms, and it's always best to understand how things are done before you play.

How to play the kill: When you have the kill, whether you act last or act in turn, the money that's in front of you — that "kill" you posted — is no longer yours. It's essentially money left in the pot from the previous hand you scooped. So think of it as your "winner's tax." And remember that you scooped everything other than the amount of the kill.

In the following discussion, we examine a $10-$20 game with a half kill to $15-$30. The amount of the kill blind is $15, and when the pot is killed, the betting limits become $15-$30. Whenever someone scoops a pot containing at least $100, you'll find the standard $5 small blind, the standard $10 big blind, and — in addition — a $15 kill. All three of these forced wagers are posted prior to the beginning of the next hand. Note: As a general rule of thumb, a kill is almost always three times the small blind, except in a full-kill game, where it's four times the small blind.

When the pot has been killed, you have opportunities to play hands you might not ordinarily play based on your usual starting hand requirements. With the two normal blinds supplemented by a kill, you have a chance to get lucky with marginal hands if you can see the flop inexpensively. And when the flop does hit your hand, you'll have a chance to win a large pot.

If no one else raises, the killer gets to see the flop for no additional investment. But if an opponent raises, the same line of reasoning applicable to the big blind applies when it's the killer's turn to act. Since he can see the flop for just one additional bet, he can call with many more hands than if he had to call the raise cold.

Also, starting hand requirements for a kill pot are somewhat more liberal than those recommended to play a raised blind. Both blinds have to put in considerably more money to see the flop than they would if there were no kill. If the blinds fold, that's good news too, because that puts dead money in the pot. That dead money increases the size of the pot — giving better pot odds — so players can enter the pot with starting standards a bit lower than usual.

The killer also has the advantage of having better position than either of the blinds. The killer acts later in the hand. Even if the killer acts relatively early — or even first, if both blinds fold — there's some strategic opportunity for crafty play with superior hands. For example, the killer can easily check-raise after others have indicated the way they intend to play a particular hand. These advantages are augmented by the increased amount of money in the pot. So the killer often has excellent positional advantage, as well as excellent pot odds. This two-pronged edge allows him to play marginal hands that might catch a favorable flop.

Raising with the kill: Deciding whether or not to raise becomes a bit more complicated when you're the killer. It's not merely a question of getting more money in the pot or trying to eliminate opponents. Other factors come into play here too.

It frequently makes sense for the killer to raise the pot so it's too expensive for the small blind and big blind to play. This eliminates competition while adding dead money to the pot. If you're the killer and decide to raise early in the betting sequence with hands you'd usually just call with, you may cause better hands to fold because of the expense.

In a $10-$20 game, a raise before the flop means it costs $20 for someone to call. In contrast, when there's a half kill in the same game, a pre-flop raise in a kill pot means it's now $30 for someone to call. And if the game is being played with a full kill, the price of play is even more expensive, since it costs $40 to call the raise. The more dramatic raise resulting from a kill puts additional pressure on your opponents. Rather than call your raise, they may fold hands they'd otherwise have played. So you should keep your raising option foremost in mind whenever you post a kill — the added clout of your raise may very well win you another pot.

But before you decide to raise, determine whether you'd really like your opponents to release their hands. In certain situations, you might prefer a pot with more active opponents. As a general rule, we prefer to call rather than raise with kill hands in any of the first six positions, but we seek out raising opportunities with kill hands in Seats 7, 8, 9, and 10. Given a choice, we prefer to do our raising from one of the last three seats in the betting order.

Will you elect to raise with a kill or simply call? This needs to be an intelligent decision, made with a specific purpose in mind. It's important to take into consideration players both in front of you and behind you, noting their various playing styles and skill levels. You must also assess the quality of your own hand: Does it play best heads-up or shorthanded? Or would you rather play it against many opponents?

As killers, we tend to simply call rather than raise because calling affords greater flexibility. As unobtrusive callers, we can play the flop and turn without giving away the strength of our hands. In other words, we frequently suppress the urge to raise pre-flop to increase our chances of check-raising on the turn — when the cost of betting doubles. Also, by taking the caller's wait-and-see approach, we save money whenever the flop misses us completely. Though our once gilded holdings are now just fool's gold, our chip stacks are none the worse for it.

Nevertheless, it's often correct to raise in early position with certain hands in a kill pot. Your hand doesn't have to be a premium hand, just the type of hand that plays well against few opponents. You can even raise with a hand you wouldn't even have played had you not had the kill. In such cases, the purpose of your raise is to keep players from coming in behind you — to narrow the field.

A good example is a hand like K-K-3-2. You wouldn't play this hand in most situations. But since there's money already in the pot from the kill and the blinds, and since you know you're going to play the hand, go ahead and raise. The idea is to force out some of the marginal A-x-x-x hands and improve your chances of winning either a piece of the pot or all of it. But such decisions should be carefully thought through, not made in a vacuum. If you're in a game where several opponents call raises with almost anything, your raise won't accomplish its purpose. As elsewhere in poker, it pays to know your players.

When to raise a kill: As a general rule, we recommend lowering your pre-flop raising requirements by approximately 20 percent in kill pots because you're able to attack three blinds with a raise, rather than two. Your raise puts severe pressure on players yet to act because to call your raise, they'll have to put more money into the pot than they're used to. This "make'em fold" raise works better in a game with a full kill than in one with a half kill or a one-third kill.

A raise pressures both blinds to either play mediocre hands in a raised pot or fold and leave dead money on the table. Just as importantly, there's less chance that other opponents will contest the pot. In the face of your raise, many will fold hands they would have played had you not raised the kill. When you raise a kill pot, you'll often find yourself playing only against the kill, or perhaps against the kill and one other player.

This is a specific application of a general rule: Plays effective in shorthanded situations should be brought to bear against random hands. It's an effective ploy, because you'll find that the killer rarely throws his hand away. For some reason, players tend to "defend their kill" even more aggressively than they defend their big blind. When they defend with weak holdings, you can clearly profit by raising and playing the pot heads-up.Remember: When you raise the kill, you're playing against a random hand. While your hand wouldn't normally be considered a raising hand, it's called up for duty in this spot because there are now three blinds — the small, the big, and the kill — and this is your opportunity to attack them. You might get lucky right now and pick up the blind money with no contest if everyone folds. But often, the kill will call, although you may succeed in eliminating one or both blinds. You've now achieved your goal of narrowing the field, possibly even making it a heads-up contest.

Confronted by a raise in a kill pot, many players in the big blind throw their hands away because they can't justify calling twice the amount of money they've already put in just to see the flop. In a $10-$20 game there is normally $10 in the big blind. When you raise the $20 kill, a ticket to play is now $40 for the big blind. That's four small bets — or two big ones — just to see the flop. This pressure forces many players to throw away hands they normally would have defended from the big blind.

Because kill pots are played at higher betting limits than the game's usual structure, these pots tend to be quite large. A scooped kill pot is usually big enough to become a kill pot too. Players like to win big pots, so some tend to call more liberally on the flop and turn than they usually do, simply because they want to win "a big pot."

These same players will also throw more hands away prior to the flop, but once involved in a kill pot, they make more bad calls because they've been seduced by a big pot's siren song. Players who are stuck also tend to play more hands than usual. Often they'll go against the grain and force the action by playing kill pots because they want to win a big pot and make their losses up in one fell swoop. They want to get even. They want to get out for the day. And when they do this, they give us an even greater opportunity to take advantage of them than we otherwise would have in a pot that hasn't been killed.

This may sound like we're saying that players simultaneously play more and fewer hands in a kill pot. And that's true — it's a little of both. Tight players tend to play fewer hands in kill pots.

They defend their blinds less often and shy away from playing mediocre aces. Poor players, and even good players who are losing and perhaps somewhat on tilt, find reasons to play more kill pots.

One of your jobs as a skilled Omaha/8 player is to observe how each opponent plays, taking special note of how he or she adjusts both starting hand selection and strategy when the pot is killed. Some players become more conservative in a kill pot, while others grow more liberal. Still others become temporary kamikazes, taking needless wild risks that burn chips because they're mesmerized by the far larger pots. You can take advantage of such propensities, but first you have to be aware of them. It's up to you to observe — and prosper.

Kill pots also offer bluffing opportunities not often found in non-kill pots. These opportunities exist in kill pots because the cost of calling seems so much higher than usual. It's much more difficult to call with a mediocre hand for $40 than for $20 against a player who has been aggressive on the flop and continues to play aggressively on the turn. This is particularly true when no low draws are available.

We like to bluff at a kill pot by betting when two high cards come on the flop. No low can be completed on the turn, so we continue to bet. Then if no low is possible on the river, we bet again.

You'll also find a bluffing opportunity when someone has raised the pot and two low cards flop. He bets. You call. If the turn and river are both high cards, you can bet and almost always steal the pot. He failed to make a low and often can't call even if he suspects you of bluffing. Once you're aware of such situations, you can take full advantage of them whenever they arise.

Raising

When you're playing Omaha, you have four different opportunities to raise: before the flop, on the flop, on the turn, and on the river. In this chapter, we'll examine reasons why you might raise at each stage.

Raising Before the Flop

Prior to the flop, there are three reasons to raise. One reason is to limit the field. Another is to increase the amount of money in the pot. Sometimes you can accomplish both objectives at the same time. After all, if a raise eliminates the blinds, two bets from each of three callers leaves you with more money in the pot and fewer opponents than single bets contributed by five adversaries.

But there's a third reason to raise. Its underpinnings are more psychological than the two reasons cited above. Raising makes you the aggressor. It makes your opponents react to you, and forces them to be continuously cognizant of your actions. They can't make assumptions about you and they won't be able to take your play for granted. Raising puts your opponents to the test and forces them to a decision, and whenever you can impose a decision on an adversary, there's a chance he'll make an error. That doesn't mean you should raise willy-nilly; but it does mean that raising is frequently a better option than quietly calling, if for no other reason than this.

You shouldn't raise just because your hand is strong. If you have A-A-3-2 double suited — hands don't get much better than that — and say, "Oh goody, I get to raise," that's not really the way to go about it. Your decision should be based on your answer to this question: *Do I want to limit the field or increase the amount of money in the pot?* This question is so important to the subject of raising, and also to your success as an O/8 player, that we're going to examine its implications in detail later in this chapter. But first, let's look at what we mean by "limiting the field" in Omaha/8.

Raising to limit the field

Should you fold, call, or raise? To decide, first assess your position in the betting order. Because the blinds occupy the first two seats, Seat 3 is the first to make a decision, while the button acts last — except during the initial pre-flop betting round, when the blinds get to bat last. When you assess the quality of your hand, examine it in relation to positions of other players in the pot and your own spot in the betting order. Then decide whether you want more players in the pot, or whether you want to limit the number of opponents.

Does your hand play best against many opponents, a few, or only one? Some hands play better heads-up. Others play well three-handed or four-handed, while still others require five or more opponents in the pot to be playable. Examine whatever information is at your disposal before making a decision.

If you're in Seat 3, you're first to act. If you raise, you're raising both blind hands — as well as the kill, if it happens to be a kill pot. Your raise forces the blinds to decide whether their hands are worth playing for the additional cost. And by raising from early position, you're essentially telling other opponents that you have a high quality hand. It's now up to them to decide whether they're holding hands worth two betting units, especially if they believe a premium hand has raised in front of them.

We've already discussed hands containing a pair of aces with not much else. It's a skeletal hand with no flesh on its bones — no low possibilities, flush possibilities, or straight possibilities to speak of. A naked pair of aces in third position must either raise or fold; it's not a calling hand. Naked aces are more valuable when you can reraise an opponent than they are if you merely put in the first raise. The reason is simple: By re-raising, you hope to play heads-up against the initial raiser — who probably has low cards — so that your pair of aces stands a good chance of winning the high end of the pot, or even scooping the pot if the board doesn't contain three low cards.

Is your hand one you want to play, but against only a few players? If so, a raise may serve to narrow the field, increasing your chances for winning the pot. A hand like A-K-K-3 plays much better heads-up or against two players than it does against a table full of opponents. Although A-3 is the second nut low, there's no backup in case your hand is counterfeited, and while K-K is a big pair, it limits you to only one straight opportunity: a Q-J-T to work in conjunction with your A-K. You need to flop three kings for this hand to become really powerful. But remember: a pair will only flop a set approximately once in eight times.

Let's assume you're first to enter the pot. With cards like A-K-K-3, it's to your advantage to play shorthanded. You don't want players entering the pot behind you. Depending upon the game's texture — the nature of the players and the relative level of aggression or passivity in the game — this is a hand that screams out, "Raise me or release me!"

It's important to evaluate each hand you're dealt, remembering that as more people release hands in front of you, it increases the chances that opponents behind you have playable hands. Poker author Mike Caro calls this "Clumping Theory," and it's in your interests to keep it firmly in mind as you make decisions in relation to your position.

If you're in a loose, passive game with six or seven people seeing each flop, and four people have thrown their hands away before it's your turn to act, your remaining opponents may very well hold quality cards. So if you have a marginal raising hand, your raise may not cause remaining opponents to throw their hands away. Any opponent who plays behind you probably has a stronger hand than yours. If that's not enough of a problem, remember that you'll also be out of position on each succeeding betting round. So please don't look at your hand, decide that it's of "raising quality," and then raise automatically.

Before raising, consider:

- players who have acted in front of you.
- opponents who will act behind you.
- the game's texture.
- how this information relates to your hand.

Take time with each hand to think through the factors listed above. Your assessment should consider all we've suggested. Once you've done that, determine your best course of action by answering this question: *Do you want to limit the field or increase the amount of money in the pot?* We've mentioned this question before. Now let's examine its implications.

Raise to increase the amount of money in the pot when you have a hand that has multiple possibilities, or, more importantly, has a chance of scooping the entire pot. Included under this guideline are one-way, high-only hands, since you can scoop if no one makes a low hand.

Here's an example. You're on the button, Seat 3 raises, four players come in behind the raise, and you see four ten-point cards in your hand — cards like K-Q-J-T — or some similar combination. Perhaps there's even an ace your hand, although with a raiser and four players coming in cold for two bets, all the aces are probably spoken for. But you never can tell.

Consider a reraise with this hand full of painted faces. Since you're on the button, you'll be building the pot; everyone who's already in the pot for two bets will call one more. The players who've already acted are telling you that most of the low cards have already been dealt, and that the remainder of the deck may very well be rich in high cards. With four high cards in your hand, it's more likely that the flop will help you than your opponents. Assuming that the flop fits your hand, if you have multiple opponents, at least one of them is likely to bet. That allows you to raise, and to do so from good position.

For all these reasons, reraising before the flop from the button with many players in, or putting in the first raise if nobody has raised yet, is your best course of action. But if you're right up front in Seat 3 with those same four big cards, you have no idea whether the deck is clumped toward the low side or the high side. You don't know how many opponents will come in behind you, either. From this early position, you shouldn't raise with that hand.

After all, the deck may be rich in low cards — not high ones — and all your raise will accomplish is to build a pot for someone else. It's the same hand, but when you have to act early, you're in a bad position from both an informational point of view and a playing point of view. You'd ideally like big cards in the cut-off seat, on the button, or in the blinds. From those positions, you can raise — and even reraise — hopefully with many players already committed to the pot.

Now let's suppose you've been dealt A-4-3-2, all prime low cards, but seven players have already entered the pot before it's your turn to act. You love your cards, and you like the fact that there's a lot of money in the pot. Even if you win only half the pot, you'll make a nice return on your investment. Based on percentages, this hand is still a raising hand. But there's a downside to all of this — with all those callers, you can assume that the remainder of the deck is rich in middle and high cards.

Now is not the most ideal time to raise. You're certainly going to play the hand, but this is a time to quietly call and hope that two or three low cards flop. If they do, you can get aggressive by raising or even reraising. But don't be surprised if only one low card flops. The deck, after all, was tilted that way and you certainly suspected it by the number of opponents who entered the pot.

However, if you're in late position, a lot of people have entered the pot, and you've been dealt A-A-3-2, or A-A-5-2, or a pair of double-suited aces with a deuce and another prime card, you certainly want more money in the pot. You should raise to increase the size of this pot because if the flop hits your hand, you're in good position even if you only get half the pot.

If a couple of players have entered the pot and you've got a high-quality hand like A-K-3-2 suited or double-suited, you should raise to get more money in the pot. These are raising hands because they're the kind of holdings that you can scoop a pot with, or take the lion's share of when you quarter someone who was playing a low hand that had no chance of winning the high side.

Omaha/8 differs from hold'em in that big speculative hands are raising hands in Omaha/8, while big pairs, such as aces or kings, are raising hands in hold'em. Because of this difference, some players have suggested that it's never a good idea to raise pre-flop in Omaha/8.

We don't agree with this, because raises should be predicated on the opportunity to take reasonably considered risks under favorable conditions. In addition, poker is such a flexible game, that it's difficult to say always or never. As a player, you're constantly making decisions, and the relationship between risk and reward can be speculative. Things are not always so clear-cut as when hopes are pinned to a clearly defined hand.

Raising on the Flop

When an opponent bets on the flop, he's saying his hand fits the board in some fashion. But suppose the flop has hit a nice chord with your own hand as well. Hmmm. To raise, or not to raise: that is the question, and suddenly it's your turn to act, thereby answering it.

Again, a decision to raise needs to be predicated on whether you want to limit the field or add more money to the pot. Is this choice of goals beginning to sound a little familiar? It should, because it's what you always need to think about when considering a raise in Omaha.

Sometimes a raise accomplishes both objectives. A raise intended to build the pot may intimidate opponents yet to act, so your raise leads them in the direction of folding. When there's a bet and you've raised, your opponent — if he's playing wisely — has a hand stronger than yours if he calls you. So when it's bet and raised to you, you need a very strong hand to stay in the pot too. When you raise, savvy opponents won't be drawing to second and third best hands. But if you do get callers who can't resist playing inferior hands, that's good news for you — they'll generally be contributing dead money to the pot.

If you have the best made hand with redraws, such as the nut straight with the nut low draw, or the nut low with a nut flush draw and a straight draw, you may not want to limit the field. By simply calling rather than raising, you may ultimately increase the pot's size. Only you can make such decisions, yet you need to make them in the heat of battle, when you're under pressure and sometimes have conflicting factors to consider.

These helpful hints can serve as a guide:

- When you raise the flop, you're far more likely to limit the field than you are on the turn or river — so limiting the field should be your primary objective. Of course, there are many exceptions. You'll run into situations where an opponent bets and gets called in one or two places before it's your turn to act. Now your raise won't limit the field, but it will increase the size of the pot.

- When an opponent bets and one or more players call, you can conclude that each player already in the pot will call your raise. It's safe to assume that your raise here won't limit the field, but instead will simply increase the size of the pot. To raise for the purpose of building the pot, you should have a very big hand or an equally big draw. For example, if your hand is A-3-3-2 with the ace suited in spades, and the flop is Q-7-6 with two spades, you should raise to increase the size of the pot. You have two huge draws, one in each direction, and if a low spade comes you'll have made the best possible hand in both, giving you a scoop. Moreover, if you make a nut low hand, it's very unlikely to be counterfeited. Here's another example: If you hold top set when there's only one low card on a flop containing three different suits — a so-called "rainbow" flop — you should raise both to increase the size of the pot and to make any opponent pay dearly to back into a flush or straight. Regardless of what card appears on the turn, no one will have completed a low hand. If a low card does come on the turn, your top set is still the best hand, and some of your opponents will still be drawing in hopes of making a low hand. Further, if you have a backdoor low draw to accompany your set, your hand is even more valuable. So raise it up!

- But: *Don't raise* only because you have the nut draw, whether it's low or high, and don't raise just because you have a set. You should be raising for a purpose — to increase the size of the pot or limit the field, or both — and you should clearly understand the import of your actions. When you put in a raise, always be crystal clear about your objective(s).

- You can also raise on the flop to bluff. If a pair flops with only one low card, and an opponent bets, he may be bluffing — particularly if he bets in early position. If your opponent really *did* flop three-of-a-kind or better and he's like most players, he'll often check with the intention of check-raising the turn. When an opponent bets a paired flop in early position with only one low card out there, this is a bluff-raising opportunity for you. Your bluff raise might knock everybody else out, and you'll win the pot right there. But if your opponent calls, then checks when a blank comes on the turn, you have another bluffing opportunity. A bet here will probably take the pot. This is a sophisticated play that normally happens in higher limit games, but it's one to keep in your arsenal.

Raising on the Turn

A raise on the turn almost always represents the nuts, but you still need to determine the reason for your raise. Again: Do you want to increase the size of the pot or do you hope to limit the field?

On the turn, a raise is usually made to get more money in the pot. Limiting the field is of secondary importance, for it's generally difficult to eliminate competition at this point in the hand. If somebody has a quality hand, your raise will be called.

Nevertheless, you're raising for one reason only: to build the pot. You're betting on the quality of your hand, for there's little in the way of sophisticated or crafty play available to you when someone bets the turn. This is neither the time nor the place to attempt a bluff-raise. You can raise the flop with such a bluff when a good opportunity comes along. But since an opponent who bets the turn is probably betting the nuts, a bluff-raise is very unlikely to succeed here. If you raise on the turn, somebody has already bet in front of you. By betting, that player was representing the nuts. So if you're a good player, your raise here generally means that you're representing the nuts along with a secondary hand that might scoop the pot, or the nuts with a redraw to an even bigger hand. A raise at this point is not designed to limit the field, although if someone behind you has only a drawing hand, a bet plus your raise will probably eliminate him anyway.

To raise the turn, you need the nuts, and, ideally, a redraw to an even bigger hand. If you make a full house on the turn, and it's the best possible full house, you aren't redrawing. But if you make a full house on the turn with top set, and have a redraw for a higher full house on the river, that's terrific, and you should raise. If you have the nut flush on the turn with a redraw to a full house, you should be raising then, too. And if you have the nut straight with a redraw to a higher straight or a flush, go right ahead — raise it up.

While you'd always prefer a redraw to the nut flush, it's not mandatory in order to raise. In other words, if the turn card provides you with a flush draw to go along with your nut straight, it no longer needs to be a draw to the nut flush. It's a quality redraw nevertheless. With a nut straight and a redraw to a flush — even if it's not to the nut flush, as long as the flush draw card comes on the turn — you're in good shape to raise.

If you have a straight with no redraws, raising is not a good idea with two players, although it is a good idea with three players and just one low card on the board. The reason for raising in this situation is to eliminate backdoor draws to a low hand. The only reason to raise with a nut straight on the turn is if two low cards are on the board and you want to eliminate the low draws or at least make them pay dearly for the chance of snatching half the pot out from under your nose. In general, you should raise the turn with nut straights only when they come fully armed with redraws to larger straights, flushes, or full houses.

Redraws should almost always be played very aggressively. If you have the nut straight with a redraw to a better straight, a flush, or a full house, be aggressive. Bet or raise. If you have the nut low with a draw to another nut low if your hand were to be counterfeited, be aggressive in that situation, too. Whenever you have the best hand along with a redraw to another big hand, you should raise if someone bets into you. But that's not all, you should reraise if it's bet and raised before it's your turn to act. After all, you have the best hand at the moment and you're free rolling to a better hand in the process. Omaha doesn't get much better than that.

Raising on the River

Raising on the river is very different from raising on the turn. A raise on the turn might come from a huge draw, a made hand with one or two redraws, a good high hand with a draw to the best low, a bluff, or a semi-bluff. A raise on the turn can be a raise based on your hand's potential as well as whatever value it has. But a raise on the river is almost always what it represents: the nuts.

Make a raise on the river for one of two reasons: to build the pot or limit callers behind you. Raise to increase the pot when you have the nuts *and* you believe you won't be quartered. This means you should either have the nut low along with a decent high hand, or have the nut high. The exception is when there are four or more players and quartering means you either break even or win a little.

When an opponent bets on the river and you have the nut high with no low when three low cards are on the board, you don't want to raise secondary low hands out of the pot. You want their money in the pot, since fifty cents of each dollar they contribute will go to you.

A sophisticated play to stick in your arsenal involves raising with *second-second*, which means you have a high and a low hand but neither one of them is the nuts, and may not even be the second or third nut hands. If an opponent bets before it's your turn to act, and there is only one player behind you, a raise is sometimes your best course of action. In such situations, you should either raise or release your hand, because calling is usually your worst option. The player who bet into you is probably betting the nuts; you're just hoping he doesn't have the nuts in both directions. Your raise is designed to deter an opponent behind you from overcalling with a better secondary hand than yours.

Obviously, if the player behind you is a perennial calling station who can't be budged out of a pot come hell or high water, and you suspect his hand is better than yours, you shouldn't attempt this maneuver. You have the green light, though, if your raise is likely to scare off a conservative, thoughtful player who would have called a single bet.

You're hoping to play heads-up with a low and a high hand against one opponent, and you're hoping to win half the pot. When an opponent bets and you have a high and a low hand, neither of which is the nuts, you don't want to call, only to have another opponent call behind you. Either raise the bettor or throw the hand away.

You can't use this play all the time because it doesn't come up all that often. So when it does come up, give it a try. But remember, do this only with one player behind you. If it's bet and you're next to act with marginal two-way hands and two or more players are behind you, throw it away. Don't call. And don't raise. If one of your opponents has a nut hand he will call. You won't eliminate anyone, and not only does the player in front of you have the nuts, but someone behind you probably has them, too. All you'll do if you raise is lose two bets.

Take our advice:

- Raise the river with either the nut high or the nut low accompanied by a secondary high hand. This raise is designed to get more money in the pot.

- If you have a secondary high and a secondary low with only one player yet to act, and you don't want an overcall, you can raise the pot unless the opponent behind you is a perennial calling station.

Omaha/8 gives you four opportunities to raise: before the flop, on the flop, on the turn, and on the river. You can raise to limit the field, build the pot, or to exploit a bluffing opportunity. But remember that bluffing in Omaha/8 is a very sophisticated and frequently marginal play. It should be used sparingly. It isn't particularly applicable in low-limit and middle-limit games, where it will often simply cost you more bets. Also, never bluff with more cards to come when two or three low cards are already on the board

Raising from the Blind

If you're the small blind: When you raise or reraise from the small blind, you provide a tremendous amount of information for your opponents. You're virtually defining your hand for every other player still in the pot. That's okay if you don't mind playing your cards face up. And you can do that when playing Omaha/8 with savvy players because the only reason to raise from the small blind is to build the pot with a quality hand, unless you are heads-up with the big blind. Sometimes you'll find yourself willing to play your hand as though your cards were face up and allow your opponents to play behind you, regardless of what they may have.

When the small blind raises, he's announcing to the table at large that he has a top grade hand. When he raises in front of you, assume he has a premium hand and play yours accordingly. After all, he'll do the same to you.

If you're the big blind: In multi-way pots, raising from the big blind also gives away information, though it's not as powerful as a raise from the small blind. Nevertheless, it's much more information than simply calling — or checking if no one has come in for a raise. Raise or reraise from the big blind for just one reason: to get more money in the pot with a hand that deserves to be played against a lot of opponents.

Players often raise from the small or big blind because they have hands containing a pair of aces — and frequently not much more. They mistakenly consider this big naked pair to be as strong as a pair of aces in hold'em. This folly has caused these misguided players to add money to pots with marginal hands while giving away the useful information that they harbor two aces. And as if that's not enough of a gift to the opposition, they also have to act first on each betting round. Gee, nothing like playing with your cards showing!

We rarely recommend raising from the blinds because the very action of raising from them gives away far too much information about your holdings. Your opponents can't put you on a hand if you just call. Calling from the blind provides the greatest amount of flexibility for crafty play. If you just call pre-flop rather than announce your strength by raising, you're in superb position to check-raise the flop, the turn, or the river. Your opponents won't be aware of the strength of your hand until it's too late.

Information is valuable and you shouldn't give it away when you're in the blind. You can build the pot by check-raising on a later betting round, instead of raising before the flop. This also allows you to save money when the flop is unfavorable, when your once potent hand has become just another piece of cheese to be thrown away.

There are a few times, relatively infrequent, when it does make sense to raise from the blinds. If you're in the small blind, no one has raised, and there's only one caller, you can raise and hope to force the big blind to fold. Your object is to play heads-up against the caller. If you're going to play your hand in that situation, you don't want the big blind in there with a random hand. You're much better off heads-up against one caller than getting involved in a three-way confrontation against both the caller and the big blind.

That's one of the very few situations where we recommend raising from the small blind. The small blind provides an ideal check-raising platform, but raising pre-flop rains on that parade. There are just a few other situations where we'll raise from the small blind, and they almost always involve hands like A-3-2-x, or A-5-4-2 with a suited ace, to be played against at least three or four opponents. These are hands with scoop potential written all over them, so we don't mind giving some information away. We recommend raising some of the time with hands like these, though certainly not all of the time. Never be too predictable in poker.

Raising With the Nut Low Before the River

If the board doesn't practically scream that there's a likely flush or three-of-a-kind or full house or straight out there, and you have top pair with a decent kicker and the nut low, you should strongly consider raising if someone bets into you. Your objective here is to play the pot heads-up, because you stand a chance of scooping the entire pot or perhaps grabbing three-quarters of it. But if there's a bet and a call before it's your turn to act, calling is usually your best play.

A Word Of Warning About
Bluffing In Low Limit Games

We've discussed bluffing opportunities and woven some ideas about propitious times to bluff throughout this chapter. Just bear in mind that tricky play — and bluffing in particular — is generally neither prevalent nor very profitable in low-limit and middle-limit Omaha/8 games. Because so many of the pots in those games involve a relatively large number of opponents, it's difficult to promote a weak hand into a winner by bluffing.

At higher limits of play, generally $30-$60 and above, where virtually every pot is raised before the flop and a majority of hands are three-handed or heads-up, you'll find plenty of opportunities for deceptive, manipulative plays — including outright bluffs. That's because bluffs and tricky plays can work only if opponents have good knowledge of the game and care to ponder what lies beyond their own hands. For the most part, that's just not the case in low-limit and middle-limit games. In smaller games, just play good, solid, straightforward Omaha, and be prepared to show down the best hand to win the pot.

Chapter 13

Playing Pairs on the Flop

I f the flop contains a pair of nines or higher — a pair of aces is
not part of this equation because they're low as well as high
cards — the hand will usually play for high only and the pot
will be scooped. Of course, if there's a low card on the flop along
with the high pair, a low hand is always possible if low cards
appear on both the turn and the river. Such a "backdoor" low
occurs only a small percentage of the time, so if you have an A-
2, you should fold after any action on the flop unless your other
two cards offer something substantial toward high.

Pursuing an evasive low in this situation is pure folly. Keep in
mind that unless you have a backup low card, neither an ace nor
a deuce on the turn or river will help you, since either will counterfeit your hand. Only five card ranks can help you, and you
must catch two different ones in succession on the turn and river
to make your low. On top of that, after the high hands put you
through the gauntlet for the privilege of pursuing your draw, you
may well end up being quartered. Drawing for runner-runner low
without additional business in the pot is a losing proposition for
you all the way around. *Our advice is very simple: Don't do it.*

When a pair of nines or higher flops, the hand will almost always
be played shorthanded, because the majority of players with low
draws will release their hands. Shorthanded, these paired flop situations present prime bluffing opportunities. When a pair of
nines or higher flops, the first or second person to act — especially one of the blinds, who could be holding anything — often
bets the hand. This player may be bluffing, hoping to take the
pot right there. And he may very well succeed: If no other player
has matched the pair on the flop, the bettor is in a terrific position to steal.

But whenever there's a call and an overcall, you can be fairly
sure that the overcaller has matched the flop. Even the initial
caller may have matched the flop, though he may have something less than three-of-a-kind. But if it's bet, called, and over-
called, you can be sure one of your opponents has trips.

Sometimes all three players have been helped by the flop. Two of them may have trips, while the other may have a full house already if a pair in his hand matches the odd card on the board.

Note: If you're the player with the full house, and the odd card on the board is of lesser rank than the pair, beware. Although you're probably in the lead right now, if either opponent pairs a card in his hand with either the turn card or the river card, you'll be beaten by a bigger full house. Also, if through your bad luck one of your opponents holds the lone remaining card of the same rank as your three-of-a-kind, your hand is very expensive toast. We're sorry, but that's part of poker. Just remember that if there's a lot of action after a paired flop, there's usually a reason.

Some Bluffing Opportunities

Bluffing in Omaha/8 is less common than in seven-card stud or Texas hold'em. But bluffing opportunities do come along from time to time. A play you might want to try is to call an early position bettor on the flop, then bet if your opponent checks the turn. This maneuver often works against a lone opponent regardless of what you have — even if you called with absolutely nothing in hopes of bluffing on a later betting round.

The play can be especially effective if the flop is atypical in some respect — all high cards for example, or three of a suit with only one low card, or a high pair with an odd card. The early position player may have a premium low hand that missed the flop, so your bet on the turn may be enough to make him relinquish the pot. More often than not, your opponent will throw his hand away.

If you call a player who has bet into a pair on the flop, and the bettor checks the turn, you must bet. Never check behind your opponent in this situation. Checking gives your adversary a free draw to a straight, a flush, or a backdoor low. If you call a bet on the flop and your opponent checks the turn, be prepared to bet in all cases.

But don't bluff in this spot if one or more players have called the pot behind you. In that case, bet the turn only if you have the nuts. This means you should be cautious about betting hands where you've matched the pair on the board to make three-of-a-kind, but haven't yet filled up. The exception is when your kicker is an ace. If you have three-of-a-kind with an ace kicker and it's checked to you, feel free to bet the turn, even with a player behind you.

When You Bet Into a Paired Board and You're Raised

If the player behind you raises when you bet into a paired board, you can often assume he has a full house. You must now evaluate your hand to determine the number of outs that can yet give you a higher full house than your opponent's. First count the number of available cards that will give you a hand strong enough to beat the raiser's. Then determine if the pot promises enough return on your call to offset the odds against making your hand.

Let's say, for example, that a pair of nines and a king hit the board and your hand is A-9-3-2. The turn card is a seven. If you bet on the turn and find yourself raised, you should assume your opponent holds the fourth nine and has filled up already, or that he may even have made kings full of nines right on the flop. Either way, things are looking very bleak for you, since the only cards available that might improve your hand enough to win are three aces. But even if you get one, you may already be beaten. This is a clear fold for you.

Omaha/8 players frequently get married to their cards. When they bet and find themselves raised, their immediate instinct is to call. But a raise usually means a strong hand. In fact, it usually means the raiser has the nuts. Bluff raising in Omaha/8, particularly on the turn and the river, is uncommon, to say the least. Players occasionally bluff by raising the flop, often hoping to save bets on the turn and river if opponents defer to them. If the bluff raise on the flop works, the bluffer may get to see the rest of the board for free.

But bluffing by raising on the turn or river is very uncommon. Trust us on this: When an opponent raises the turn or river, he usually has a very strong hand. In this spot, it's okay, even if you have a fairly good hand, to throw it away. You'll probably save money, or, at the least, not miss out on much.

If you have the second best low, and a draw of some kind, or a small set, remember you're not married to the hand. Don't feel compelled to see it through hell or high water regardless of cost. Without an excellent high hand, you're likely to wind up being quartered at best. Chances are that the raiser has a nut low, very possibly with counterfeit protection, plus a high hand and possible scoop as well. Fold and wait for better opportunities where you have the raising hand.

When Your Opponent Raises Before the Flop and Then Bets Into a Low Board

A pre-flop raiser generally bets if the flop contains two low cards. You can almost count on it. Yet a player who limps in from early position with a quality starting hand like A-A-4-2 will sometimes check this kind of flop. Psychologically speaking, it's as though he realizes that since he isn't expected to bet, he won't. But had he raised before the two low cards flopped, you can be sure he would have come out betting.

The very act of raising pre-flop sets up an expectation that the raiser will take the lead on the flop by betting, no matter what appears on the board. But many hands, even premium hands, are rendered worthless, or nearly so, by an uncongenial flop. Nevertheless, the pre-flop raiser will very often grit his teeth and bet anyway. He's expected to bet, so he does, though he may have nothing at all. This nugget of information is valuable to your future profits in Omaha/8, so remember it well.

When a brick — a high card, such as a nine, ten, jack, queen, or king — falls on the turn, the initial raiser who also bet the flop may now put on the brakes and check. What does this tell you? It almost screams, "Low draw at work!" That most often means a hand containing an ace and, usually, a deuce. If it doesn't include a deuce, it has a trey. Moreover, if your opponent is a good player, he also has another prime card as a backup.

If he's a very aggressive opponent who plays too many hands and frequently raises pre-flop, he may bet on the flop with nothing but a bargain basement low draw like A-4. Nevertheless, if a brick comes on the turn, Aggressive Al often reverts to Cautious Charlie. Confronted with a turn card that doesn't help his hand, he meekly checks. Now that you can follow his betting pattern, you pretty much know his hand. But he doesn't know yours, so if a third low card fails to arrive, your bet on both turn and river will often take the pot.

While surmising his hand based on his play, you should evaluate your own hand against the board and determine whether to be aggressive or passive here. If you have just one or two opponents — the pre-flop raiser and perhaps one other player — and the river card is a brick, you can bluff at the pot and frequently pick it up — particularly if you're first to act. Your bet may win you the pot right then and there.But what about a skillful, crafty player who raises before the flop? He bets when he flops two low cards, only to catch a high card on the turn. What does he do now? Answer: He'll evaluate his hand, then follow through and bet the turn if he has possibilities of scooping the entire pot. For example, he may have a flush draw to the same ace he's using for his draw to the nut low hand. And the truly good player won't simply base his wager on an A-2 combination and an ace-high flush draw. He probably has a backup low card too, so if a deuce comes on the river, he'll still make a low hand — even though it may not be the nuts.

Your bluffs will have a higher batting average if you bet the turn when a brick appears that's unlikely to help anyone else, then follow through with another bet on the river. Bluffs in Omaha/8 are more likely to succeed when the bluffer is able to make two successive bets rather than just a single bet on the end.

If the bluffer bets the turn and bets again on the river after two consecutive bricks appear, it's easy for callers going low to throw their hands away. Though some loose players will call a bet on the end with far less than the nuts, it's difficult for someone holding a thwarted low hand to call just for high with something like one small pair when a bluffer has made two successive bets into high cards. This is one of the few good bluffing opportunities in Omaha/8.

But remember: It usually won't work unless you bet twice. A bluff on the river, especially if it's the first bet you've made in the hand, is seldom successful. On the other hand, when you make your hand on the river after calling all along, you'll almost always get called when you do bet.

Chapter 14

Different Betting Limits Make For Different Style Games

Some old bromides are just that, but others are truly right as rain. Take the one about "different strokes for different folks." It might not be valid in every case, but it sure is around the poker tables. Games do differ, and one crucial distinction lies in the size of the bets. Bigger games are different than lower limit games. That's just the way it is. With that in mind, let's look at some of the common game structures and describe what you can expect to find in typical games at various betting limits.

Low-Limit Omaha/8 — $1-$2; $2-$4; $4-$8

Sometimes you'll find a $4-$8 game played with $1 and $2 blinds. In them, you can call two dollars and raise it to $6. The idea behind this structure is to allow players to see the flop on the cheap, and to encourage action. Such games tend to played in a very loose, passive style, and you'll typically find five or more players seeing every flop. Sometimes you'll find all of them seeing the flop. But most $4-$8 games are played with $2 and $4 blinds, where it's $4 to call before the flop and $8 to raise. These are a notch or two tighter than games where the blinds are $1 and $2, but they're still fairly loose.

Raises are infrequent in these games, particularly before the flop. But when someone does raise, it's done with only a few select hands — A-4-3-2, A-A- 2-x, and A-A-4-3 with a suited ace are typical examples — so it's pretty easy to deduce the raiser's hand. In these games, when someone raises before the flop, it's almost like he's turning his cards face up at the very moment he raises. On the other hand, it's extremely difficult to know what other opponents may have because so many of them see the flop with just about anything, even though it means calling the raise.

Loose, passive games like these don't lend themselves well to tricky or crafty plays.

Bluffing is usually futile and the best hand almost always wins at showdown. On the other hand, when the river is checked all around, as it sometimes is in these passive games, that's a pretty good indication that no one has the nuts. Play at the river is usually quite straightforward.

Whenever there's a bet at the end, it usually means someone has the nuts. Profitability in these games comes from holding the goods at the showdown, because you'll generally find at least three players calling with less than the nuts for either high or low. They came to play, and they won't fold until they've paid to see the winning hand.

As a related point, aggressive play, while quite effective in higher limit games, doesn't offer any particular advantage at these low limits other than to put more money in the pot. If that's your objective, raise, re-raise, or check-raise at will. Just remember that most opponents won't stop to ponder the meaning of your aggression, and you'll rarely be able to force them out of the pot. You can beat these games with solid, straightforward poker, but slick play, bluffing, and tricks won't get the job done, nor will naked aggression. To come out a winner, you'll have to win more money with your good hands and lose less on your poor ones by saving bets, most often through judicious folding.

Bigger Than Baby Steps — $6-$12; $9-$18; $10-$20

As a general rule, these games, like their lower limit brethren, tend towards fairly passive play. But there are some important differences. One primary difference between this betting tier and the lowest is that there are fewer pre-flop callers now. Many players at this second level do throw away their weaker holdings. They don't do so often enough, mind you, but they've learned not to play just anything. Play in general is much tighter here too, and it's somewhat easier to deduce an opponent's hand since players are both more selective and more skilled. But as in the very lowest limit games, the best hand is almost always shown down at the end.

Middle-limit Omaha/8 — $10-$20; $15-$30; $20-$40

Here's where many skill factors discussed in this book come into play. On this third tier, you'll find high-quality Omaha players sharpening their skills while earning a solid hourly wage for their play. At this level, the best hand is not necessarily shown down to win the pot. A solid player of this category can change gears, wear multiple hats, and take full advantage of the theories and approaches discussed in this book to increase his or her win rate.

Big Games — $30-$60 and $40-$80

$30-$60 Omaha games are inconsistent, teetering in texture like a ride on a see-saw between middle-limit games and those played for higher stakes. The direction of the slant at any given moment is dependent upon the exact player mix. Play at this level is sometimes like that at $20-$40 and other times like games of $50-$100 or more. The determining factor is generally based on other games in the room. If $30-$60 is the biggest game available, it will play more like a very big game. But if there are bigger games spread in the room, it will play more like $15-$30 and $20-$40 games.

Quite often there is a distinct advantage to playing in the second biggest game in the house, because the biggest game tends to attract the best players. So if you walk into a cardroom and spot a huge full game, especially one with known tough players, take a hard look at the game just under it in limits. Chances are it's far more beatable!

Quite often, $30-$60 Omaha/8 is played with more chips on the table than you'll find in a $50-$100 game. That's because lower denomination chips are used. As a result, players feel like they're wagering more than they really are. This is an important, but somewhat unobtrusive, psychological consequence of game structure. Pots look bigger when smaller chips are used, and this tends to encourage loose play and plenty of action. It's harder to maintain discipline in such games because it's tempting to chase those apparently larger pots with inferior cards, hoping to get lucky.

This insidious power of smaller denomination chips has equal impact in many other games. Never underestimate the significance of the prevailing denomination used in your game. For example, in Southern California, $9-$18 games have all but replaced $10-$20 games. Why? Pots in $10-$20 games with their five-dollar chips look smaller than those in $9-$18 games, which are played with three-dollar chips. In fact, because the three-dollar chips lead to pots that *look* bigger, these games are actually played much more loosely. More players are lured into action because of the *perceived* size of the pot, leading to games that not only look bigger, but are bigger as a result of all the loose play. What was initially erroneous perception has become reality.

Marshall McLuhan wrote about becoming what we behold. He may not have been a poker player, but with this observation McLuhan was never more spot-on accurate in his understanding of poker players than he would have been if he'd studied the game for 100 years.

High-Limit Games — $50-$100 And Higher

Play in these games is at a much higher overall skill level. Players exhibit much more variety in their strategy and conceptual understanding — although you'll find some very weak players here, too.

At this level, as at all others, keep track of the chip denomination used. As we've pointed out, the smaller the denomination, the bigger the pots appear, the looser the games are played, and the more mistakes players make. At this level of play, you might think psychological factors are implausible, that big-game players would be immune to this sort of stuff. But they're not. Trust us.

A $60-$120 game played with $20 chips tends to play much more loosely than a $50-$100 game played with $25 chips. If you're going to play in one of these games and have a choice, pick the game with more chips on the table and a lower denomination chip. All else being equal and given the choice, we'd always prefer a $40-$80 game with $10 chips over one played with $20 chips.

A $15-$30 game almost always plays with $5 chips, and there are more chips on the table than you'll find in a $10-$20 game. This very compelling visual factor encourages loose play. There are, consequently, more players in each pot, and you may be sorely tempted to join them. It's here that you must exercise great self-control and refuse to lower your standards. If you keep your discipline, the contagious psychological desire to win big pots can be a boon to your winning ways

After all, big pots seem more determined by the number of chips in the pot than by their total value. Imagine five large-denomination chips stacked neatly in the center of the poker table, versus a raggedy, dribbling mound, five inches high, of small-denomination chips. The tiny stack of chips just doesn't get that old adrenalin flowing the way that humongous pile does, does it? It's that perception thing again, but it's powerful.

Even solid players who know better may succumb to the temptation of playing inferior hands in early position, simply because the pots are so large in games affected by the "small-chip illusion." If you're choosing between several such games and can observe them first, watch carefully at showdowns to see what cards turn up, especially those held by players in early positions. This can help you categorize adversaries as well as prove useful in choosing the right game.

Big Fish In Small Ponds — Killing Time In Smaller Games

Always be on the lookout for higher limit players playing at lower limits, especially if their usual game isn't available. Usually they're just killing time until their usual game starts up. You'll frequently find $50-$100 players in a $20-$40 game while waiting for the bigger game to begin.

Special Beginners' Alert: You'll occasionally find $20-$40 players in a $4-$8 game because it's the only one available. It may be late at night or very early in the morning, or, for any number of reasons, there aren't enough higher limit players to spread the bigger game. Although this isn't the kind of competition you want, we don't mean you shouldn't play if you spot such players in your game. Just respect their bets and raises and take advantage of this opportunity to learn all you can from their play.

Then again, these higher limit players often play differently at lower limits than they do in their usual game. They may play more hands, play them loosely, and be more aggressive. They may, for example, raise with inferior hands because they're playing in what for them is a less serious or even recreational game. If they lose at this much lower level, they can rapidly make up their losses when their usual game gets underway. Money at these lower limits just doesn't have the same value to them, and you can often use this to your advantage.

For example, sometimes these players are frustrated because they'd really like to play more aggressively in their usual game. They may lack the stomach for it there, so when they move down in limits to the only game available, they suddenly start splashing chips all over the place and playing a style that's totally out of character for them. If you see this sort of behavior, take advantage of it. While it's almost counterintuitive to think that someone who can hold his or her own at higher limits might be a fish in a lower limit game, that's exactly what can happen.

But beware: The higher limit players may splash chips for a round or so, then shift gears and tighten up considerably, just in time to take a few racks of chips out of your game before moving on up. So stay alert, and always play your best game against them. Never forget that these particular fish are really sharks, and that they can revert to shark-like behavior whenever they choose.

Also be aware of other good players in your game — opponents who have the tools that you do, who know what's going on when players move down in limits and take advantage of it. You can take advantage of them too, because you know exactly what they're doing. Savvy opponents who realize that high-limit players are throwing extra chips away may be changing their own play too. And as long as you're aware of it, you can take advantage of them also.

Chip Management

Regardless of what betting limits are comfortable to you, it's important to have a sufficient number of weapons on hand to fire at the target when you have a hand that warrants action. From a psychological viewpoint, it's also important to have enough chips to ensure that their scarcity doesn't affect your play. We recommend buying into the game for 25 big bets. If you're going to play $20-$40 Omaha/8, you'll need two racks of five-dollar chips, a total of $1,000. If you're going to play $4-$8, you'll need $200 in chips.

If you're having a bad day but decide to keep playing, consider rebuying when your stacks get down to about half their original size. We've noticed that players who are very short-stacked — so close to the felt that they may have to go all-in the next hand they play — tend to play differently than they do when they have a full arsenal at their disposal.

Some players who are very disciplined — but in all honesty it's a precious few — know how to use short-stacked status to optimum effect. They might, for example, go all-in with a hand featuring multiple secondary draws. They'd ordinarily pass such a hand if it appeared necessary to invest too much money in it, but they'll play it short-stacked, knowing it's a low-risk, high-reward situation. But those disciplined enough to do this are very few, and there's no guarantee that a situation affording that kind of parlay opportunity will come up at the right time.

Instead, most players who go all-in simply tend to make kamikaze calls with their remaining chips, then rebuy once they lose them. Though they intend to revert to playing their best game with the newly acquired chips, this psychological posturing normally doesn't last very long. After just one bad beat at the river, or one high-quality starting hand that miserably misses the flop, that new complement of chips may dissipate even faster than the initial buy-in. Please don't let this happen to you.

If you're short-stacked and the blinds are approaching, we recommend that you rebuy only after you've acquired the button. Deferring the rebuy means you won't have to risk a lot of chips when you're out of position in the blinds, and can simply hope to get lucky. In this one specific situation, it's advantageous to be short-stacked, which, of course, is one of the reasons players are not allowed to remove chips from the table.

Chapter 15

Runner-Runner: Dream Street or Nightmare Alley

R unner-runner is a parlay of sorts. It occurs in all flop games whenever a player catches a perfect card on the turn and another on the river to complete his poker hand. Let's say a player holds two cards of a single suit. When one card of the same suit flops, another comes on the turn, and yet a third arrives on the river, completing the flush, that's runner-runner.

Another typical runner-runner situation yields a straight. Many times this happens when a player already has a good low hand and "backs into" a low straight or a wheel to accompany it. Such cases often constitute a scoop. Runner-runner to a full house is also possible, though it's not as common as catching two perfect cards to complete a straight or a flush. Perhaps the most common runner-runner event in Omaha/8 is when one low card flops, another comes on the turn, and the river brings still another, making a low hand for the fortunate recipient.

But playing for runner-runner can be very costly unless the two perfect consecutive cards happen to arrive through luck, incidental to a bona fide hand. You might, for example, get lucky enough to catch two running flush cards while drawing to a nut low hand after two babies appear on the flop. This sort of serendipitous event is a far cry from calling a bet on the flop with nothing but the scant hope of catching two perfect cards for some other type of hand.

Here's another example: Assume David raised before the flop with A-K-3-2, double-suited — a very strong starting hand, but the flop presents T-9-3 of different suits, a complete mismatch. David stifles a sigh. He knows deep down that this is the time he should give up the ghost by checking and then folding if someone bets, but he does nothing of the sort. Because our hero raised before the flop, and remains "... in love with his hand," he's frustrated with the "garbage flop" but decides to play on anyway. He checks. Someone bets. He calls, hoping for a low card in order to draw at the nut low for half the pot.

If a low card does come, David's committed to the hand and will probably call any number of bets or raises just to see the river card. So what's happening here? Does he have legitimate business in this pot after the flop? No. He's hoping to catch runner-runner with little else going for him. Whether he gets lucky this time or not, he's playing loser's poker here.

Although David's play may seem totally irrational as you read this, in the heat of battle you may succumb to the same temptation he did. Most Omaha/8 players have found themselves in similar dilemmas. Premium hands rarely come along, and when you do get one and then catch an ugly flop yielding but one lonesome low card, it's all too easy to say, "I'll just take one off."

Bottom line: When you act on this impulse to see another card, you're hoping for a low card on the turn so you'll be able to rationalize investing two additional bets in the pot. And for what? Why, just to draw for yet another low card on the river. You may miss that second perfect card, of course, and lose all you've wagered in the hand. But even when you do get lucky and catch runner-runner low cards this way, you'll take down just half the pot.

So fortify yourself against future temptation right now. Read our lips: Drawing for runner-runner low despite an unfriendly flop is very costly and extremely silly. In the vast majority of such situations, you should simply fold when your premium low hand marries the wrong flop. Here's an exception: If you have a suited ace with a deuce and another prime card, you can continue past the flop if it includes one low prime card and one card of your suit, and two of your three prime cards haven't been counterfeited. This kind of hand, although still requiring two running cards, has good scoop potential. So if pot odds are right, it actually makes sense to take one off.

To justify "…taking one off" as an exception to the general rule against pursuing runner-runner draws, you should have at least four, and preferably five, players in the pot, plus backdoor draws to the nut flush *and* nut low. For example, with five opponents, suppose you hold A♣-Q♣-Q♦-2♠ and the flop is J♦-9♣-4♥. In this situation, you can see the next card under the guidelines just given. You're looking for a low club or possibly a queen on the turn. Even though a queen carries the distinct possibility of a made straight for the opposition, you can still scoop if the board pairs on the river.In this instance, the perfect runner on the turn is a low prime card that's suited to your ace and doesn't counterfeit your low hand. Second choice is another low card — though not prime — that's suited to your ace. And third best is either a high suited card that matches your ace without pairing the board, or any low card — even if it's a different suit than that of your ace. With luck, you'll get one or more of the following: a draw to scoop with the nut flush on the river, a draw to the nut flush and the nut low, a draw to scoop with both a wheel and the nut low, or, at least, a draw to win half the pot with a nut low only.

Remember, your goal in playing runner-runner hands is to either scoop the pot or win half of a very large one. Anything less makes the draw too expensive. Hands like these require either lots of players or lots of money — or both — to be in the pot before the flop. When that's the case, "...taking one off" is playing good poker. But we can't put this warning strongly enough: Avoid taking more cards, as so many players do, out of anger and frustration because the flops keep missing your starting hands.

Chapter 16

A Bet Saved Equals A Bet Earned

In every poker book ever written and at every poker seminar ever presented, you'll find this same, simple, commonsense mantra presented: *A bet saved is just as valuable as a bet earned.*

If you're playing $10-$20 Omaha/8, or any other game for that matter, and you don't call a $20 bet that you would have lost — and therefore have $20 more in your stack of chips — that's just as valuable to you as winning a $20 bet. You're twenty bucks to the good either way, and that $20 spends the same whether it's money won, or money you didn't lose.

This makes an awful lot of sense and seems very logical, doesn't it? But it begs this question: Why do Omaha players in particular make so many bad calls, yet fail to make good value bets? If this seems like a self-inflicted case of "heads you win, tails I lose," you're beginning to get the picture, and it's not a pretty one.

A Bet Saved

When we talk of bets saved, we're not talking about those bets saved because you decided not to play certain starting hands. Since you now have a better understanding of the game of Omaha, we're going to hold you to a higher standard, and we both know you're going to play fewer starting hands than you played before picking up this book. So this chapter deals with the quality of your decision-making *after* you've decided to play a hand.

Once you've decided to play, you have four basic decisions to make:

- Am I going to play the hand on the flop?
- Am I going to play the turn?
- Will I see the river?
- Will I check, bet, or raise on the end?

The second and third decisions cost twice as much as the first. A bet on the flop is just one unit, while bets on later rounds are two units. For example, if you're playing $10-$20 Omaha/8, all bets on the flop are in units of $10, but wagers made on the turn and river cost $20.

So our latter two decisions cost twice as much as the first one. Nevertheless, while the flop is relatively bargain priced, that's when most really bad decisions about saving bets are made. Fact: More bad calls are made on the flop than on any other betting round. Implication: Over time, many players lose a good deal of money unnecessarily on the flop.

Now that you're armed with this information, you can resolve to better decisions on the flop. But it's harder than you think. One problem is that it's easy to become quite ego-involved with those first three board cards. Your ego leads you to seek reasons to keep playing — and find them — even when the flop doesn't fit your hand at all.

In fact, the worst mistake you can make on the flop comes when you've raised before the flop. Because you've taken the initiative, everyone tends to react to you, and your first instinct is to show the table that you're still the one to beat. So you bet the flop, even when it's not to your liking.

Let's look at a specific case. Suppose you've made a marginal raise before the flop with an unsuited A-T-9-2 and Q-6-3 shows up on the flop. Although you have a nut low draw, you have no draw to a straight or flush, and no pair that might improve to a set or better. The best you can hope for is to make a low hand and win half the pot, while hoping someone else doesn't quarter you with the same low hand. But because you were the raiser and two low cards flopped, you feel compelled to bet on the flop, partly from ego. But perhaps it's a better idea to check not only your ego, but the flop too.

Deciding not to bet in such situations can save you money, perhaps as much as three betting units on some hands. Checking the flop may even get you a free card on the turn, since opponents may either fear your check-raise or not like the flop themselves. Then if the turn doesn't help you, it's easier to get away from a weak hand when someone else bets.

Contrast that to what may happen if you bet the flop and check the turn, only to have someone else bet. Your ego may push you to call, even though you're calling for only half of the pot with no backup to your ace and deuce. You're counterfeited if an ace or deuce comes, and what's worse, if you catch an ace — giving you a pair of aces and nothing else — you may even call out of frustration in hopes of winning half the pot with that measly, lonely pair of aces. Of course, there are situations where the pot odds make it appropriate to play for half the pot, and you need to be conscious of the size of the pot and know when it's large enough to play for half of it.

Unfortunately, in this game you'll lose the high side most of the time with one big pair — even if it's a pair of aces. At this point, your low has come to naught, and your pair of aces for high will probably drown at the river. Meanwhile, you've invested several bets you could have saved, and those unwisely invested chips will find their way to players with better hands.

Another money-eating situation occurs when you make a mediocre call before the flop and the flop fits your hand, but poorly. Perhaps you pickup a draw to the third or fourth best flush, or the second best straight, and you're angry with yourself for investing money in this hand before the flop — although, if you're honest, it's more than likely that you threw it away rather than "invested" it. Now trouble abounds and you bet or call or even call a raise out of ego. You're angry with yourself and want to prove that your pre-flop decision wasn't that bad, but you're simply throwing good money after bad.

This is commonplace. We believe more bad calls are made for psychological reasons in Omaha/8 than in any other poker game. By being aware of this insidious Omaha minefield, you can make more of an effort to control your decisions, saving bets you'd lose otherwise.

Face it: The best time to ditch hands foiled by the flop is on the flop. If the flop doesn't hit your hand, it must provide possibilities for either scooping the pot or getting a positive return on your investment if you win just half of it. Otherwise, you need to get away from your hand and you need to do it right now. Every dime saved spends the same as a dime won. And while saving bets is far less enjoyable than dragging a big pot, at the end of the day that old adage holds true: "A penny saved is a penny earned."

When you play Omahas/8, the most difficult decisions you'll make are those related to playing or folding once you see the flop. One of Omaha's biggest traps occurs in three stages:

1. You make a mediocre or bad call on the flop, although you know better.

2. The turn card improves your hand, but only slightly. You call here, too, although you know better.

3. On the river, you make a one-way hand that turns out to be second or third best. You make a crying call here, although, again, you know better. (This is starting to sound predictable, isn't it?) But this time you rationalize your added double bet investment by telling yourself it's justified by the size of the pot. Well, sometimes it is and sometimes it isn't. But when you make such calls out of frustration and stubbornness — when you tell yourself that since you've gone this far, you may as well go the rest of the way — you're really hoping that divine intervention will save you from your parade of bad choices by granting you a miracle. But miracles, of course, rarely happen — even in poker.

If the three little steps above sound like stairs you've climbed once too often, you've identified a huge leak in your game. That's good. Naming the problem is half the battle. But now you must take measures to win that battle. But what measures, exactly?

We guess you could try praying to the Omaha gods that you'll never make a bad call again. But they might not answer. Or you could just go on hoping to get lucky when the cards are turned up. Probably you've tried that, and it's even worked on occasion. But in your heart of hearts you know that players who live on hope generally wind up broke. Over the long term, reliance on luck doesn't work because Lady Chance is notoriously fickle. So what does work? Answer: Informed decision-making.

Omaha can't be played well in an information vacuum. Every decision you make needs to be based on such factors as:

- your assessment of possible hands held by opponents.
- the number of players in the pot.
- your position in the betting order.
- the sequence of cards already dealt.
- your opponents' betting patterns and actions.

That's a lot to consider in the heat of battle — which is why you're allowed to call "time" and spend a few seconds analyzing things — but once you've got the process down pat, you simply need to make correct decisions most of the time if you want to be a consistent winner.

At the risk of being repetitive, we're going to repeat this point because it's so very important to your success as an Omaha/8 player: The biggest decision you'll encounter is making the right decision on the flop. It's the biggest decision because it's the one you most hate to make when the flop doesn't fit, and it won't fit much of the time. Once you've discarded your starting cards, nothing can bring them back, though you may occasionally have a twinge when your unwanted dog would have won a big bone. But when you have an active hand, it's very hard to let it go if the flop helps a little — just enough to give you a bit of hope that it can win.

But in this game, a little hope, like a little knowledge, is a dangerous thing. It's easy to toss a hand on the flop if it misses completely, and easy to play on with gusto if it hits hard. But a tepid match of your hand with the flop is like any other tepid relationship — you aren't thrilled, but you stay anyway, hoping it might get better and hating to let it go.

But in poker, as in life, you have to make those hard decisions and cut your losses. In a typical four-hour session you shouldn't decide to "...take one off" more than two or three times, if that many. You should only do so if your hand has good scoop potential. If you catch runner-runner to win the pot, it should be because you made a cost-effective choice to play on, not because you acted on a hunch.

Bets Earned and Saved on the Flop

When the flop hits you perfectly and your hand is complete — maybe it even has redraws to a better hand — there's no anguish associated with your decision. You'll either bet the hand in complete comfort, or try for a check-raise. You'll make your play, and you'll be comfortable with it because your hand is complete.

With several players in the pot, you may also decide to try for extra bets with come hands, where many cards can complete your hand on the turn or the river. Under these circumstances you can bet or even raise for value on the turn. It's time to get more money in the pot because your hand's potential justifies it.

It's essential, though, that several players see the flop, so that the amount of money promised by the pot will more than offset the odds against making your hand. Conversely, you probably won't be offsetting the odds against making your hand when you're up against only one or two players. Remember: You can earn extra bets on the flop by betting on the come whenever the number of opponents in the pot justifies it.

You should be on the lookout for hands with multiple possibilities — hands where you've got the nut low draw, the nut flush draw, and a backup card for your low as counterfeit protection. Perhaps you've got the nut straight draw and wraps to bigger straights. Perhaps you've got a flush draw in addition to your straight.

So although your hand may not even be complete at this juncture, you've got options galore. You're in a position to scoop the pot, win three-quarters of it, or maybe only half of a big pot. In any event, there's enough money in the pot to justify your investment. You should be betting all you can to build that pile of chips and obtain a big return. But like any investment, the potential reward has to outweigh the risks you take on the road to winning. Like so much of poker, this is a case of comparing the potential reward at the end of the rainbow with the cost of getting there.

Sometimes your ability to read your opponent's hand will allow you to save a bet or two. When your opponent checks and calls on the flop, then bets the turn, he almost always has the nuts and frequently the turn card is the key. For example, if two low cards and two spades flop, and your opponent checks the flop and then comes out betting the turn when a third high spade appears, he almost always has the nut flush. You shouldn't call with smaller flushes unless you also have the nut or second nut low draw.

Although this is a simple and rather obvious example, it does illustrate a point. Skilled Omaha/8 players are always on the lookout for transparent actions such as these. Although expert players will mislead their opponents through deceptive play, in lower limit games you won't find much trickery. You can often deduce your opponent's hand by reviewing the board cards in light of the action your opponent took — or didn't take —on the various betting rounds.

Bets Earned and Saved on the Turn

Even if you made a poor decision earlier in the hand, you should get away from a bad situation on the turn and save yourself two betting units in the process. The turn is expensive; calling a bet there is twice the price of calling on the flop.

Most of the time you play the turn, you should have either the nuts or a draw to the nuts, *and you should also have a chance to scoop the pot.* Drawing for just half the pot on the turn is usually a bad idea. Ideally, you'd like your hand to have several possibilities. The very least you should have on the turn is a low draw with a third prime card to insure against being counterfeited, and there ought to be enough money in the pot to justify it.

With drawing hands, if we call the turn, we hope to scoop the pot if we get lucky *but also* have some outs that can give us at least half of the pot. We don't want to call bets on the turn — or worse yet, call raises — without such multiple options. And we most certainly don't want to call bets or raises on the turn with second nut draws or worse.

Remember to stop, think about those hands your opponents might have, and anticipate your own actions based on the turn and river cards. And while you're at it, be sure to get a rough fix on your potential return on investment. After all, the relationship between risk and reward should drive most of your actions. Make logical decisions. Value bets on the turn should be based on a complete hand — and hopefully it's one with redraws to a bigger hand, or a completed one-way hand with chances of picking up the other half of the pot, too.

Bets and raises on the turn should be based on value and upon making it costly for opponents to draw cards that will beat you. Here's an example: If you have the nut straight, but with no low or redraws, and an opponent bets into you, it's appropriate to raise if there's someone else in the pot. You need to forestall a third opponent from drawing to a second or third flush or to a backdoor low hand. Even though you're in a defensive posture, you should force opponents to fold by making it too expensive for them to call with marginal hands.

Players who bet into situations where it's obvious they'll be called are usually not bluffing. In order to call or overcall in situations like this, you should have the nuts, a draw to the nuts, or a sufficiently large overlay from the pot to make it correct to call.

Suppose you hold a pair of sevens among your cards and flop a set when K-Q-7 appears on the flop. An early position player bets and you decide to "…take one off." The turn is a nine and your opponent bets again. Because you called the flop, unless your adversary is in a stupor, he's figuring that you'll call the turn, too. But he still came out betting. Unless you're drawing to more than your set, you're often drawing dead, and it's OK to fold.

Bets Earned and Saved on the River

The river is more easily played than other betting rounds. A bettor on the river usually has the nuts. The caller's actions and those of any overcallers are usually based on both the size of the pot and reasoned assessment of the bettor's likely hand.

Your options on the river are generally straightforward. These plays are more easily determined than all other decisions you've had to make thus far:

- Should you bet the nut high?

- Should you bet the nut low with nothing at all toward high?

- Should you raise or try for an overcall when an opponent bets and you hold the nut high?

- Should you raise with the nut low and a quality high hand?

- Should you raise with a nut hand and a secondary hand in the other direction in order to eliminate overcallers and enable you to scoop or win three-quarters of the pot?

- Should you raise with a mediocre low and a mediocre high hand when one opponent bets into you and there's one potential caller behind you, in order to give yourself an opportunity to win half the pot?

One of the biggest mistakes made on the river occurs when a player has the nut low against several opponents and is so concerned about being quartered that he decides not to bet. When four or more players are in the pot, such reticence is silly, because the value of that bet far exceeds the risks.

When you're quartered and four players are in the pot, you get your money back, so it's essentially a risk free proposition. It's only a problem if there are *two* other players who also hold the nut low. But that's rare, and to win consistently at poker, you have to avoid what poker maven Barry Tanenbaum calls the MUBS, or "Monster Under the Bed Syndrome," where you consistently refrain from taking the most profitable action because you fear an opponent might hold the one hand that can beat you, regardless of how improbable that hand might be.

It's often appropriate to bet the nut low with nothing else when there are three players in the pot. To do so, you must conclude it's at least even money that yours is the only nut low. But even if you're wrong, and wind up getting quartered, you'll lose only a *small percentage* of your last bet. The upside is that you'll gain *half* of that last bet if your assessment was correct and neither opponent has a nut low hand.

If you were to keep records of such events, you'd see that the nut low wins half the pot more often than it gets quartered when three players remain in the hand. It's the "Three Player Left In The Hand Decision." With four players in the hand, it's a no-brainer. At worst, you get your money back; at best, you'll show a profit. (Yes, we know that if you bet, and someone throws his hand away, and then it's raised, only three players will remain and if you get quartered, you'll lose money. It does happen every now and then, but you have a bad case of MUBS if you refrain from taking action based on that sequence of events.)

Whenever there are four players, you'll make much more money in the long run by betting the nut low. And you'll make more money by betting the nut low when there are three players, too. But it shouldn't be done automatically. Do it with thought and evaluation. And then, if you conclude that one of your opponents also has a nut low, especially if he's a very conservative player who seldom goes to the river without the absolute nuts, just check and call.

Chapter 17

Playing Styles

If you want to master this game, you'll need to evaluate the playing styles of your opponents, and you should be able to do that within the first 30 minutes of sitting down at the table, even if you haven't played against any of them before. It's not difficult to categorize opponents based on generalities, on the way they play most of the time. But that's not enough. Since generalities are rife with exceptions, you'll need to bear in mind that players aren't robots. Their play will vary based on their moods, on whether they're winning or losing, and on a variety of other factors.

While you can categorize players in a wide variety of ways, here are a few broad categories you might want to use when you play:

The Rock

This player enters fewer hands than most others at the table. When he does play a hand, it almost always has an ace in it, unless he's in one of the blinds or he's killing a pot. Even then, he usually folds hands from the small blind that don't include an ace, and he makes no extra bets or raises unless he holds quality cards. The Rock raises infrequently, but when he does, his hand almost always contains an ace, a deuce, and another prime card. More often than not, the ace he's holding is suited as well.

Most of the time, the Rock will also raise with two aces, as long as they have a deuce or a trey to go with them. But some Rocks refrain from raising at all, even with very high quality hands. Instead, they often prefer to wait and see what happens on the flop. When these very tight players do raise, they're practically announcing what they have, because the number of hands they raise with is extremely small.

The Rock rarely bluffs. In fact, he'll rarely bet a hand without the nuts. He tends to check and call both the flop and the turn, but leads out at the river if — and only if — he has the best possible hand. In this instance, best possible hand means a possible or probable scoop. This player seldom bets with only a nut low on the river because he fears being quartered. If he bets out on the river, it's almost a sure bet that he'll take down at least half the pot, and possibly more, or even all of it. It's not too difficult to determine which players at your table fit this super-tight archetype.

The Will Rogers Player

Will Rogers was famous for saying, "I never met a man I didn't like," and some Omaha players never met a hand they didn't like. These guys have *come to play*, and want plenty of action. A Will Rogers player normally plays six of every ten hands, possibly more. Some opponents in this category play as many as ninety percent of the hands they're dealt.

Will Rogers is usually passive. He very rarely raises pre-flop, and visibly agonizes when someone raises in front of him. He wants to play every hand so badly that it hurts when he has to call a raise to enter the pot. He'll call every chance he gets, but raise only with hands he likes for one reason or another. Such hands may diverge from those shown in poker books as premium raising hands, and may be somewhat idiosyncratic, so carefully observe the cards he turns over at showdown.

Although Will Rogers' raising hands don't always contain an ace, they probably do contain two prime cards. They may also be hands with a high pair, such as kings, queens, or jacks. Bulletin: Will Rogers has never quite successfully made the transition from hold'em to Omaha, so he tends to get excited over any big pair in his hand. Don't fail to file this fact away for future profit, or to save some bets when such a player check-raises a board containing any face card.

Here's one last tip about Will: He tries with all his might to find some justification to play a raised pot, but he doesn't require any reason at all to call with almost any four cards as long as nobody's raised the pot yet.

The Maniac

The Maniac is easy to spot: Just look for a wild and crazy player who raises at every opportunity. He seldom just calls. He may not play as many hands as Will Rogers, but he still plays far too many. And he's way beyond aggressive. He's a full-blown maniac when he plays, hence his name. This is a crazy player, an action junkie who wants to be table boss by betting his ego as well as his chips every chance he gets. He wants opponents to react to him regardless of the cards he's holding. You'll frequently find this guy at your table. When you do, be glad, and treat him kindly: One Maniac can make the difference between a so-so game and a great game.

Some players are maniacal every time they sit down to play. But ordinary players can turn into short-term Maniacs too, and they'll play this way until they reset to their default position. The Temporary Maniac may be a player who's just taken a bad beat and gone on tilt. He may be a guy who has played very well for hours but has somehow blown through a full rack of chips. When he buys that second rack, it triggers his Jekyll and Hyde syndrome, and that nice, pleasant, reasonable player turns into a full-fledged Maniac right before your eyes. Just watch him as he starts raising with everything and anything in a desperate attempt to get even, though he usually gets buried even deeper as he journeys through the dark side of his playing style.

The Fish

Everyone wants this guy in the game. Call him the Sucker, the Fish, or the Pigeon, but be sure to call him whenever you see a game about to begin. Then be nice, as nice as you can be. Make him feel welcome at all times, no matter how difficult it may be when he gets lucky and beats your much-favored premium hand. That will happen sometimes, because he won't surrender if he has anything at all — even if it's nothing but hope for a one-out miracle card. Every once in a while, he'll snag one on you and take down a mound of chips. When that happens, be happy, for he'll be back to play again.

The Fish doesn't really know a whole lot about Omaha — usually just enough to be a danger to his bankroll — but he wants to play. He loves to play. But he has a difficult time reading his hand, and he can neither analyze nor assess the strength of his hand against the opposition.

He calls most of the time, never puts in a value bet, and makes bad percentage calls. He'll play if he flops two middle pair, or top pair with an ace kicker and no other draws. If he has two cards to a flush, regardless of how high those cards may be, he's locked in to the bitter end whenever two more cards of the same suit flop. You can't drive him out of a pot, either, because he's oblivious to the meaning of bets and raises from opponents. He's taking this hand to the showdown, regardless, and that's that. This player will call all bets on the flop with nothing but an inside straight draw. He'll also call with a draw to the third, fourth, fifth, or sixth best low hand.

You don't want to emulate his play, but boy, do you ever want him in your game! And the more fish, the merrier. In fact, there's nothing you'd like to see more at your Omaha table than a school of fish with large stacks of chips. Think of it this way: Fish and chips = delicious game. Yum yum!

The Tricky Player

He's smart and clever, though usually a tad too clever for his own good. He's fond of what poker expert Mike Caro calls "the Fancy Play Syndrome." He thinks he's smarter than everyone else at the table. And to show you just how smart and tricky he is, his favorite play is the check-raise. He'd rather check-raise than do just about anything else, although he seldom raises before the flop, and rarely, if ever, makes it three bets. And when he check-raises, he invariably comes out betting on the next round. If he check-raises the flop, you can be sure he won't check-raise the turn. Instead, you can count on the fact that he'll bet out.

If he check-raises the river, you can take it to the bank that he's got the nuts, and it almost always will be the high end. He won't check-raise the nut low on the river because he doesn't want to find himself quartered — he sees such an inglorious finale as a blow to his outsized ego. A Tricky Player doesn't like it one bit when he's the one carved up into little pieces — he's the one who likes to carve the turkey, thank you.

The Aggressive Player

He usually raises when he enters a pot. If it's already been raised, he likes to make it three bets. This player will not allow a betting round to be checked around the table. If it's checked to him, he bets. If he's first to act, he leads out. He never checks behind opponents who don't bet.

His philosophy is to force other players to make decisions based on his actions. He's hoping his opponents will err, which they often do. There are two styles of aggressive play.

- Some players are aggressive so opponents will react to them. This provides an edge because other players can make mistakes when reacting to aggressive play.

- Very Good Aggressive Players — the kind you find in middle-limit and high-limit Omaha games — may play more hands than most others, but confine their play primarily to the flop and secondarily to the turn. The VAGP allows the river to play itself. He's aggressive when circumstances support it, but won't force the action by betting or raising when his hand doesn't warrant it. The VAGP is selectively aggressive, and that selectivity differentiates his game from a maniac's unmitigated aggression.

  He reads other players accurately and always knows just when to bet or raise with two pair. He also knows when it makes sense to bet or raise on the come because he's always aware of pot odds and their relationship to the card odds against making his hand. Others are constantly marveling at how lucky he is; but it's not luck at all. He's able to evaluate cards, position, and other players at the table, and his skill is predicated on this knowledge.

To be this kind of player, you need to develop two skills:

- Learn to recognize your opponents' traits, and to categorize their play. You'll need to recognize when a player's style changes, because a style change during a poker session generally signifies deterioration in play, not improvement. It happens like this: Your opponent is playing quality cards and making the right decisions, but he's just unlucky. The cards aren't breaking even for him and he's getting frustrated. Suddenly he's playing more hands, calling far more often, and raising out of sheer frustration. He so desperately wants to win pots that he's changed his style of play. Basically he's no different from an opponent who starts drinking at the table. The Drinker is an interesting case study too. Just watch and see how alcohol changes his play. We'll give you a hint. Drinking usually won't turn him into a tight, tough opponent.

As you can see from the various player personas we've just discussed, you'll see a variety of playing styles at the Omaha table, but not all of them are winning styles. We've identified four playing styles that are successful in the long run. They appear to separate winning players from losers.

The Quality Starting Hand Player (QSHP)

He sticks to quality starting hands, and seldom, if ever, varies from this approach. His primary strength lies in his ability to evaluate starting hands and make consistently good decisions about whether to play them. In loose games — and "loose" characterizes a surprisingly wide variety of Omaha/8 games, particularly lower limit games — he simply plays better starting hands than most of his opponents do, then makes rational decisions on the flop, turn, and river. His adherence to conservative guidelines, though unimaginative, is enough to ensure his long-term success. Sometimes it's just that simple.

The Very Good Aggressive Player

You met him above as a special case of the Aggressive Player. This player rarely calls. When he plays, he raises. When he's not raising, he's reraising. He puts in many pre-flop raises, and he's willing to cap that round of betting if he has the opportunity. He then bets or raises on the flop and the turn — and also on the river — *when he thinks he has the edge.* Knowing when to be aggressive is important in all forms of poker, and Omaha/8 is no exception. As long as aggression is tempered with selectivity, it generally has a big edge over passive play. Note: We're not talking about maniacal aggression here — that's a sure way to go broke in a hurry. We're talking about aggression based on logical decisions and good judgment.

The Evaluator

This quick-thinking player is skilled at evaluating opponent playing styles. Within minutes of sitting down to the table, he knows how everyone plays. He doesn't miss a thing.

He's also a master of assessing and evaluating both his own pre-flop position and the positions of his opponents. He then astutely applies that knowledge on the flop, turn, and river. He can quickly and accurately count possible outs, calculate pot odds, and assess his hand against those likely to be held by his opponents.

This player is somewhat less concerned than the QSHP with selection of starting hands. The quality of his play is superb on all betting rounds, so he can generally outplay his opponents. Because he plays so well, he typically plays more hands than the QSHP, and as a result, it's somewhat tougher to deduce, or "read," his likely hand.

The Evaluator, the guy who plays far more hands than his opponents do but always seems to come up a winner, is the one players always shake their heads over. They can't understand why — or how — he wins. "Did you see the garbage he turned over on the end? Boy, is he lucky." But he's no luckier than anyone else. He's just very, very good.

You might initially mistake the Evaluator for a loose, clueless player. That's exactly what he wants you to do. The lesson here is: Don't rush to judgment about opponent playing styles until you have quite a few hours of playing experience.

But after you've learned to spot him, you'll see that the Evaluator always knows exactly where he stands in relation to his opponents. He gets maximum possible value out of his winning hands, and when he loses, it's usually for the minimum necessary. He has the ability and discipline to get away from hands easily. He seldom finds himself trapped, and when he does, he manages to slip away — usually by releasing his hand and awaiting a better opportunity. He has an uncanny ability to put every player in the game on a hand, and he's right most of the time. Sometimes you'll think his opponents are playing with their cards face up.

The Crafty Player

The crafty aspects of the game are a large and essential part of an expert's playing style. Although a Crafty Player might resemble a Tricky Player at first glance, there's a world of difference between these two archetypes. Tricky Players are often too tricky for their own good, while Crafty Players are frequently too tricky for your *own* good. A Crafty Player check-raises to maximize his return on investment. Sometimes he check-raises to slow down an Aggressive Player who constantly bets behind him. This player always thinks about gaining additional bets when he's got the best of it, and saving bets when he doesn't. He also knows when to bet for value, and when to check-raise for value, too.

Here's an example of crafty play from Omaha/8 expert Mark Gregorich:

"Let's examine how two different hands might be played into the same flop. In the first instance you have A♠-T♥-4♣-3♠ and on another occasion you're holding A♠-T♥-6♣-5♠. In each case the flop is Q♣-J♠-2♠.

"With the first hand, your best play is to call a bet, rather than raise, because you have some scoop potential. You want more players in there with you in case you catch a high spade or two running low cards, one of which is a spade.

"With the second hand you would raise because you'd prefer to play it short handed. If you don't make your flush, you might escape with a backdoor low hand, and you don't want better backdoor low hands to take one off."

This is a terrific example of thinking through the play of a hand. You must first know your objectives for the hand, and then carry out the actions needed to bring them to fruition. It doesn't always play out the way you envision, but Omaha/8 players who think this way and make plays like this are light years ahead of their competition.

The Crafty Player is also adept at modifying his playing style to take advantage of any given set of table conditions. He's a chameleon, a master of roles and disguises, and he knows exactly when to shift gears — it'll be right around the time you think you have a fix on him. He's part Evaluator and part Very Good Aggressive Player, but he can mimic any of the other archetypes whenever it suits his purpose. Just when you think you have him trapped, he'll spring a surprise and play back at you, costing you a stack of chips.

The Crafty Player is every poker player's hero. Top players in this category win a large percentage of the gold bracelets at the World Series of Poker. Study the Crafty Player at every opportunity if you want to be a highly successful Omaha/8 player.

Forging Your Own Winning Style

You'll want to find a style you're comfortable with as you grow into your Omaha persona. Once you've forged a winning playing style, you're the boss. You'll be the player who *takes action*, so that everyone else is forced to *react*, whether to you or simply to their cards. Reactors are the opponents you really want to play against.

As you continue to play Omaha/8, as your confidence grows and your skill increases, you might even become a player who combines all four winning styles described above: the QSHP, the Very Aggressive Player, the Evaluator, and the Crafty Player. You'll be able to beat most games, if not all of them, if you grow into a player with the discipline to play quality starting hands *most of the time*, as well as one who is willing to take a mediocre hand on occasion and play it superbly through each betting round. Mix in aggressive play when your hand warrants it and shift gears on occasion to confuse the opposition, and you'll be tough to beat.

You can become this kind of player, but to do so, you'll have to exercise your mind. You'll have to think when you play. Give it a try.

Chapter 18

Thinking, Calculating, Evaluating

Players make decisions in a vacuum more frequently while playing Omaha than they do in any other poker game. Sometimes they become so focused on their four starting cards that they're simply unaware of what other players are doing in the course of each hand. They don't stop to think what draw or made hand an opponent may have, what a bet or raise may really signify, or how many times the player in Seat 5 has raised pre-flop. They simply don't think about any of those things. They've gravitated to Omaha/8 mostly because they want to play more hands. So lucky you! What this means is that you can use the skills you've learned here to win their money.

Becoming a successful Omaha player takes discipline as well as thought, and you're the only one who can supply either one. We can help some. We can supply the theories, concepts, and guidelines for you to think about. That we can do. But while we can preach the value of disciplined play, we can't offer you a pill that supplies discipline's minimum daily dose. You'll have to find that deep within yourself, and once you do, you'll have to commit to using it all the time.

You're also going to have to exercise that handsome part of yourself perched above your shoulders. That means using it to think, evaluate, and make good judgments. Most of the time you'll have to base your decisions on incomplete information. Poker is a game of incomplete information, and there's no getting around that. Nevertheless, when you make a decision, it should be informed and logical. As you exercise your mind and the quality of your decision-making improves, so will your results. That's as true in poker as it is in life.

Some Thoughts on Position

If you're a former hold'em player making the transition to Omaha/8, you'll notice a striking general difference in playing styles. Good hold'em players always seem to be aware of how their starting cards relate to their position in the betting order, yet many Omaha players tend to play their starting cards as though they're in a vacuum — with no regard for position.

Is position *more* important in hold'em than in Omaha/8? Absolutely. But is position nevertheless an important factor in Omaha? Yes. It certainly is. Don't let anyone tell you differently. While position may not be *as* important in Omaha/8 as it is in hold'em, it's still very important. Just think about playing in an Omaha/8 game in which you'd always be first to act. Betcha wouldn't like that very much, would you?

Position is always important in poker. First, there's the obvious advantage of acting last. In the back, you can assess the real or purported strength of opponents' hands through the betting action before you act. But position in relation to the playing styles of your opponents is also important. Much about positioning is idealized, of course, because you can't just come to the table and revise seating arrangements to suit yourself. Nevertheless, you will have the option to change seats as players leave the game. Bear these thoughts in mind when considering a move:

- In Omaha, as in hold'em, you want tight, predictable players on your right because you can easily deduce their hands. Acting after them is advantageous. In addition, tight players in the cutoff and button seats will allow you to see more flops inexpensively when you're in the blind, which is a decided advantage. But when Ms. Rock immediately to your right *does* raise your blind, you can safely assume she's holding a big hand. This knowledge allows you to alter your own play accordingly — forewarned is forearmed. If it's heads-up and you know Ms. Rock raises only with premium low hands, when the flop comes Q-J-9, your bet might just take the pot right then and there.

- In Omaha, *unlike* hold'em, you want loose, aggressive players on your left. If you play the right starting hands, you'll have a chance to see what action they take, and then decide whether to call or reraise. You'll also have lots of profitable opportunities to check-raise, enabling you to create much larger pots when you have the best of it. But don't forget that you'll have to play high quality starting hands when aggressive players are seated to your left. When you do play correctly, you'll seldom be at a loss about what to do on subsequent betting rounds. You'll generally know right where you are in the hand, so when you do have the dominant holdings, you'll be able to punish your overly aggressive opponents with two or three bets instead of one.

There's Value in Value Betting

According to poker authority Mike Caro, one should "...value bet more when winning than when losing." When you think about this, it makes good sense. Most of us don't play as well when we're losing. When we're taking our lumps, we tend to play more marginal hands and to make more marginal bets and raises in a driven attempt to win — or to at least get even.

Here's what you really should do instead: When losing, tighten up on your starting standards and pull in the reins on your creative plays, including value bets, which you're likely to make with weaker-than-usual hands. There's not much you can say about a valueless value bet. It generally costs money and when you're already stuck, there's no point in throwing good money after bad. This is the time for lots of traction and not much speed. When you're playing your "A-Game," which you're much more likely to do when you're ahead, you can value bet more because your judgment is likely to be sharper and your value bets will be just what they are named.

Many players often miss the opportunity to value bet on the river with a hand that's worth a call. Suppose the board is K-Q-9-3-2 with no flush possible. You're holding "three pair": K-Q-9 and an irrelevant fourth card. Your best poker hand here is two pair, kings and queens, since you can use only two cards from your hand. But you can bet. Yours may very well be the best hand. If you're raised, just throw your hand away. But it won't cost any more than checking and calling, and when your hand is good you'll be called by two lower pair, and often by a player holding only A-A if you're heads-up.

And you needn't worry about a straight draw, either. The play of the hand ought to tell you if one of your opponents has flopped a straight. If you analyze the betting patterns and can read your opponents reasonably well, whenever you suspect a straight, save this play for some other time when your chances look a bit better.

Changing Gears

Good Omaha/8 players are skilled at mixing up their play. They've learned to avoid responding to similar situations as though they're merely playing on autopilot. Since many people tend to "play to form" in Omaha/8, it's easier to read your opponents in this game than in most others. And because it's easier to surmise the hands of other players, you'll have to take steps to disguise the strength of your hand. One way to do this is to consciously change gears from time to time.

Shifting gears works best, though, against opponents who are aware of what you're doing. As a general rule of thumb, the higher the betting limits, the more sophisticated you can expect your opponents to be. If your adversaries only pay attention to their own cards, or are otherwise brain dead at the table, then you've really no need to change gears at all. In games of clueless, loose-goose players, you'll do better by sticking to a straightforward, workmanlike style. For a full discussion of this topic, peruse the chapter entitled "Reading Hands" in Ray Zee's *High-Low-Split Poker For Advanced Players*.

You often shift gears, consciously or unconsciously, just because you're winning or losing. The more you're winning, the looser your play can become — although it should never become too loose — while the more you're losing, the tighter you should play.

The vast majority of poker players flip-flop this commonsensical advice and loosen up considerably when they're losing. Many players hate losing so much that they'll play far too loosely in a usually ill-fated attempt to get even. Even those who record their results are prone to this folly. They want to avoid recording a losing session, but usually make things far worse by taking foolhardy risks. All too often, what started out to be a relatively minor loss is compounded into something ugly.

Whenever you change gears without realizing it, you're likely to be loosening up, not gearing down, and you'll probably be doing it right when you shouldn't. Remember: Although changing gears is a good technique to use selectively, you should only shift your playing style consciously, and for good reason, and not just float into some other gear in a frustrated or blissfully soporific state.

Applying Your New Skills

We've talked about many of the skills and techniques you'll need to practice to become a winning player. Here are three you should emphasize:

- Develop the ability to wear more than one hat during a session. Learn to change gears. Play quality starting hands most of the time, but occasionally put on another playing style hat and be aggressive when it's appropriate. Aggression allows you to take advantage of position. This is all part of being crafty and clever. For example, try check-raising from early position when you're quite certain someone will bet if you check.

- Become selectively aggressive, particularly from late position when all action is in front of you, giving you the perfect opportunity to get more money in the pot. Learn when to bet on the come. By increasing the amount of money in the pot, you can put pot odds to work in your favor.

- Learn how to play multiple draws, and how to play made hands with redraws. You won't win every time, but you should always have a game plan. Learn to put each of your opponents on a hand; then, as your skill increases, you'll learn to put them on secondary hands too. When you're able to do that, you'll be able to play your own hands to maximum advantage, garnering every bet you possibly can.

Playing Shorthanded

You'll frequently find yourself in shorthanded situations when you're playing Omaha/8 in a casino. Sometimes games are short early in the day, when players are still arriving and others want to begin playing. Games are also often shorthanded in the evening, particularly late at night, when many of the players have gone home, but a few still want to keep playing.

Many players just don't like shorthanded games and try to avoid them at all costs. But these games can be fun as well as profitable. You get to play more hands, although the blinds come around more rapidly. To play well in a shorthanded game, you'll have to make some strategic adjustments when it gets down to five players or fewer:

Hands change value: In shorthanded games, hands with aces increase in value exponentially. For example, in a full game A-8-6-x is usually unplayable. But any hand with an ace and two low cards, regardless of the fourth card, becomes a premium raising hand in shorthanded games. Two-way hands like these — though far too weak in either direction to consider playing in a full game — frequently create scooping opportunities because they allow you to "back into" either the low hand or the high hand. Remember, an ace is like two cards in one — it's simultaneously the lowest and highest card in the deck. The fewer players there are in the game, the more pronounced is its versatility, and the more its value rises.

But just as hands with aces go up in value in shorthanded games, high-only hands begin to sink. In a full Omaha/8 game, position is just one factor to take into account. But in shorthanded games, position is critical. In a shorthanded game, A-8-6-x is a raising hand in all positions other than the blinds. In the big blind it's a calling hand against a raise. But it's a folding hand in the small blind against a raise unless the ace is suited — then it's a calling hand. It's also a calling hand in an unraised pot in the small blind, and a raising hand if you're heads-up against the big blind.

Unless you're in the blind, never enter a shorthanded pot by calling: Either raise or release your hand. This is a major key to shorthanded Omaha play.

Hands having two-way possibilities are critical in shorthanded Omaha/8 play. Just as full-handed Omaha/8 is a game of scoops and flushes, shorthanded play is a game of two-way hands, regardless of whether they're the nuts or not. Most of your important decisions are not whether to play the hand, but how to play on each of the betting rounds based on your position.

Many hands that are typically losers in a full game, such as bottom set and two pair, are hands that should be played aggressively in shorthanded games. Middling high and low hands should usually be bet for value in heads-up situations on the river, and you can call with them if your opponent bets into you.

Draws and pairs: Drawing hands decrease in value in a shorthanded game because even when you make your draw, you don't figure to get enough calls to make it cost effective in the long run. On the other hand, high pairs, particularly aces, should be played aggressively if your other two cards are low.

Timing is everything: We've emphasized thinking and evaluating when playing Omaha/8. There's just not as much time to think when the game is shorthanded. So if you're just learning the game, be kind to yourself. We recommend that you avoid shorthanded play until you've mastered the strategic concepts outlined in this book and can react quickly in the heat of battle. You must be able to evaluate situations quickly and then act on them without becoming confused. In general, shorthanded play makes for a loose, aggressive game, and it's not for the fainthearted.

Common Omaha/8 Errors and Traps

There are a number of errors we see players make all the time in low-limit and middle-limit games. Maybe you've been making them too. But, we hope, not any more. After reading this list, do yourself a favor and take a pledge to never again allow yourself to be lured into these common traps:

Praying for runner-runner: You have a premium starting hand, catch a bad flop, and call a bet hoping to catch a turn card that will give you a draw to the river. When you do this, you're clinging to hope, and hope is the death of many Omaha/8 bankrolls. Let your opponents try to catch runner-runner, not you. The attempt to catch runner-runner is essentially a parlay of looking to pick up a draw to another draw — and plays like this are very bad news. How bad is it? Bad enough that if you took the world's best Omaha/8 player and convinced him to play his usual scintillating game with this one exception, he'd no longer be the world's best Omaha/8 player. He probably wouldn't even be able to beat the game.

Drawing for a high hand when three low cards flop: When three low cards flop and you have naught but a draw to a high hand — and draws include flopping middle and bottom set as well as straight draws — you're chasing half the pot, but the cost to draw is the same as if you were chasing the entire enchilada. It's OK to see the turn if you flop top set or a draw to the nut flush, but even these hands ought to be pitched some of the time. We realize this is difficult to do, particularly for hold'em players who come to Omaha/8 with a much higher opinion of a set's value (which in Omaha/8 is only that of a drawing hand). But you must learn to bite the bullet and fold fool's gold hands if you want to become a consistent winner and promote yourself up to higher limits. Before we forget, when you do begin pitching these hands into the muck, please don't crow about it to your neighbors. Don't let them know you have the skills necessary to make plays like these.

Failure to value bet: When you fail to value bet the river, you can wind up leaving money on the table. Much of the time, value betting the river is revenue neutral. You bet, someone else calls, and it's not much different than it would be if your opponent came out betting and you called him. But by betting, you attract some calls from players who hold lesser hands and would gladly check it down on the river. On some of these occasions, an opponent may raise when you bet, and when that happens you can usually toss your cards away. Because most opponents raise on the turn, a river raise is fairly uncommon. It usually signifies a miracle card for the raiser.

Draws and traps to avoid: We've discussed all of this elsewhere in the book, but just to make our list inclusive, here are some draws you should avoid and some trap hands to beware of:

- Top and bottom pair
- Third best flush

- Second best straight
- Second best low hand
- K-Q-Q-x whether suited or unsuited, and similar holdings
- J-J-T-x whether suited or unsuited, and similar holdings
- 7-6-5-4 suited or unsuited
- 6-5-4-3 suited or unsuited

Some Miscellaneous Tips

Here are some miscellaneous tips to improve your Omaha/8 game. We've covered many of these suggestions elsewhere in this book, but we've listed them here, so you can access all of them in one place.

- If you're playing $10-$20 Omaha/8 or lower, after the flop you should generally draw only to the nuts or have multiple, high quality draws.

- If you're in a loose, passive game, where lots of players typically see the flop, you should play very tightly on the flop. If you're in a tight, aggressive game, be certain you're playing fewer hands before the flop than most of your opponents, unless the deck is running over you.

- Early position and late position in Omaha/8 is fine; you'd prefer not to be in middle position. The advantages of late position are obvious. You get to act after you've seen the real or purported strength of your opponents' hands. Early position gives you an opportunity to check, see what transpires, then fold, call, raise, or reraise. Middle position has very few options and should be played in a straightforward manner.

- If you've been dealt A-3 or 3-2 with nothing else of real quality, you ought to throw it away if you're in early position. In late position, A-3 is almost always playable in a pot that hasn't been raised, but 3-2 is not.

- While late position allows you to play more hands, middle cards, such as 9-8-7 — particularly hands with nines in them — should not be played. If you're on the button and the pot hasn't been raised, you can consider playing hands such as Q-J-3-2 double-suited, A-K-T-4 suited, J-J-4-2 suited. If no one has entered the pot when it's your turn to act, you should either raise or release your hand.

- As a general rule, the larger the pot, the looser your play can be on the flop; the smaller the pot, the tighter you should play.

- High hands lose more value against low flops than low hands lose against high flops.

- When you've made a nut low on the flop and you're sure you're going to be quartered, you have our permission to muck your hand, particularly when you have no back up to protect you against getting counterfeited, and no possibilities of making a high winning hand. If you're holding A-K-Q-2, it may look good if the flop is 6-5-4, but if you suspect one of your opponents also has an A-2 in his hand, the best you can hope for if there are three others in the pot with you is that you'll get your money back. It's sort of like, "Heads they win, tails you tie," and that's not a rosy picture, is it?

- On the river, you can raise if you're holding a nut low when it's four-handed, but just call if you're playing three-handed. However, if you backdoor the nut low, it's a raising hand.

- As in all poker games, most of the money you'll make playing Omaha/8 will not come from your genius, but from the poor play of your opponents.

- The higher the stakes, the more important redraws become. Possibilities like backdoor flushes, straights, and low redraws are critical when you apply your foot to the gas.

- When you're in the cutoff seat — that's the seat immediately to the right of the button — or on the button in a pot where no one else has come to play, either raise or release. Do not call.

- High hands with no low possibilities do well in heads-up play, three-handed play, and pots where many players are there to take the flop. When there are a gaggle of players already in the pot, intimating that many low cards are already in play and that the deck is rich in high cards, you should raise with your good high hands.

- According to Ray Zee, "Most players will form an opinion about your hand and not deviate from that opinion throughout the play of the hand. A little deception is good. It gets you calls or folds when you need them." You should be putting players on hands on every betting round, and you should be flexible enough to change your opinion about what they might be holding. Revise your assessments in accordance with their actions and the cards they show down. Don't get married to your initial conclusions about what cards opponents might be holding. While this idea is easy enough to understand, putting it into practice is anything but easy, though it's essential for expert play.

- In multi-way pots, position goes down in value; in short-handed pots, it's critical.

- In multi-way pots, bet early position strength. The object is to attract paying customers. Deception is unimportant. When your opponents see the flop, many of them will find any possible excuse to call and see the turn — and the river too.

- If a player in early position bets into a raiser, don't call with anything other than the very best fitting flops. In this situation, it's really OK to throw your hand away.

- Because Omaha is a game of flushes, flushes are much more threatening than straights. Whenever the board pairs with a flush card, your straight is generally worthless. If the river makes a low, a flush, and a straight, your set is worthless too. But if only a low and a gapped straight are possible on the river, your set is playable.

- The ace is the most important card in Omaha/8. Next in importance is the deuce. Nine is the worst card, and if you hang around an Omaha/8 table long enough, you'll find that more nines, eights, and sevens appear in losing hands than any other cards.

- The flush factor: In a 10-handed game, you'll be dealt a suited or double-suited hand most of the time. So will your opponents, so when you draw to a flush without a nut low or a nut low draw, be certain the flush stands a good chance of winning the high end of the pot if you complete your draw. In most cases, that means drawing only to the nut flush unless you have other possibilities working for you.

- According to World Series of Poker bracelet winner and Omaha/8 expert Linda Johnson, 6-5-4-3 is the worst starting hand combination that most Omaha/8 players consider a good hand, and one they'll play in error on a regular basis.

- When playing heads-up, any hand with two unpaired low cards is playable. No hand in Omaha/8 is more than about a 25 percent favorite over any other hand. (The exceptions, of course, are the obvious ones: quads, or three-of-a-kind in your hand.)

- Professional poker player Roy Cooke says, "I make my decisions when it's my turn to act. If I make my decisions based on more information than my opponents have, I'll make better decisions."

- Don't soft-play your friends. You should play as aggressively against your friends — and your grandmother, for that matter — as you would against any other opponents.

- Play hours, not results. Make good decisions and let the results take care of themselves.

- Promote poor play; don't berate it. Remember, in hold'em it's better to be feared, but in Omaha/8, it's better to be loved. The looser you're perceived, the more calls you'll get. And in Omaha, the best hand usually wins.

- Be a sponge. Gather information constantly while you're playing.

- It takes a bigger hand to call a raise than it does to raise in the first place. And it takes a bigger hand to overcall than to be the first caller.

- World Series of Poker Omaha/8 champion Steve Badger says, "You can get by on a smaller bankroll in Omaha/8 because the game is more profitable than hold'em. That's because there are more weak players playing poorly."

- Although many players think of Omaha/8 as a game of draw-outs, it's worth remembering that seven-ninths, or 77.7 percent, of your hand is known on the flop.

- The river card is the least important card in Omaha/8. All of the important action takes place prior to the river. If you have the best of it before the river, you'll win more often than not. *Get your money into the pot when you have the best of it, and save your bets when you don't.* While that sounds simplistic and obvious, many players don't follow that axiom.

- High stakes poker player Annie Duke names these top mistakes in Omaha/8:

  - Playing stranded pairs. Hands like K-K-8-4 are unplayable, but hands like Ks-Kc-2s-3c and K-K-Q-Q can be played.

  - Overestimating the value of small pairs, deuces through eights, since these sets become very vulnerable when hit.

  - Overestimating the value of A-2.

  - Overestimating the value of A-A.

  - Underestimating the value of big connecting cards, because you can't get trapped with them.

- Some of Omaha/8 expert Steve Badger's favorite Omaha myths: (The authors' comments — and we are in complete agreement with Badger — are in parentheses.)

  - *Myth:* Omaha/8 is a complicated game. (*Reality:* If you play properly, you'll rarely find yourself in complex situations.)

  - *Myth:* Starting hands run close in value. (*Reality:* Only heads-up!)

  - *Myth:* Don't raise before the flop. (*Reality:* Why not? We've already shown you, for example, how four high cards can be a raising hand in some situations.)

  - *Myth:* Never raise with just a low hand. (*Reality:* If you've got the only low hand and you suspect your opponents of holding high hands, *not only can you raise, you should raise* — and you ought to do so *every chance you get.)*

- *Myth:* You can play more hands in Omaha/8 than you can in hold'em. (*Reality:* Nope, you can't. And here's why: It's a lot easier for two starting cards to combine and work together than it is when you've got four of them in your hand.)

- *Myth:* You can't bluff in Omaha. (*Reality:* Small pots in early position are bluffable. So are boards with two low cards when a third low card fails to arrive.)

- *Myth:* You can't win with a set. (*Reality:* You can. But remember, sets are drawing hands.)

Consistent application of these tips will allow you to accomplish your objectives: to control the game, to become the master of your universe, and to control your environment. You'll become the best Omaha/8 player you know by mastering three key ingredients of solid play discussed extensively throughout this book: discipline, awareness, and good decision-making.

Part 3:

Other Poker
Skills

Chapter 19

Money Management and Record Keeping

What's Money Management All About?

Money Management is one of those concepts that make their way into far too much gaming literature. Much of what's said about money management is based on the timeless adage, "Quit while you're ahead." In other words, once you've won some predetermined amount, get up and leave the game a bit wealthier and a lot happier than when you walked in.

There's a flip side, too, which tells you to set stop-loss limits and quit once you've lost some predetermined amount at a given session. Fifty dollars might do it for some people, five hundred for others, while a five-thousand dollar or even a fifty-thousand dollar loss might be the trigger point for a high-rolling few. "Give it up and go home," is what the money managers tell you. "You won't make it back to even today, so come back tomorrow. Lady Luck cold shouldered you, and you ought to know better than to chase your losses."

Does any of this make any sense? Should you quit while you're ahead? What about once you've lost some predetermined amount of money — should you go home then? After all, if you quit when you're ahead as well as when you're losing, you'll only play when your results are banded between arbitrarily established stop-loss and stop-win limits. If you set them tight enough, you'll almost never play.

Even money management adherents agree when you tell them that a poker game never actually ends. It's a lifetime event extending over every session you ever play. So if that's the case, does it really make any difference whether you play four hours today and four hours tomorrow, or just play eight hours today? And what's the compelling logic behind all these money management theories? Or isn't there any logic to them at all?

Does Quitting While You're Ahead Make Any Sense at All?

Those who advise you to quit while you're ahead will tell you that their advice allows you to take your winnings out of the game, and avoid giving back money you've already won. But this makes sense only if you decide to quit playing poker entirely. If you just decide never to play poker again, and you're ahead today, quitting does ensure that you'll put today's profit into your pocket.

But if you quit winners today and lose tomorrow, are you any worse off overall than if you simply play on today, and lose what you won earlier in the session? You know the answer. It's "No!" You're not any worse off at all. Coming back tomorrow simply allows you to pocket those winnings for a few more hours. More than likely, today's winnings rest right on your nightstand while you're sleeping, so what's the difference between playing a few more hours today, and playing tomorrow, the day after tomorrow, or even next year?

Should You Set Stop-Loss Limits?

The same logic applies to *stop-loss* theory. If you're losing and leave the game, ask yourself whether you plan to play tomorrow — or next week, for that matter. If you answer "yes," and you plan on playing again — it doesn't really matter when, since the game never really ends — and believe you can beat the game, is there any real difference between quitting now and quitting later?

We don't think so. If the game is so tough that you don't think you can beat it, you shouldn't play at all. If you play in a regular Omaha/8 game and all the other players are more skillful than you are, it's time to find a different game. Even if you've been on a hot streak and you're beating that game, you can expect to eventually lose all your money if you play against more skilled opponents — and it makes absolutely no difference whether or not you practice money management.

But if you're a favorite, why not keep playing, regardless of whether you're ahead or behind at any given moment? When it *doesn't* pay to keep playing is when you have other commitments, you've lost so much that you can't afford to keep playing without wagering the rent money, or you're so whipsawed from your losses that you're emotionally beaten down. A good night's sleep will restore your emotional equilibrium so that you can once again play sound, winning poker.

All You Need to Know About Money Management

Here's the only facet of money management that's true: If the game is good and you're a favorite, keep playing. If the game is bad and you're an underdog, quit! Never mind whether you're winning or losing.

Of course, the game can be terrific, but you might not be a favorite for any number of reasons unrelated to your skill level. You may be tired, stressed out, unable to concentrate, or knocked off your stride by any of a number of threats to the sanctity of the human condition.

You will save yourself a lot of money over the course of your poker playing career by following this simple rule: If you're not playing up to your best abilities, go home. That's the beauty of playing poker in a brick and mortar casino or in an online casino located somewhere in cyberspace; the game will still be there tomorrow.

Game Selection and Money Management

Gambling successfully is based on putting yourself into situations where you have a positive expectation. That's why you won't find any professional craps or roulette players. In the long run they have no chance of winning because the odds are fixed and stacked in favor of the house. But poker players can find games where they're favored, through skill, over other players. While favorites do have losing nights, they show profits in the long run.

Since one of the key concepts of winning poker is choosing the best game, why would you voluntarily take yourself out of a good game just because you've won or lost some arbitrarily predetermined amount of money? If it's one of those nights when nothing seems to be going right, you might want to quit even though the game is good. That's OK with us, but only if you're quitting because you've lost your groove and are no longer in the right frame of mind to continue playing to the best of your ability. But you shouldn't quit just because you've reached some arbitrary stop-loss limit, as long as your losses haven't caused your game to deteriorate.

What if you're in a good game and you're $1,000 ahead? Or $1,000,000 ahead? The amount doesn't matter. If the game is that good, and you have no other pressing commitments, why not go right on playing? After all, you're a favorite. Chances are you'll win even more money.

But whether you win or lose from that point on isn't predictable. Your future results are always up for grabs, regardless of whether you keep playing or pack it in and return to the game tomorrow. The game goes on, and the segments of time during which you play are only arbitrary delineations.

Summary

Here's the last word on money management, and it's simple:

- Money management, as a strategy for maximizing winnings or limiting losses, is meaningless.

- Stop-loss limits, and quitting once you've won a predetermined amount of money, will neither stop your losses if you're a losing player nor protect your profits if you're ahead.

- Poor players will probably go broke no matter what they do. Good players will establish an expected hourly win rate regardless of whether they quit after they've pocketed a certain amount of winnings.

- If you're playing in a good game, and you're playing your best, stay in the game unless you have other obligations.

- If you're in a bad game, leave it now. Whether you're winning or losing at the moment should have no bearing on the situation.

- If you're emotionally upset, stressed out, fighting the flu, or otherwise not at your best, you're better off not playing, since your malady will ultimately take itself out on your bankroll.

Keeping Records

If you don't keep records, how will you ever know whether you're a successful poker player? Without accurate records, you'll never know how good a player, or how bad a player, you might be. While most poker players don't keep accurate records, they'll also tell you they're winning players. But there's a lot of self-deception out there.

If you're serious about poker, you have to treat your Omaha game like a business or profession. Every business keeps records. Without them, no business would have any idea of what it costs to make, sell, or inventory its products, and no way of knowing whether the bottom line will be written in black or red ink. Perhaps it's easier for the vast majority of poker players to avoid looking truth in the face. But if you intend to win money by playing poker, you must keep accurate records of your results.

Fortunately, the kind of records you'll need to keep as a poker player are a lot simpler than the records maintained by business owners. In fact, they're much simpler than the kind of records you have to keep to prepare a simplified income tax return.

What Kind of Records Should I Keep?

You'll need to be concerned about two basic statistical parameters — your win rate, which is expressed as the average amount of money won or lost per hour, and another figure — called the standard deviation — that measures those short-term fluctuations you face on the road to establishing an average hourly expectation.

Next time you play poker, take a small pad with you, and record the amount of your buy-in.

Then record the following information each hour:

1. Amount won or lost during that hour.
2. The game you're playing in (e.g., $4-$8 Omaha/8).
3. Total number of hours played that session.

When you get home, you'll also want to record this cumulative information:

4. The amount won or lost for the entire year.

5. The total number of hours played during the year.

The calculations are actually quite simple, even for the mathematically phobic. Computing your win or loss rate is simple. Just divide the amount of money won or lost by the number of hours you've played. This calculation represents the average amount of money won or lost each hour. In statistics, that figure is called the mean.

If you play in different games, you might want to keep records on a game-by-game basis (to determine whether you're doing better at hold'em, or Omaha) as well as on an overall basis.

Knowing how much you're winning or losing on an hourly basis is important. But it's also important to know whether the mean is representative. In other words, is your mean, or average win or average loss, an accurate barometer of your overall playing data?

If that sounds complex, here's a simple case in point. Let's say San Francisco and Kansas City each have an average annual temperature of 65 degrees. But in San Francisco, the temperature rarely gets very warm or very cold, while Kansas City is extremely hot in the summer and bitterly cold in winter. While the mean annual temperature might be the same for both cities, there is greater variability in Kansas City than in San Francisco. Consequently, the mean temperature of 65 degrees is more representative of San Francisco's temperate climate than of Kansas City's highly variable weather.

In poker, two players might each win an average of $15 per hour. One might have big wins and big losses only every now and then, while the other player might experience substantial fluctuations to arrive at the same average winnings. The player who can achieve that win rate while putting less of his money at risk is generally better off.

To get at this measure of variability, we need to know more about those *observed values* (the amounts you won or lost each hour and recorded in your notebook) that were used to calculate your average win or loss. Once we do, we'll know just how well the mean represents them. That's where the *standard deviation* comes in.

How Does the Standard Deviation Work?

If you haven't taken statistics, that term might seem intimidating, but it's really not that mysterious. Try thinking of the standard deviation as though it were an adjective modifying a noun (your hourly win rate). Here's an example: "She's wearing a dress." Dress, of course, is the noun. Now modify that sentence by adding any one of the following adjectives: "She's wearing a (sexy, blue, business-like, grandmotherly, clinging, revealing, scandalous, see-through, designer, hideous, glamorous) dress. You can see how substituting one adjective for another can radically change the meaning of the sentence. It's much the same with the relationship between the standard deviation and the mean.

If there were no dispersion at all in a distribution, all the observed values would be the same. No observed value would deviate from the mean. If, for example, it were exactly 64 degrees Fahrenheit for 6 days in a row, the mean temperature would be 64 degrees for that period, and there would be no variance at all between the high and low readings — just the way things should be in a wine cellar. But, with dispersion, observed values do deviate from the mean — some by a little, others by a lot. The standard deviation is a way of indicating an "average" amount by which all the values deviate from the mean.

How to Calculate the Standard Deviation

Which of these sets of values would you expect to have the larger standard deviation?

"A"	"B"
6	111
24	114
37	117
49	118
64	120
Mean 36	116

The values in the left-hand column are more dispersed (they deviate more from the mean) than those in the right hand column, so we can expect the standard deviation to be larger. Let's see how this works out.

Value	Deviation	Value	Deviation
6	-30	111	-5
24	-12	114	-2
37	+ 1	117	+1
49	+13	118	+2
64	+28	120	+4

We can't simply take an average (arithmetic mean) of the deviations because they will always add up to zero — since the negative deviations cancel out the positive. To overcome this difficulty, we square each deviation ("squaring" means we multiply the number by itself — thus 5 squared is equal to 5 times 5, or 25). This gets rid of the minus sign, since a "minus" multiplied by a "minus" is a "plus." So for the right hand column, we have:

Deviation From Mean	Deviation From Squared Mean
-5	25
-2	4
+1	1
+2	4
+4	16

The mean (average) of these squared deviations is called the Variance:

The variance is a measure with uses of its own. But it does have one disadvantage for everyday use: If the original values were in dollars — as they would be when you're calculating your hourly

$$Variance = \frac{25 + 4 + 1 + 4 + 16}{5} = \frac{50}{5} = 10$$

winnings or losses in a poker game — then the variance would be in dollars squared. To get the *measure of dispersion* back into the same units as the *observed values*, we take the *square root* of the variance — and this is what we call the standard deviation.

Standard deviation of the distribution shown above = 3.16

The same calculations for the left-hand distribution yield a variance of 399.6, and a standard deviation of 19.99. Now that you've walked through the process of calculating a standard deviation and understand the process, here's how you can simplify the calculations.

Get yourself a pocket calculator that performs statistical functions. A calculator can be purchased for under $25, and will eliminate these time-consuming arithmetical steps. Better yet, if you have a personal computer, use any of the popular spreadsheet programs to store your data, or you can purchase inexpensive software specifically designed for keeping records of your poker play. All you'll have to do is enter your hourly winnings or losses, then use the spreadsheet's statistical capabilities to calculate your average hourly results (mean) and standard deviation on a cumulative basis.

Using the Standard Deviation to Analyze Your Poker Results

When you begin to analyze your poker results, you'll see that you'd really like to maximize your hourly winnings while minimizing your standard deviation. In other words, you'd like to win as much as you possibly can, while subjecting your bankroll to the smallest possible fluctuations. Winning lots while risking little is nice work if you can get it.

That, of course, is a real conundrum. If you choose to take the risks required to maximize winnings, such as getting all those extra bets in whenever you believe you have the best of it, you tend to increase bankroll fluctuations because you're not going to come out on top in every one of those marginal situations. In fact, because many of these situations are very close calls, you'll probably wind up losing a lot of them. Let's face it, if you flop four-of-a-kind, or the nut flush with the best possible low hand, or some other equally huge hand, it's never a close call. You're going to get all the money in the pot you possibly can, because you're going to win.

But when you're out there on the edge, you'll lose nearly as many as you win. You're hoping, of course, to win more often than not, in order to maximize your winnings. But you're bound to experience fluctuations as you navigate this precarious path.

The game you're playing in can be inherently high in variance or not, and there's little you can do about it, other than pack it in and wait for a more placid game. If your game is very aggressive, with most of the pots raised or reraised, that's a game with an inherently high variance. Games with inherently low variance are those that lack a significant amount of unmitigated aggression.

Life On the Edge: What's My Risk Tolerance?

From a statistical viewpoint, when you live on the edge you're flying in the face of a high standard deviation — meaning lots of risk. Because of this, you must come to terms with your own risk tolerance and decide how much of your bankroll you're willing to risk to gain marginal boosts in earnings. If you're not comfortable with a certain level of risk, or if you're playing on a short bankroll, you'd be better off minimizing your variance rather than trying to maximize your winnings.

By avoiding marginal situations requiring you to put additional money into the pot when it's close, you can play on a shorter bankroll. If you're a winning player, you'll eventually win just as much money. It will just take more hours at the table to reach your goals.

There's no right or wrong here. Some people are comfortable with a high level of risk and have the bankroll to accommodate the fluctuations that inevitably accompany this kind of play. Others are not. In fact, you'll frequently hear players bemoaning the fact that they're at a table with all live ones. "I wish there were two or three good, tight players at the table," they'll say, "because they bring more stability to the game and my good hands tend to hold up more often."

From a statistical perspective, this comment is nothing more than a cry for a smaller standard deviation, and a willingness to accept the slightly smaller win rate that accompanies it. Even without a knowledge of statistics, these players have learned that when you operate on the edge, or when you're in a jam-up game with a lot of maniacs, the price you pay for an increased win rate is usually a significantly larger increase in the fluctuations you can expect.

How Should You Balance Your Win Rate Against the Standard Deviation?

What does this mean to you as a player? Do you live on the edge, or seek whatever safety net might be available? As long as you can afford to play the game you're in, this becomes a matter of personal choice. Only you can decide how much uncertainty you're comfortable with. If you elect to push every advantage, no matter how small, expect significantly higher fluctuations than you'd experience if you were willing to trade off a relatively small fraction of that win rate for a bit more stability.

The texture of the game you're in can also affect your standard deviation. In an aggressive game, where lots of pots are raised and reraised before the flop, you can expect a lot more variance in the results you achieve than you would in a passive game, where the majority of pots are quietly called and raising is relatively rare. If you elect to maximize your win rate, then you'll need a larger bankroll to play the game.

Keeping Up With Record Keeping

One of the toughest things about keeping records is simply keeping up with them. After a tough loss, it can be very difficult to record it, only to have it stare you in the face each time you make a new entry. But if you don't keep records, you'll only delude yourself about your results.

If you're playing just for enjoyment, and don't really care whether you win or lose, then by all means, excuse yourself from the drudgery. But if you're a winning player, or aspire to be one, you must consistently record and analyze your results. Sometimes the truth hurts and sometimes it can be painful to look it in the face. But that's what has to be done if you want to know how you're doing. Awareness, after all, is the first step along the road to improvement, so if you don't keep good records, you may never improve at all.

Chapter 20

Playing Poker Online For Play-Money and For Real Money Too

What's Online Poker All About?

I f you have a computer and it's connected to the Internet, there's a world of poker opportunities awaiting you just a few mouse clicks away. You can play online in both tournaments and cash games for a variety of stakes, from pennies to hundreds of dollars. But if you don't feel ready to plunk your money down on a cyberspace card table, or Internet wagering isn't allowed where you live, you can give it a go for play-money instead. The games are very real. You may be in cyberspace, but the other players are living, breathing opponents who may be anywhere in the world. They won't be in the same room with you, but they're real folks like you, looking for a game.

You'll have to make a few adjustments when you play online. Rather than sit at a table in a brick and mortar casino, you'll play in a universe of electronic connections that is at once everywhere and nowhere. At first it may be a little disconcerting to have your cards yanked away by an invisible dealer instead of folding them yourself!

As with any other computer game, the designers have done all they can to simulate poker's real sights and sounds:

- You see yourself represented as a pictogram — an icon, of sorts — seated at a virtual table with other pictograms, whose real counterparts may be anywhere in the world.

- Your player name or "handle" and the amount of chips you have in play are listed above or beneath your virtual representative.

- Vibrantly colored cards, tables, chips, and player costumes mimic the visual elements of real casino poker.

- An invisible dealer deals the cards, keeps track of bets and raises, and declares winning hands. He does all this and more with one hundred per cent accuracy, and in just milliseconds. Even better, you don't have to toke him if you win a pot.

- You hear the familiar poker sounds of clacking chips and cards being shuffled and dealt.

- You can communicate with other players in the "chat window" by typing messages back and forth on your keyboards. It's just like sending instant messages on AOL.

- To check, bet, or raise, you click on-screen choices with your mouse. Help and hand histories are easily summoned by clicking other options. Want to leave the game or go to another? That's easy. Just click!

But it Isn't Real Poker, is it?

Internet poker is real poker, as long as you're playing for real money. But even in play-money games, you can practice many skills before you feel ready to promote yourself to cash games. For instance, you can brush up on

- Evaluating hands
- Reading hands
- Folding, betting, calling, raising, and reraising
- Categorizing opponents
- Figuring pot odds

Nevertheless, there are some differences when playing online:

- You won't be able to detect most tells — those involuntary physical and emotional slips that often give away a player's hand — unless you're psychic. But there are ways to get an idea about another player's hand. You can get to know his or her style of play from observing it during the game, and you can sometimes tell a lot about the quality of another player's hand by how long he takes to check or bet, fold, call, raise, or reraise.

- You won't be able to practice tricky strategies in play-money or low-limit cash games. To win any pot, you'll probably have to show down the best hand after all the cards are out. Fancy strategies? Fuggedaboutit. Players will usually call with anything in a play-money or mini-limit cash game. After all, playing is lots more fun than folding, and there's not much at stake in these games.

- Real-money games on the Internet are faster than games in a brick and mortar casino. The shuffle and deal are much faster, and other dealer tasks, such as the verification of bets and raises and the awarding of the pot, take place in microseconds. Also, cyberspace players are able to act faster online than in a brick and mortar game because they don't have to cut out chips or count money.

- Once they've played online for a while, many players take to playing two or more games simultaneously. While you can't do that in a brick and mortar casino, in cyberspace an auditory prompt alerts you when it's your turn to act in each of the games you're involved in. In addition, the programming yanks you back and forth between game screens as though you're on an electronic leash. While it's difficult to get any sort of fix on opponents when you're table hopping, if you have an edge in each game, the added amount you win may well make up for any edge you lose through failure to scrutinize game texture at each table.

What the Internet Play-Money Games are Like

Internet play-money games are loose, action-filled games. Players enter pots with guns blazing, firing bets and raises at will — after all, they've really nothing to lose. So don't expect to win a pot without a struggle!

There are many *family* pots — pots in which all players participate in the action. No one sits on the sidelines hand after hand. Betting is frequently *capped* as players put in the maximum number of allowable raises. Players call, and even call raises, with cards they should have folded after the deal without a moment's hesitation. But don't you do this. Your challenge in these games is to keep from joining the party!

After all, if you're going to play poker, you should try to play it well. Otherwise, you might just as well play roulette or some other game of pure chance. If you always strive to play your best game even in a play-money game, your good habits will carry over when you play poker for real — meaning, of course, for real money.

If you're lucky, you'll have a choice between Omaha high-only and Omaha/8. The trend is toward a wider selection of games at online poker sites. You can also find tournaments.

Game menus change with popular trends, and even game sites themselves come and go. To find out what games are currently available, post an inquiry at the Internet poker newsgroup Rec.Gambling.Poker (RGP). We'll tell you more about RGP, as well as how to find it, later in this chapter.

How Play-Money Games Help You Improve

Play-money games are full of players who are learning the game. But most of them play strictly for fun. You won't be. And therein lies the difference. You'll be playing good, solid poker, just as we've taught you, while most of the others will be mired in bad habits because they either don't care or don't know any better.

Play your best — always. That's the key. Play like it's for keeps, as though your cyberchips will be cash in your pocket when you win. But when you promote yourself to real-money games, you'll have some challenges ahead of you. While you'll have more Omaha/8 knowledge than most other players in low-limit games, winning won't be as easy as you might think. Once the initial rush wears off, after about the first thirty or sixty minutes, you'll find yourself fighting the 3F factor: *frustration, fatigue*, and far too much *fun*. The 3F factor often leads you to join in the loose play and have a better time. So lick temptation *now*, while there's no cost.

Keep records so you can make these sessions count. Determine how long you can play without yielding to the temptation of playing inferior hands, calling when you shouldn't, or getting emotional when someone draws out on you. Remember that the hardest victory in poker is conquering yourself!

If you find it hard to take an Internet play-money game seriously, remember that for you, the game really does count. It counts as preparation. Eventually, when you play in a game with cash stakes, you'll be facing many of the same factors you face in these cyberspace play-money games. Here's why:

- Unless money is no object, you'll be playing your first cash games for low limits. In many places, low-limit games are almost as loose as the play-money games you'll find online. Even though there's real money at stake, many players call, bet, and raise in low-limit games as though they're risking nothing but play-money!

- If you can maintain discipline in a play-money game, you're even more likely to keep your gambling gremlin in check when there's real money on the table. What's a gambling gremlin? Why, it's that little voice — and we all have it — that keeps popping up to urge us to stay when we should fold, or to see one more card when we know the odds don't justify it. Keep this in mind: Losing players indulge their gambling gremlin. Winners don't!

The Best Internet Play-Money Sites: Internet Poker Casinos

Online poker casinos offering real-cash games often offer introductory play-money games. These are a great place to start. Here's why:

- Play-money games let you get used to the graphics and procedures of cash games. They're user-friendly by design. You're a potential cash client, and the online casino hopes to expand its business by making you feel welcome and comfortable enough to "move on up" later on.

- Although the games are remarkably easy to use, the programming and graphics are almost identical to those used in the site's money games. Moreover, in overall sophistication, these games are far superior to games offered at Internet sites intended strictly for entertainment.

- Players here are somewhat more serious than those you'll find at sites meant strictly for fun. Notice we say "somewhat more serious." You'll still see eight out of ten players calling the flop. But at least it won't be ten out of ten!

If you wish, you can watch the cash games. If the procedure for doing so isn't clear, don't hesitate to ask about it. Ask other players by typing in the chat window or send e-mail or an instant message to the designated helper to get directions.

At Internet poker casinos offering real-money games, you don't have to pay to practice at the complimentary play-money tables. You may have to go through the motions of setting up an account, though. Although you might not have to provide a credit card number, you'll probably have to give your name, address, e-mail address, and telephone number when you register.

Getting Started

First, you need to download the game site's program files to your computer. Then you'll need to supply a user name or handle by which you'll be known in the games. Some people use their first name or initials, or an amalgam of parts of their first and last names. Others adopt imaginary, literary, or humorous names, so feel free to be creative here.

Once you've chosen your handle, you may not be able to change it easily, so choose carefully. Your handle is the only way opponents will be able to identify you to remember how you play, so it wouldn't be fair to keep changing it.

Participating in the Future of Poker at Rec.Gambling.Poker (RGP)

Think of the Internet newsgroup Rec.Gambling.Poker (RGP) as your one-stop poker newspaper, discussion club, information bureau, and personal advisor. Like all Internet newsgroups, RGP is a global, interactive electronic bulletin board serving thousands of people interested in the same subject — in this case, poker.

As with other newsgroups, you can read messages already there, then respond to them with either private e-mail to the author, or a public message called a *post* that's meant for all RGP readers. You can also create your own messages on new topics.

RGP is not a chat room; you can't conduct real-time discussions in newsgroups. You can also expect a slight delay between the time you post a message and when it actually appears onscreen because newsgroup messages are relayed through a series of servers before reaching the site that appears on your monitor.

Finding RGP

RGP is located in the part of the Internet called Usenet News, or Usenet. It's in a different part of the Internet than the World Wide Web, so you don't get there by typing a www address. Think of Usenet as a huge electronic bulletin board hanging in cyberspace. It has thousands of subdivisions called *newsgroups*, all organized into categories called hierarchies. You can find RGP under the *category* or *hierarchy* "rec" (short for recreation), under *subcategory* "gambling," where it's devoted to the *specific topic* "poker."

As you can see, newsgroups have nothing to do with the daily news. On AOL, they're found under keyword: *Newsgroups*. Other ISPs handle newsgroups much the same way. If you don't find RGP easily under "Newsgroups" from your ISP's home page, try typing *Rec.Gambling.Poker* into the Internet address window and clicking "Enter." You can also access RGP through the Internet, by going to www.google.com and navigating your way from there.

Another poker forum, located on the World Wide Web, is the United Poker Forum. While smaller than RGP, this forum is moderated and the posts are strictly about poker. It's well worth reading, and you can find it online at www.unitedpokerforum.com, or you can link to it from www.cardplayer.com.

Benefiting from RGP

RGP represents the entire poker community, from experts to rank beginners. As an open forum where one can exchange ideas, theories, opinions, and personal experiences, it's like a healthy extended family whose members agree to disagree sometimes. All members learn from each other's mistakes and experience.

Here are some of the key ways RGP will help you become a better player:

- If you're looking for specific information, someone in your extended poker family either will have the answer or know who does. Looking for a home game in Missoula, Montana; Marblehead, Massachusetts; or Magnolia, Mississippi? Want to find out which Internet poker casinos are the most reputable? Seeking info on the best games in your area or an upcoming tournament? Just post a new message and ask.

- If you give an opinion or propose a theory, you're likely to get a cheerful little earful of the opposing view. This causes you to think through your ideas to define them clearly enough to defend them, and to benefit from counter-arguments and the experience of other players.

- In the course of defending their own viewpoints, in answering questions, or just as a service to the rest of the group, members often include links to other Internet poker sites in their posts. The text of these links, called hyperlinks, may appear underlined and in a different color than the surrounding text. Another way to recognize a hyperlink is to rest your mouse pointer over a spot without clicking on it — if it's a hyperlink, the pointer will change into a tiny hand. By clicking on hyperlinks, you can explore sites they lead you to and bookmark or "save to Favorites" those that intrigue you.

- Players looking for feedback describe many game-specific and hand-specific situations in detail. You can participate in these discussions or just read any responses posted by experts, who often respond to interesting posts.

Such "superthreads" are the crown jewels of RGP. By following their strands from message to message, you'll reap a whirlwind of poker knowledge, insight, and vicarious experience — three factors that translate into profits when it's time to cash out your chips at the cage!Posing an interesting question or theory in a new message may spawn a lengthy thread (the initial posted message plus its trail of responses). If the subject is interesting or controversial enough, the thread may go on to weave a life of its own, generating responses from responses to the point where everyone from world champions to railbirds chimes in with his or her two cents. You'll wonder how in the world your seemingly innocent little post wound up causing such a fuss!

Virtual Poker for Real Money: Internet Cash Games

Using state-of-the-art computer technology, thousands of people play poker online for real money. By linking their computers to the Internet, players living as far apart as New York, London, and Tokyo are able to play together simultaneously in computer-generated poker games for real cash.

Until recently, such games weren't feasible. The challenge was to invent poker software that would enable strangers to play against each other in live games from different locations — and with enough confidence to back their mouse clicks with cash.

Without real money at stake, online casinos can't make profits since they take a rake from each pot just as a real casino poker room does. Advances in computer graphics, sound, and programming made Internet cash games possible. On January 1, 1998, Planet Poker was the first Internet poker casino to offer poker for cash stakes. Others followed quickly, and the market for Internet poker continues to grow at a steady pace.

But is it Legal?

The answer depends on which side of the business you're on — supplier side or client side — as well as where you live. To our knowledge, no one has ever been arrested for playing poker online, so there's no reason to worry about a midnight raid by the local authorities. But don't even think about starting an Internet poker casino in the United States. You'd be prosecuted for operating such a business, since federal law prohibits it. To satisfy the demand for online poker, foreign entrepreneurs rushed in to fill the void. Internet poker casinos are based where laws are more lenient, such as the Mohawk Reservation in Canada, or Costa Rica.

Our Advice to You

Our advice is to stay abreast of new developments in federal and state laws by inquiring about them regularly on Rec.Gambling.Poker. Then let common sense dictate. You also need to be concerned about your legal rights if you play for cash in online casinos.

Consider the following:

- *Bankrupt Casinos:* If an overseas-based casino goes bankrupt, you could lose any money you have on account without recourse.

  Our advice: Check out an online casino's reputation with the Internet poker newsgroup Rec.Gambling.Poker. Once you start playing, keep good records and cash out your wins frequently. Leave no more on account than you can afford to lose. After all, businesses in the good old USA go belly-up too. Money on deposit in cyberspace is at risk no matter where in the world it is.

- *Be alert for collusion:* Dishonest players may play in the same game while using cell phones, instant messages, or even adjacent computers. *In any of these ways, cheaters may be sharing information unfairly against you.*

  Our advice: The best online casinos have extensive programming that monitors and tags unusual betting patterns that indicate collusion, and they have "online cardroom managers" whose jobs include reviewing hand histories when collusion or some other form of online cheating is suspected by players. Choose a well-known online poker casino and ask about it on RGP before you start playing for serious money. Also, if you're a beginner lacking the necessary experience to detect unusual betting patterns yourself, stick to the lowest limits available. Cheaters usually play for higher stakes.

- *The easiest way to open an account at an online casino is to use a credit card, a debit card, or an online service, such as Neteller.com, to make a deposit:* You should be concerned any time you submit credit card numbers and other personal information through the Internet. If you're not comfortable making a credit card or online finance service deposit, arrange to wire money or send a cashier's check or money order. Even a personal check may be acceptable. When in doubt, ask by sending an e-mail inquiry to the online casino you have in mind.

Our advice: Take the time to check out the financial reputation of your chosen site at the poker Internet newsgroup Rec.Gambling.Poker. Look for messages listed by subject headings concerning online poker casinos. After you've read the related threads, start a new one by asking if anyone has had problems with an account at casino X. Also, once you've played online for cash, carefully monitor your credit card or bank statements each month to make sure you're not being overcharged or assessed hidden fees, and to verify that any cashouts have been properly credited to your account.

Finally: If you're really interested in online poker, you might want to point your browser to www.conjelco.com and pick up *Internet Poker: How to Play and Beat Online Poker Games*, by Lou Krieger and Kathleen Keller Watterson. It includes a CD containing interactive hands that, with the accompanying text, prepare you to play Omaha/8 and Omaha high-only, as well as several other popular Internet poker games. Also on the CD are links to informative Internet poker sites and several popular online poker casinos.

O ccasionally the truth is so apparent, so patently self evident, so abundantly clear, that having to mention it at all seems unnecessary, almost comical — like Mom reminding you to pack warm clothes when you tell her you're headed for Chicago in the dead of winter.

But at the risk of belaboring the obvious, we'll say it anyway. "Play your best all the time." Now, before consigning your authors to the scrap heap of redundancy, ask yourself whether you always *do* play your best, and if the answer is "No," perhaps you'd like to know why not. The sad, simple truth of the matter is that few of us *always* play our best. Not all of the time, anyway, and here's why:

Playing Omaha Is Too Much Fun

Omaha/8 is fun. We love it. That's why we haul ourselves to the card table *every* chance we get. It's so much fun, in fact, that we'd much rather play a hand than fold it. When we get in a game with a lot of loose players, and see K-J-7-6 run down a hand like A-A-3-2 double-suited, or witness the unadulterated joy on the face of a winner raking in pot after pot with hands he really shouldn't have played, the lure can become undeniable and the gambling fever contagious. In other words, we drop those pesky starting hand standards and just play, play, play. Any four will do, so long as we don't have to fold. Where's the fun in folding?

Yes, we get caught up in playing far too many hands, and we do it simply because it's fun. We enjoy it. We love it. And when we lose more than we should have, what do we do? All too often we loosen up *even* more, in an attempt to scoop a big pot and get even in one fell swoop.

We Call Too Much

Not only do most players call too frequently, but they're not as aggressive as they should be when they *do* have good hands. They enter far too many pots and hate to fold even when they miss the flop. Then they compound these errors by failing to raise in situations that clearly call for it.

Suppose you hold K-K-Q-J in an unraised pot. The flop is K-8-4 of mixed suits, and the big blind comes out betting. If there are players to act after you, this is an automatic raising situation. Yours is the best possible high hand right now, and you certainly don't want to let the low draws, or anyone who might have a draw to a straight, get there without paying the price.

Even though this hand is vulnerable to a low draw that might cost you half the pot and a straight draw that could cost you the whole shebang, you're better off raising than calling. Here's why: Not only do you have the best of it right now, but you also have a chance to improve to a full house or quads. If you do, you hope an opponent makes a straight and feels compelled to pay you off to the river.

Moreover, even though there are two low cards on the flop, there's no guarantee that a low hand will get there. After all, if you manage to get lucky, one of the next two cards will pair the board and the other will have a rank of nine or higher. You'll then scoop the pot and rake in all the dead money contributed by those who were chasing low draws. Last but not least, raising also increases your chances of winning if it eliminates someone who would have called the single bet with a marginal hand, then gone on to beat you by snagging a miracle card on the turn or river.

We Tend to Play to the Level of our Competition

We'll bet that if you found yourself in a game with the last eight winners of the *World Series of Poker*, or even with the eight best players in your local cardroom, you'd play better than you usually do because you have a lot more respect for those players.

But if you were in a game with the eight biggest fish in the world, you might find yourself playing almost as poorly as they do.

Indeed, many top players have been quoted as saying that they don't play well when they drop down to lower limit games. Keep this in mind: Not only is poker inherently seductive, but it often seems to lead us down a primrose path where we find ourselves playing just like our "loosey-goosey" opponents — even when we know better.

Don't Play When You're Psychologically Weakened

Poker is tough enough to beat when you're at your best. If you're tired, sick, or dealing with issues that command your thoughts, don't play. One of the biggest benefits of playing in casinos, in public cardrooms, and on the Internet is that the game never really ends. It's usually there whenever you're ready for it, so please don't make the costly mistake of taking your troubles out on your bankroll.

Monitor Your Own Play for Weaknesses; Then Act On Them

There have been times that we've played when tired or psychologically weakened. We all have. We recognized the condition but instead of acting on it, we ignored it, or denied it altogether. On those occasions we've generally lost money. In fact, the act of pretending they're in tip-top game shape when they're not is the single biggest flaw in many players' games. Many experienced poker players, when not at their best, have played in what should ordinarily have been very profitable games, but lost because they allowed their egos to seduce them into believing they were still big favorites.

But playing less than your best game at times is no reason to despair. If that journey of one thousand miles begins with the first step, why not take it now? You don't have to wait until New Year's Eve to pronounce your resolutions. If today is the day you elect to shout your good intentions to the heavens, if now is the hour you've selected to forgive yourself for past failings and transgressions at the poker table, if the moment has come to vow with all the resolve you can muster that you're going to make things better — go ahead. Do it.

But remember, in poker, as in life itself, talk is cheap. It's achieving a goal that takes unrelenting effort. Here are three simple poker resolutions you're cordially invited to adopt as your own if you believe they will help improve your game.

• *Never Go On Tilt; Never Play Less Than My Best.*

Controlling emotions in the heat of battle is a never-ending endeavor. When your senses are rubbed raw by a bad beat administered by a particularly obnoxious player, you might want to get up and walk away from the table until you've finished devouring your own innards. Even a slight tilt, playing just a wee bit poorly, is enough to upset the delicate balance needed to win consistently.

Poker, after all, is a very subtle game. Playing at the $20-$40 level, just a small loss of balance is enough to turn what should have been a $500 win into a loss of similar proportions. Small decisions can have a major impact on your bankroll. Making a bad decision about playing a hand can trap you for a significant loss. Folding when you should call, just because your senses aren't fully attuned to all the game's nuances, may cost you a pot large enough to turn an otherwise winning session into a losing one. When you're not at your best, avoid turning what should have been a nice win into a loss. Go to the movies instead. After all, popcorn is still cheap whether you're on top of your game or not.

It's very easy to steam or go on tilt when you're playing Omaha/8. Here's what'll happen if you do: You'll convince yourself to play many more starting hands, and you'll find it very difficult to get away from those hands after the flop. In hold'em, when you miss the flop it's an easy fold because the miss is so patently obvious; but in Omaha you can rationalize almost any flop into one that's playable.

It's also more expensive to go on tilt in Omaha/8 than in hold'em. That's because drawing hands are often the name of the game in Omaha/8, and you'll frequently find yourself calling all the way to the river with them. If you want to play

Omaha/8 well, stop yourself from succumbing when you feel the urge to "...take one more off." If necessary, imagine us applauding vigorously in the distance. But remember: We applaud only for good decisions, not for lucky flukes when you catch cards you really shouldn't have seen. So we hope you'll hear us booing if you administer bad beats to opponents, rather than the other way around.

Naturally, there'll be times when you've made a sound decision to fold, only to see the turn or river bring the exact card you needed. But more often than not over the long run, that won't happen. And the long run is what poker's all about.

Next, be on the lookout for steamers. They tend to bet, raise, and call early. But if they bet and raise on the turn and river, most likely they've stumbled into real hands and have what they're representing. It's pointless to try outplaying steamers, and keep in mind that if you're heads-up, the steamer's hand is never that much of an underdog, even against a premium hand. If you're up against a steamer, just let the cards guide your play, since you'll almost certainly have to show down the best hand to win the pot.

• *Make Myself a Narrow Target.*

If you make yourself a big fat target for opponents to shoot at, don't expect to win much money. The idea of narrowing the target (you!) means that if you take the worst of it too often, you're putting too much money at risk in unfavorable situations — and you won't win if you persist in doing that.

Avoid hunches. If the flop brings three — or even two — low cards, you can't afford to flop bottom set and convince yourself that a miracle will enable you to scoop the pot. Also: Don't play marginal starting cards in early position, and don't try to prove what a tough, tricky player you are by attempting to bluff perennial calling stations.

Fact: You'll earn more money in poker through opponents' mistakes than through your own skillful play. Though it takes skill along with a bit of luck to maneuver a decent player into making a serious error in judgment, it takes no skill whatsoever to collect extra bets from players who call when they shouldn't. So don't make things tough on yourself. There's no need to give opponents a handicap and then have to rise to extraordinary heights to beat them, especially when well-executed, solid play will take the pot.

- *Model Successful Behavior and Play.*

We've never thrown cards, insulted dealers, or otherwise acted like jerks in casinos or public cardrooms. After all, this isn't life and death. Nor is it God, country, apple pie, motherhood, or the flag. It's a game. Yes, that's right. Poker is only a game, not life itself. Our egos and self-esteem aren't so fragile that we become unglued by a losing session.

We've always modeled our behavior, deportment, and playing styles after players we admire — and we've continued to learn from them. Those players are wholly professional in their approach to the game. They don't curse, throw cards, or insult dealers or other players. They also play well; they've been winning players over the course of their careers. We've learned by watching their play, by reading their books, and by talking with them. We constantly attempt to discern the secrets of their success, in hopes that it will rub off on us — and you.

The truth is deceptively simple: If you're not ready to play your best, don't play. And when you do play, keep your standards foremost in your mind. Don't tumble down to the level of your opponents. Tell yourself it's OK to play your best. Then do it. Omaha/8 is a game where patience is rewarded, but given the design of the game and the nature of most players, it's a rare attribute.

Since whatever is possible in Omaha/8 is frequently probable, be prepared to fold when your low is counterfeited, or when the turn and river bring cards sure to complete opponent draws. Discipline and patience ward off those costly losses that occur when you know in your heart of hearts that you're beaten. In such cases, losers call anyway. If you don't, you'll be one step further on the road to becoming a consistent winner.

Chapter 22

Fighting Through Emotions

S erious students of poker view learning as a process of acquiring more knowledge — getting smarter, as it were. To accomplish this we read books, work with poker software, watch videos, scrutinize TV coverage of poker tournaments, and play poker. Then we analyze our play against our study material to see where we might have gone wrong. We talk to other players, read all the postings on the Internet Newsgroup, Rec.Gambling.Poker, and watch players we respect and admire, just to see the kinds of decisions they make when playing their cards.

We'll let you in on a secret. We all know more than we think we do. Each and every one of us. Even beginners. Often we see other players — sometimes even top-notch professionals — make what we consider egregious errors during the heat of battle. Sometimes, when we analyze their play, we can't seem to grasp why they played a hand a certain way. So we write it off to the pro mixing up his play, or setting a trap he intends to spring sometime later that evening. But sometimes it wasn't a sublime and sophisticated move at all; it was simply a mistake. You spotted it and he didn't. But because that move came from an expert, you gave him more credit than he deserved. Often, when you observe someone make a poor play, you're correct and he's wrong — even if he's an acknowledged expert.

How can that be? How can you, the amateur player, the recreational poker aficionado, know more than someone who earns a living at the game? While you don't know more than he does, you did know enough to spot his error and analyze it. He didn't see it. You did. Why did that happen?

It happened because the pro, just like you and me and everyone else who plays this game, let his emotions come to the forefront of his consciousness. All of us are guilty of this. Some of us lapse into this pattern more than others, but when it happens, logic and reason are left in the dust, and decisions are made solely on our emotions. Quite often these decisions are wrong.

Our minds are complex. When dealing with issues, we draw freely on many different attributes, and employ them in varying combinations. If we gave you a series of numbers and asked you to add them up, you'd draw on your arithmetical knowledge. No emotional investment would be needed to solve this problem.

But if you turned on the evening news and film footage showed some 12-year-old kid shooting up his junior high school with an assault rifle, your response would be emotional. You'd have plenty of targets for your anger too. There's the kid; he's anger target number one. But what about the ease with which weapons like these — with no sporting value whatsoever — can be acquired? They're apparently so easily obtained that even a 12-year-old can score. What about the parents? Can't you direct some anger toward them for the abysmally poor job they did of instilling any morality whatsoever into their offspring?

Isn't that the way your mind reacts when you play poker? You sit down at the game and play correctly for a while. Then, for one reason or another — perhaps it's a bad beat or maybe an unexpected win — your emotions come to the forefront and push logic to the back. Isn't that why so many players believe in hunches? Isn't that why they "...just have a feeling" that the card they need will come on the river? Does it ever happen? Sure. If it's a one in five shot, in the long run it figures to occur about once every five tries. No more, no less, and none of us can predict the future with any certainty regardless of what we may be feeling or hoping for at the moment. You get the point. Some things are logical. Other things grab you by the gut. Think of your mind as a computer. You can open a number of programs at once, and depending on your needs you can work with a word processor, a spreadsheet, or a graphics program. Whichever one you select comes to the forefront. It takes precedence at your command, sending the others into the background for the time being.

Your authors take walks when bad beats trigger disruptive emotions. We don't like to play poker on emotion; we prefer playing on logic and whatever intuitive assumptions we can make at the time. Getting emotionally caught up in the game, needing to win so we can get back to even, needing to avenge some perceived insult thrown our way by another player, needing to impose the strength of our will on the entire table — these are irrational urges and impulses that invariably cost money.

When emotions take over, many players like to get up and go for a walk. If they can't let it go, it's a sure sign that it's time to get up and go home. Although you may have a deeper knowledge base than any other player at the table, when your emotions take the wheel it's not easy to draw on that knowledge. And guess what happens to your logic when that narrowly focused tunnel vision of emotion takes over. There's no room in that tunnel for logic, so it goes right out the window. You hone in on one thing and one thing only, the emotion of the moment.

Winning poker requires us to process information from a variety of sources. If, for example, you're hell-bent on getting even, you'll seldom be able to read your opponents with any degree of accuracy. In fact, you'll only see whatever enters your narrowly focused perspective, and invariably that's not enough.

Sometimes that narrow focus fueled by adrenalin is a good thing — but usually not when you're playing Omaha/8. It's a fight-or-flight mechanism. It allows us to concentrate on one enemy, and to deal with immediate threats to life and limb. It was, and probably still is, very necessary for the survival of our species, but it won't help you win at poker.

When your emotions leap to the forefront of your mind, that's the time to seize control of yourself. Plant your knowledge, not your emotions, firmly in the forefront of your thinking, so that you can draw on it as needed during the game. Only if you can analyze play while involved in a hand as clearly as you can when you're a disinterested observer, can you truly say you have conquered your emotions.

Until that time, you'll have to work with all the ability you possess to keep your knowledge in a prominent place. Knowledge is a reservoir, to be drawn on when needed. When applied, that reserve of knowledge becomes "know-how." If it isn't utilized because you choose not to draw on it or you're so consumed by emotions that you find yourself unable to apply your skills, the result is usually the same, and it's not one you're gonna like.

When you reach that point, it doesn't matter one whit whether you actually know anything about the game or not — you have effectively rendered yourself incapable of thinking. If you can't convert your knowledge base into practical know-how at the table, you're running on emotion alone, going on tilt or already there, and heading for another in a series of losing sessions. It's not a pretty picture. But only you can establish control over yourself and your game — and to accomplish this, you must force your emotions into the background and bring your reservoir of knowledge up where it belongs, firmly in the forefront of your mind, where you can tap into it as needed.

Fighting through your emotions so you can play with a cool head may be the single hardest thing you'll ever have to do to become a winning poker player. If that particular yoke is draped around your neck, you can either exert the Herculean effort required to remove it, or give in. It's tough, but it's decidedly not a Hobson's choice. The work is hard but your efforts will bear fruit. Your game will grow from it and so will you. Giving in is easy. All that's needed is to continue down the same old road. Yes, giving in to emotions rather than fighting through them is easy, but the consequences are raw, hard, and unforgiving — and all you'll have to look forward to is the sight of your bankroll bleeding away.

Chapter 23

Back To Basics

When the game gets tough, when things just don't seem to work out the way they should, when big hands get cracked with regularity and your nut low seemingly gets counterfeited on the river every time, when unplayable hand follows unplayable hand and you find yourself racked from pillar to post in a game you should beat, what do you do about it? How should you fine-tune your game to regain your edge?

Many poker players are notoriously remiss about redirecting their game when it appears to be in trouble. They're frequently first in line to whine and bemoan their bad luck; but whining, of course, is fruitless. Players who happen to be winning are quick to brag about their skills, but losing is a different story — one frequently attributed to an interminable, against-all-odds series of bad beats. Yet very few players realize they can play poorly and win just as they can play well and lose. Fewer still will candidly attribute their losses to poor play.

Athletes, in this regard, react quite differently than poker players. Golfers are famous for occasionally taking time off the tour, going back to their favorite teaching pro, and realigning their swing — or even breaking it down entirely and starting from scratch in an attempt to get back in that groove where all drives are dead solid perfect, each approach shot is pin-high on the green, and all putts are drained effortlessly.

Golfers aren't alone. Slumping baseball players take extra batting practice. Basketball players become gym rats and shoot jump shots for hours to recover their stroke.

But unlike poker, an athlete's craft is visible. With cameras, computers, and sometimes even with the naked eye, athletes can see what's wrong and make corrections. In poker, however, skill isn't physical, it's mental — and can neither be captured on videotape nor measured. Because poker players have no physical evidence to show them why they're running badly, it's easy for them to live in the depths of denial, and blame poor results on dame fortune, circumstance, and bad beats.

The inability of many players to acknowledge their own poor play is a rather subtle trap. It's also a major reason why many players never show improvement from one year to the next. While they may have played for years, the same mistakes persist unabated deep within their games. Some mistakes are never corrected. Week after dreary week, month after dissatisfying month, and year after miserable year, the results are remarkably similar.

But improvements can be made. Many of your opponents are better players today than last year. One key to improving your game, while deceptively simple, takes perseverance and effort along with a commitment to change. Here's how to go about it:

Back to basics is the key, and there are a few ways to accomplish this. One method involves finding someone whose poker judgment you respect and asking him to audit your game. Perhaps he could spend an hour or two over the course of a few days looking over your shoulder, evaluating the hands you play and the decisions you make during the game. But it's tough to find someone willing to act as your coach. Even if you do, chances are you'll play differently knowing someone is evaluating every decision you make.

But there's another way. You might just pick someone whose game you respect and imagine he or she is looking over your shoulder. Then pretend that your coach has promised to bankroll you for a year if you pass an audition. That audition, while seemingly simple and straightforward, won't be easy. The sole requirement for passing is to make correct decisions at the poker table. You won't even have to book a win. Make good decisions and you'll be free rolling courtesy of your coach. Make poor decisions and it's, "Don't call us; we'll call you."

While you're considering which decisions to concentrate on, give some thought to those that are most important. After all, you can't expect exceptional grades just for flopping a full house and winning with it, or for mucking a hand like K-9-8-3. It's the marginal situations that come up frequently, as well as those that can result in a significant amount of money being won or lost, that should attract most of your attention.

Perhaps you call too frequently. That's a common mistake. Many Omaha/8 players call far too often with hands that don't warrant it. They call when the potential payout offered by the pot isn't sufficient to overcome the odds against making their hands. And when they play weak hands, that's a likely possibility.

Here's a way to overcome that costly habit. Whenever you're inclined to call, ask yourself this: Instead of calling, is it better to raise, or would folding be my best decision? Many players look for reasons to call. Though they call almost reflexively in certain situations, raising or folding would frequently be a better choice. And of those two choices, folding is the appropriate act more often than not.

Try this exercise: For one hour, either raise or fold every starting hand. *Don't call — not even once.* We guarantee you won't be making marginal plays, and who knows — it may do wonders for your table image. Just accept the idea that you'll be folding lots of hands.

This concept goes against the grain of many recreational poker players. After all, they came to play, not to fold; they came for the action, not for repose, and they came to have fun, period. They may say they came to win too, but they're deceiving themselves. They've never accepted the requirements of winning poker because they're too busy having a good time.

Granted, sitting on the sidelines folding hand after unplayable hand is nobody's idea of a terrific time. But that's sometimes what winning poker requires — fold after fold after fold — repeat as many times as necessary. When hands like A-J-6-5 in middle position begin to look good, and a hand like A-8-7-4 under the gun looks unbeatable, you've got to suck it up and resist that temptation to call because "...I just had a hunch." If you want to play winning poker, you'll have to learn to fold each and every time your cards dictate, not only when you haven't run out of patience.

So where does that compelling inclination to call these marginal hands come from, anyway? Certainly not from the hands themselves. Their value hasn't increased in the least. It's your perception of them that's changed — a distorted perception shaped by comparing these latest arrivals with those really ugly dogs that came before them. Sure, an A-8-7-4 containing all four suits looks potent compared to Q-9-8-7. But someone else may be holding far better cards. Do you really want to put your rainbow-colored, mediocre hand up against A-A-4-2 double-suited?

Remember: Just because you're experiencing a run of bad cards doesn't mean your opponents are suffering the same fate. To the contrary, some of them might even be having a particularly good run of cards — and that's exactly why, if you lose your discipline, you're most likely to lose your money as well.

So what about that audition we mentioned? Care to give it a try? Just remember you're only rewarded for good decisions. If you're flying on autopilot, reflexively calling instead of actively analyzing each hand you're dealt and each situation you encounter, you'll find yourself flunking the audition. You'll be playing hands the top-notch player who offered to sponsor your efforts wouldn't dream of playing in those spots.

We want you to learn how to pass that audition every day. Pretend you're under the scrutinizing eye of the expert. Ask yourself over and over what he would do in your shoes, then enact your answers. Remember that the result of any given hand is frequently beyond your control. All you can do is make correct decisions. Do that and results eventually take care of themselves. Luck, in cards as in love, is a miraculous thing. It eventually finds its way to those who are deserving. They've earned it. Now, go out and pass that audition!

Chapter 24

Ten Keys To Success

Seminars and self-help books abound. They can teach you how to be a winner in business, in love, and in your personal life. Regardless of the field of endeavor, the core principles of self-improvement are remarkably similar, and they can help to make you a winner at the poker table as well as in life. Here are ten you may want to think about:

1. Be Aware of Your Own Strengths and Weaknesses.

An outrageous image at the table may work for some people but not for others. Some players are better suited to tournaments, others to cash games. Play your best game and play within the confines of your own comfort zone. In other words, know yourself, and do what you do well.

2. You're Responsible.

The results you achieve are the product of your own play. Yes, short-term luck is a factor in any poker game, though over the long haul results mirror skill, effort, and discipline — nothing more, nothing less. But until you acknowledge that you and you alone are accountable for the results you achieve, you won't have enough control over your game to ensure success.

3. Think About the Game.

Unless you're consistent about doing your poker homework, you're only marking time, since you have neither plan nor strategy. You need to keep up with current poker literature, and you need to think about the game. Think about it while you're at the table and when you're away from it. Analyze hands you've seen, then decide if you would have played them differently — and if so, why. Omaha/8, like all other forms of poker, is a constantly evolving milieu of strategy, tactics, and playing styles. The message here is simple: Think, analyze, modify your game, and repeat as needed. Do it from now on.

4. Have a Plan.

What are your goals when you play poker? Do you want to have fun and just break even? Do you want to be a top tournament player? Or do you want to be the best $20-$40 Omaha/8 player around? How much are you willing to risk? You need a definite plan to get it done, and in order to work, that plan must be a lot more than wishful thinking. Remember, if you don't have your own agenda, you are most assuredly part of someone else's!

5. Set Deadlines

If your goal is to play an average of 30 hours per week, then do it. If you plan to read one new poker book every two weeks, then set a deadline for yourself and do that too. If you've lost all your poker money and need to rebuild your bankroll, plan how long it will take until you're back in action. Once you have a plan, go out, get yourself a job, and earn the money that enables you to play.

6. Be Realistic.

If your goal is to win an Omaha/8 event at the *World Series of Poker* next year when you've never played a big tournament in your life, please don't expect to achieve that simply by reading this book. Instead, start with a challenging but reachable goal. Once you achieve it, you can set the next, more difficult goal. You might decide to play in one or two inexpensive tournaments per week, or in the satellites preliminary to major tournaments. If you don't do well there, keep trying. But save your money. You're not yet ready to invest big bucks in entry fees to major events.

7. Expect Difficulties.

You'll succumb to all of your flaws during the period you're struggling, growing, and reaching for higher levels of skill. Just because you've read all the books by all the experts, don't deceive yourself into believing you can play as well as they do. Every top-notch player struggled through difficulties to reach success. You'll have to do the same. Golf videos won't turn you into Tiger Woods, chess monographs won't turn you into a grandmaster, and *Super System* won't turn you into Doyle Brunson. The best poker books can teach you how to *talk the talk*. You'll have to learn to *walk the walk* on your own! And that takes practice, as well as the willingness to be brutally honest with yourself as you assess your game's shortcomings and learn to overcome them.

8. Build On Small Accomplishments.

If you're not a winning player today, but begin to study hard, put into practice what you read, and continuously integrate this new knowledge into your own style of play, you'll find yourself improving. You may not be able to make your living playing Omaha/8, but at least you'll no longer be a contributor to others at the table. Keep doing what works for you, and you'll notice that success builds upon itself. And whatever you do, don't let small setbacks put you on tilt. Train yourself to expect difficulties. If you occasionally play poorly, don't berate yourself. Just make up your mind to correct things next time instead. However, if you find yourself saying, "Just this once won't hurt me," or, "I'll just take one off," as you play yet another weak hand on a hunch, you're on the wrong track. This behavior will hurt you. Taking the worst of it on a hunch, or doing something else that's clearly wrong just for the fun of it, is nothing more than premeditated backsliding. Do it and you'll have only yourself to blame. Learn to focus on what produces positive results, and skip the rest.

9. Persist.

You must sustain. The old adage, "Ninety percent of success is just showing up," has a great deal of validity. You need to keep playing, practicing, and building on small successes. Each time you reach one of your goals, savor the moment. Then quickly set another goal. Try visualizing. Golfers visualize their putts dropping; baseball players visualize the bat connecting with the ball; basketball players visualize the hoop growing and the ball dropping through — hitting nothing but net. In your mind, watch yourself making the right plays at the poker table. When you're able to visualize strategies in action, you'll see your winnings accrue in the process. Keep showing up, always play your best game, and keep moving forward. Some of your opponents will be improving too. Remember: If you're not consistently moving forward with your own game, you're probably moving backwards in relation to theirs.

10. Have Fun.

Enjoy yourself. Have a good time playing Omaha. Otherwise it's just a big waste of time. Your poker time is discretionary. No one says you have to play poker. You play because you enjoy it; you want to play. While there are lots of bitter pills we all have to swallow as part of life, we ought to enjoy what we *choose* to do. If you can't enjoy yourself when you play, perhaps you should find another outlet for your time and money.

It's always amazing to hear players constantly griping and berating others when they play. Some of them have been doing this for years. They never seem to be happy. It's tempting to ask why they bother to play, since they obviously get no enjoyment from it. But we don't really want to know the answer. Nor do we want to ask philosophical questions that can cause these lifetime contributors to question their motives and — heaven help us — start to improve.

We're always happy to see a malcontent or two at the table, and you should be too. They represent profits, and if they choose not to take the easily accessible advice found in this and other poker books, we're not about to spoon feed it to them on an individualized basis at the tables. So enjoy yourself when you sit down to play or find something else to do. You won't succeed as a poker player if you have to fight yourself as well as your opponents.

Finally, to sum up: If you want success in poker, or in life, there's no mystery to the process you'll need to follow to achieve your dreams: Look inward, look outward, set goals, deal with the inevitable setbacks, show up, have fun, and always do your very best. We promise that you'll reap the inevitable rewards.

Chapter 25

Bad Game, Good Game

Game selection is one of the most important decisions you'll make in poker. Assuming you play well and with discipline, wise game selection should be your top priority. But just how do you go about determining what makes a good game, or a bad game?

In this chapter, we provide some guidelines to help you look the games over and decide for yourself which you ought to be playing in, and which you're better off avoiding. But before going any further, take a moment to jot down some of the factors you consider important in determining whether a particular Omaha/8 game is one you should want to play in, or one you ought to avoid. Don't spend too much time on this; four or five factors should suffice. When you've finished making your list, read on.

Poker is about winning money. Stripped bare of its other desirable qualities, that's what poker's all about. But we all know that while people play poker to win money, they also play because it's fun. Although winning money and having fun aren't necessarily the same thing, there's usually a direct correlation where poker is concerned. The most enjoyable games are usually those in which you can win the most money. It follows, then, that if you want to be happy and have fun with poker, you must play in games where you're favored to win, not in those where you're up against Savvy Shark and Serious Sally.

So important is this concept that author, poker teacher, and *Card Player* magazine columnist Roy West coined the following rule: *Play happy, or don't play at all.* If this is true on an individual basis, and we have no doubt that it is, we can extrapolate from Roy's Rule to say: Play in a *happy game*, or don't play at all.

After all, if playing poker were like having a root canal, how many of us would play on a regular basis — even if we could win money? Probably not many. Flip that question around and the answer comes up the same. Regardless of how much fun it might be, would you play poker knowing you'd lose money each and every time you sat down at the table?

Since winning money at poker and having fun are positively correlated, we've identified a strong telltale association that helps us determine which games are good, and which aren't: Good games are happy games, with players acting like they're at a party. Bad games are somber or even angry games, full of grim, serious players. Let's take a closer look:

Loose Games, Lots of Chips

Two hallmarks of a good game are lots of money on the table, and lots of players in every pot. Since winning money is your objective, it stands to reason that games with players who have plenty of chips and contest far too many pots, are games you want to play in. In fact, these are ideal money-winning situations.

Tight Games, Few Chips

Contrast those prime, happy-go-lucky, money-winning situations with somber, tight, silent games, especially those where most players are short-stacked. When very few players get involved in pots, and most have only a stack or two of chips in front of them, this is a game you're better off avoiding. Not only is this a table full of rocks, but even when players do commit to a hand, they're not going to give away very much. While you can make money in extremely tight games by taking advantage of rigid play, if you have a choice between a loose game and a tight game, choose the loose game every time.

Happy Players, Gambling Players

Games with happy players are *gambling* games. When there's lots of cross-table chit-chat, bantering, and laughter, and a couple of players are drinking, or betting on sports or horses, you know you've hooked up with opponents who have *come to play*. What does this mean? It means there'll be players calling each pot who really should have folded. Instead, they casually flip their chips into the pot, seemingly without a care. They are having *such a good time*. They're gambling while you're ready to play solid poker. This is a good game.

After all, players who call without a *care* are really calling without a *thought*, and calling without thought is sheer gambling, not smart poker. Gambling players who toss chips into the pot as though on autopilot make ideal opponents. This is exactly the kind of opposition you want, for such games are highly profitable. If you can't beat folks who bet and call without thinking, you're either having an absolutely horrible run of luck, or you can't beat anyone.

Angry Players

A game with lots of arguing at the table is probably one to avoid. Sure, you can take advantage of players who are *on tilt*, and *steaming* their money away. Anger begets loose play often enough for the astute player to take advantage of it. But not always. Sometimes the opposite is true. Rather than steam off their money, angry players can also hunker down and seethe while waiting for premium hands. So before you sit down with a table full of angry players, take stock of things. Get a fix on what's coming out of all that anger. If Angry Al is hunkering down, seething, and not putting any money into play, you should pass on this game. But if Steaming Sam is angrily tossing in unwarranted bets and raises, you may have found a place to call home.

Maniacs

Angry players sometimes raise too much. In fact, they often start raising wars, and in the process change from guys who are just a little bit on tilt into full-fledged maniacs. With a maniac or two at your table, pots are often three-bet, and frequently capped. Whenever raising wars become prevalent, you can win a substantial amount of money in a short time — *if* you happen to be catching cards. If you're not, or if several of your premium hands lose on the river to miracle draws, you're likely to see big fluctuations in your bankroll. If you can stand some wild, roller-coaster swings, just hang in there, play solid hands, and you ought to find these games profitable in the long run. Just expect to be bounced around quite a bit in the process. If you're not comfortable with big fluctuations, avoid these games.

Calling Stations

The softest games — those easiest to beat — feature players who call too frequently, but are too timid to raise with their good hands. This is really the best of all possible worlds for you. Big pots accrue because most players see the flop and then keep calling with hands they should have folded. They're in there drawing to the second best or even third best low, when the most they can do is win half the pot — though in all likelihood, they won't *win* any of it. Sometimes these very loose, passive players even call with a straight draw despite the presence of three cards on board of the same suit, or a board that has already paired.

They'll call when you raise, regardless of what they're holding, simply because they don't know any better, or because they love to play so much that they're reluctant to surrender a hand under any circumstances. But because they're timid, they'll seldom raise. As the lucky recipient of their passive playing style, you'll get maximum value from your winning hands but also lose the minimum possible amount on those that fall short. That's because your opponents will neglect to punish you when they have the best of it. They either don't know how to or don't care to, but, either way, it'll save you money.

Players who fall into this category are, invariably, recreational players, out to gamble and have a good time. They want to have fun, fun, and more fun, and your job is to allow them to do just that while taking advantage of their largess. You should never do anything whatsoever that raises their hackles, gets them upset, induces them to tighten up their play, or, worse yet, causes them to leave the game entirely. Quite the contrary; you should do everything within your power to encourage and prolong their loose play. Listen sympathetically to their tales of woe. Engage them in conversation. Make life enjoyable for them. After all, they came to play and to have fun. So help them out. Here's how:

- Never rub it in when you win.

- Never make insidious or sarcastic remarks designed to flaunt your superior play or call attention to another player's deficiencies.

- Don't assume that your whispered commentary to the solid player on your right goes unheard by the fish on your left. People have an uncanny knack for realizing when they're the focus of derogatory patter.

- Watch your facial expressions too. A disgusted grimace at a player who just made a miracle draw may be more offensive than words.

- In short: Never give lessons at the poker table. When you're playing with geese who are busily laying golden eggs, why in the world would you want to drive them away?

It's extremely rare to find a game in which all opponents are meek, timid calling stations. If you do, think about propping your eyelids open with toothpicks because it's surely a game you should never leave. Always look for a game with happy, jocular players who call most bets and seldom raise. After you get into that game, keep monitoring other games to make sure yours is still the best — and don't hesitate to change tables whenever it's to your advantage. Wait-list for several other games at a time, if necessary. Enjoy your current game and have fun, but if you want to be a winning player, don't forget your primary goal is to make money. That's the reality of poker.

Now go back to the list you made earlier. If you've put happy, timid calling-stations on the good side of the ledger, and angry, tight, and testy players on the other — you're on the right track to selecting good games and avoiding bad ones. It's a common-sensical approach: Avoid the gloom and doom tables. If that's all you can find in your favorite cardroom, go elsewhere and seek out a better game, or simply play another day. Look for the fun and laughter, the big stacks of chips, the nonchalant, freewheeling ambience of happy opponents. When you see such a game, invite yourself to the party. Take a seat!

Chapter 26

How Big A Bankroll Do You Need?

E very poker player needs a bankroll. You can't play without one, yet the size of a bankroll needed to outlast any bad run of cards and ensure that you'll never go broke is a complex issue that can't be resolved through rule or formula. Nevertheless, you can bank on one fact with absolute certainty: If you're not a winning player, your bankroll will never be large enough.

To completely eliminate the possibility of ever going broke, a losing player needs a big enough bankroll to outlast his life expectancy. Otherwise, he'll find himself regularly infusing his playing stake with fresh cash.

Some players really *do* have bankrolls substantial enough to outlast their life expectancy. After all, the world really does have a lot of wealthy poker players, many of whom are derisively referred to as "*trust-fund pros.*" Some of these folks play every day, and will swear to you that they're long-term winners. But these trust-fund pros seldom deceive their opponents, no matter how strongly they claim to be winning players. They only delude themselves, and their opponents know it.

But the price of self-deception can be high. Consider a 40-year-old trust fund pro who plays $10-$20 Omaha/8 and loses an average of one big bet per hour. If he plays 2,000 hours a year and lives to be 85, he can expect to lose $1,800,000 playing poker. To most people, that's a lot of money.

But suppose this particular player isn't really that bad and loses only three dollars per hour. He'll still run through $270,000 before keeling over at the table. It's not as bad as a million-eight, but it's still a healthy chunk of change to most folks. The best thing you can say about this player is that he did a bang-up job of financial planning since he started with a $270,000 bankroll and lost his last dollar on his last day of life. (If he did a *perfect* job of financial planning, he'd work it so close to the nub that his check to the undertaker would bounce.)

While there are more than a few trust-fund pros out there, most recreational poker players underwrite their hobby with their paychecks. Playing Omaha/8, to the majority of them, is recreation — just a hobby — and if they lose today, it's no big deal. They can supplement their bankrolls on payday, and as long as their losses don't exceed their discretionary income, they don't need to concern themselves with having adequate bankrolls.

For all players who aren't lifelong winners — and estimates suggest that 85-90 percent of all players do not beat the game — an adequate bankroll means either a trust fund ample enough to sustain a lifetime of losses, or a paycheck that can cover losses from one week to the next without risking the rent money.

But suppose you're a professional card player, or you aspire to be one, and poker is your paycheck? How much of a bankroll do you need to keep from going broke?

Professional poker players realize that every dollar won won't be added to the bankroll. After all, poker players have to pay rent and buy groceries just like anyone else, but their only source of income is the money they win. Lose, and the pro pays bills the only way he or she can — by drawing down the bankroll. But there's a limit to how deeply one can dig without getting into jeopardy.

Reducing your bankroll converts *capital* into *income* — and that distinction is an important one. If you change too much capital into income it's like eating your seed corn. When a player on a short bankroll hits a protracted losing streak, he has only a few choices. He may have to get a job in order to build up his bankroll — that reverses the process and converts income into capital. Or he can become a *horse* for someone else and play on his backer's money, but if he does, he will retain only a portion of his winnings. The other alternative is to quit poker entirely. None of these are very desirable options for working professional poker players.

Bleeding off capital and converting it to income to make the balance sheet look better isn't limited to poker players, either. Businesses do it all the time. Years ago, when Pan-Am was on the rocks, the company sold off its flagship building in New York City. As a result, the financial statements made it appear as though the airline had had a good year. But you can only convert capital into income once. Then it's gone. A poker player's bankroll is his capital.

When poker is your business, you don't need money to build factories, or to buy office buildings, trucks, machine tools, or banks of computers. Money — in the form of a playing bankroll — is your capital. If you lose some of your bankroll, you should drop down and play at smaller limits, put the screws to your personal spending habits, and grind out small but steady winnings until you have an adequate bankroll again. Remember: If you lose too much of your bankroll, you run the risk of becoming so undercapitalized that you're unable to compete as a professional poker player at all.

We've always used the figure of 300 big bets as a reliable bankroll — but even that may not be enough. If a bankroll of $6,000 to play $10-$20 Omaha/8 seems like a shockingly high number, it's important to remember that the vicissitudes of fate can produce some extreme results in the short run. Even $6,000 may be a conservative estimate.

But that's not the whole story. If you're an outstanding player in a regular game that's made up of absolutely horrendous, extremely passive players — who seldom raise but always call until all hope, no matter how small, is completely dissipated — you can probably play on a much smaller bankroll without the risk of going broke. But few among us are lucky enough to find a regular game filled with players who play that badly.

Even when you're a favorite in your game, you're probably not a prohibitive one. If you regularly play in a tough game, you might even need more than 300 big bets as a hedge against going broke. For the average working professional player — the guy who plays every day trying to win between one and one-and-a-half big bets per hour — there's no reason to deviate from the conventional wisdom of a 300 big-bet bankroll as a minimum requirement.

Can you still take occasional shots at bigger games without a 300-bet bankroll? Sure — and you probably ought to — as long as the game looks good and you know you're a favorite. If anything, it will help you prepare for the next move up the poker ladder, once your bankroll grows large enough to play there regularly.

Limit poker, after all, is like a job. As long as you're a winning player, the more hours you put in, the more money you'll earn. And if you give yourself a pay raise by jumping to a bigger game, you ought to win more in the long run. Just make sure you don't take risks you can't afford — like playing on a short bankroll. Without a sufficient cushion, all it takes is a few big losses to find yourself terminally downsized.

As for using money management concepts — like setting stop-loss limits and quitting once you've won some predetermined amount of money — and thinking they'll shield you against the possibility of going broke, forget about it. If you're a favorite, just keep playing. The more you work, the more money you'll make. But if you're tired, or that once good game is now full of tough opponents, get up and go home. The game will be there tomorrow. Poker, after all, is a marathon, not a sprint.

Chapter 27

Afterword

Y ou've come to the end of the book and your natural question is, "Where do I go from here?" Having read this far, you might think you've learned enough to knock 'em dead at the tables. If this were true your authors would be wealthier men, Omaha players the world over would pay handsomely for our advice, and those who have read this book would trundle up to the table and easily squeeze every last dollar out of any opponent who hasn't read it.

But it's not that simple. Few things in life ever are. There's more to learn, more to read — and you'll need hours and hours at the poker table playing Omaha to convert your book learning into real know-how. To progress as an Omaha player, you'll need to do a few more things. They're all interrelated, and each one of them supports the others.

You won't improve without playing. That's a given. Time at the poker table is absolutely necessary to integrate the content of this book into your game. Your first goal is to play skilled, efficient, and mechanically effortless poker. Once your mind is freed from having to think about the mechanics of the game during the heat of battle, you can begin observing opponents and determining strategic and tactical lines of attack — and that's where creative poker play really begins. But before you can hope to accomplish that, you need to know the basics and know them cold.

You have to think about the game too. Set up your own internal instant replay camera, so you can review those things you did well as well as those questionable decisions you might have made during your last Omaha session. This self-analytical review of your game is the only way — outside of hiring a poker coach to sit at the table with you and review how you played the hands you were dealt — you can learn to overcome your mistakes and capitalize on your strengths.

It also helps to think about each session you play in terms of what you've read in this book. Go back and review your day's play to see how it comports with the information we've presented and the suggestions we've made in these pages.

Read other books too. Ours is not the only Omaha book on the shelf, and you should read them all. Fortunately, that's not a very long reading list. There are a relatively small number of books about Omaha poker on the bookshelves, especially when measured against the dozens and dozens of books that have been written about Texas hold'em. In fact, that's one of the reasons your authors wrote this book. We saw a real and compelling need for a book designed to teach beginners and experienced players alike about how to become winning Omaha players, and although we're pleased that you have chosen to read our book, we really hope you read all the others too.

Reading, playing, and thinking about the game is sufficient to give you an undergraduate degree in Omaha. But the "real world," as any recent college graduate will attest, is always different, and education at an entirely new level begins at the poker table. And if you're really dedicated to improving your game, that education will never end. If you're new to Omaha, our book provides the basics along with more sophisticated ideas you won't fully grasp until you've added some real world experience to the concepts you've read about. Learning is a never-ending process, and it's seldom that a single book will teach a reader all he or she needs to know to conquer any field of endeavor, including poker. That's why the bookstores are filled with scads of self-help books on every conceivable topic: from how to fix your love life, to taking charge of your financial affairs, to improving your golf. And most readers will avail themselves of a variety of books and approaches about a subject that piques their interest. Poker isn't any different. And anyway, reading all the Omaha books in print is hardly a daunting challenge.

Some facets of Omaha are very simple. Others are very sophisticated, and you probably won't grasp all of their implications in one reading. In fact, the more you learn, the more applicable many Omaha books become. You'll find yourself reading and digesting them in an iterative process of "read, play, and think."

Never stop. Becoming a winning Omaha player demands continuous learning. The process of learning and thinking about poker should never cease. And you know what? The more you learn, the more you'll win, and the more enjoyment the game provides. So study up. Then go out and play some Omaha and knock 'em dead. Have a wonderful time. May you flop the nuts in both directions...and may they hold up!

Index

About the Authors

Mark Tenner is an entrepreneur with advanced degrees in communications, business, and law. He is a partner in *Card Player Cruises*, a gaming industry consultant, and a semiprofessional poker player. He has been playing and winning on a regular basis for 40 years, and can generally be found playing in the highest limit games.

For the last several years, Mark has played Omaha/8 almost exclusively, and has lectured extensively on this game in such venues as the *World Poker Players' Conference*, and for special interest groups, various casinos, and cruise ships.

His peers consider him one of the finest minds in the game because of his almost uncanny feel for how Omaha/8 should be played. It is this special gift, along with general expertise, that Mark Tenner brings to this book. Because he is also a skilled communicator, he succeeds in imparting not only tips and techniques but his unique process of analysis and thinking. Mark's guidance will assist you, the reader, to develop a similar feel for the game.

Lou Krieger learned poker at the tender age of seven, while standing at his father's side during the weekly Thursday night game held at the Krieger kitchen table in the blue-collar Brooklyn neighborhood where they lived.

Lou played poker throughout high school and college — it was seven-card stud back then, since Texas hold'em and Omaha weren't even on the horizon — and managed to keep his head above water only because his cronies were so appallingly bad. But it wasn't until his first visit to Las Vegas that he took poker seriously, buying into a low limit seven card stud game where he managed — with lots more luck than skill — to break even.

"While playing stud," he recalls, "I noticed another game that looked even more interesting. It was Texas hold'em. "I watched the hold'em game for about 30 minutes. The pots were bigger, there was a lot more action, and the players seemed to be having a lot more fun. I got my courage up, asked for a game change, and sat down to play. One hour and $100 later, I was hooked. I didn't mind losing. It was the first time I played and I expected to lose. But I didn't like feeling like a dummy, so I bought and studied every poker book I could find.

"I studied; I played. I studied and played some more. Before long I was winning regularly, and I haven't had a losing year since I began keeping records."

A few years later Lou discovered Omaha. "I was spending a week in Palm Desert, and the only place to play poker back then was a small club in a run-down building near Indio. The two hold'em games were both small limit affairs, but the club had a $10-$20 Omaha game that was flourishing. "I bought in," Krieger said, "and began to learn the game by trying to use what I knew about Texas hold'em and apply it to Omaha. It didn't work all that well, but by week's end I had broken even, learned the rudiments of the game, and knew I had a lot more to learn if I ever expected to play it well."

In the early 90's Lou Krieger began writing a column called "On Strategy" for *Card Player Magazine*. He's also written four books about poker: *Hold'em Excellence: From Beginner to Winner*; *MORE Hold'em Excellence: A Winner For Life*; *Poker For Dummies*, coauthored by Richard Harroch; and *Internet Poker: How to Play and Beat Online Poker Games*, coauthored by Kathleen Keller Watterson. Along with Richard Harroch and Arthur Reber, Lou also coauthored a book about casino gaming, *Gambling For Dummies*. Lou is also a columnist for *Casino Player*, *Strictly Slots*, and *Western Player*, and is a host for the Internet poker site, *www.royalvegaspoker.com*.

But flash back for a moment to that week in Palm Desert, when Krieger was struggling to learn Omaha by the arduous — and often costly — process of applying what he knew about Texas hold'em. "There was a woman in that game who seemed to win every night, so it was clear to me," said Krieger, "that she played the game very well indeed. Her personality illuminated the game as easily as her skill took the money out of it. She was friendly and approachable, so we chatted a bit and wound up as friends by week's end. Back then I had yet to write a book or even an article about poker, and she hadn't yet done anything in the poker world either, other than to win money from all of us. So wasn't I surprised a few years later when I learned that my old